MARX AND THE INTELLECTUALS

LEWIS S. FEUER was born in New York's East Side, the son of an immigrant Jewish worker. After graduation from the City College, he studied at Harvard University, where he later helped found the Harvard Teachers' Union. He was professor of philosophy at the University of Vermont and for nine years professor of philosophy and social science at the University of California at Berkeley, where he was chairman of the Social Science Integrated Course. In the spring semester of 1963 he was invited to Moscow as an exchange scholar at the Soviet Institute of Philosophy and since 1966 he has been professor of sociology at the University of Toronto. He is author of, among other works, *Spinoza and the Rise of Liberalism, The Scientific Intellectual, The Conflict of Generations* and editor of *Marx and Engels: Basic Writings on Politics and Philosophy* (A185).

MARX AND THE INTELLECTUALS

A Set of Post-Ideological Essays

by

LEWIS S. FEUER

ANCHOR BOOKS

Doubleday & Company, Inc.
Garden City, New York
1969

The Anchor edition is the first publication in book form of
Marx and the Intellectuals

Anchor Books edition: 1969

Library of Congress Catalog Card Number 69–15214

To
KATHRYN FEUER

ACKNOWLEDGMENTS

"The Character and Thought of Karl Marx: The Promethean Complex and Historical Materialism" was originally published in *Encounter*, Vol. XXXI, No. 6, December 1968. Reprinted by permission of *Encounter* magazine, London.

"Marxism and the Hegemony of the Intellectual Class" was read at a symposium at the Fifth World Congress of Sociology, Washington, D.C., September 1962, and published in *Survey*, No. 49, October 1963. Reprinted by permission of *Survey*.

"What Is Alienation? The Career of a Concept" is reprinted from *New Politics*, Vol. I, No. 3, Spring 1962.

"American Travelers to the Soviet Union 1917–32: The Formation of a Component of New Deal Ideology" was originally published in the *American Quarterly*, Vol. XIV, No. 2, Summer 1962. Reprinted by permission of *American Quarterly*.

"Marxian Tragedians" was originally published in *Encounter*, Vol. XIX, No. 5, November 1962. Reprinted by permission of *Encounter* magazine, London.

"The Alienated Americans and Their Influence on Marx and Engels" was originally published as two articles, "The Influence of the American Communist Colonies on Engels and Marx" and "The North American Origin of Marx's Socialism," in the *Western Political Quarterly*, Vol. XIX, No. 3, September 1966, and Vol. XVI, No. 1, March 1963. Reprinted by permission of the *Western Political Quarterly*.

"Neo-Primitivism: The New Marxism of the Alienated Intellectuals" was originally published in *The New Leader*, Vol. LI, No. 21, November 4, 1968. Reprinted with permission from *The New Leader* of November 4, 1968. Copyright © 1968 by the American Labor Conference on International Affairs, Inc.

"A Neo-Marxist Conception of Social Science" was originally published in *Ethics, An International Journal of Social, Political, and Legal Philosophy*, Vol. LXX, No. 3, April 1960. Reprinted by permission of the University of Chicago Press.

"Generational Conflict among Soviet Marxists" was originally published under the title "Meeting the Philosophers" in *Survey*, April 1964. Reprinted by permission of *Survey*.

"Indeterminacy and Economic Development" originally appeared in *Philosophy of Science*, Vol. 15, No. 3, July 1948. Reprinted by permission. The Williams & Wilkins Company, Baltimore, Maryland, 21202, U.S.A.

CONTENTS

Introduction

In the history of thought the last decade might well be called the Age of Neo-Marxism. The essays in this book, written with one exception during this time, arose from my effort to come to terms with the emerging ideology. My hope is that the experience of a generation has imparted some significance to them, and that they have perhaps probed beneath the phrases, slogans, and facile sentiments that stand in the way of understanding.

Almost thirty years ago, I wrote a series of articles defending historical materialism and its philosophy against what I believed were superficial criticisms. The Marxist philosophy, I felt, possessed certain truths its critics tended too readily to overlook. My arguments of that time I still think were largely valid. But as my own experience and reflection deepened, I found there were flaws in the Marxist philosophy and sociology of a far more profound sort than the critics of the thirties had ever suggested. With the decline of Marxism, however, after the Second World War, the discussion of its philosophy and sociology lost its immediate relevance. Around 1960, however, a revival of interest in Marxism began to take place in the United States which was coeval with the beginnings of a student movement. As I watched the reviving Neo-Marxism, I was disquieted by what I considered the irrationalism and amorality of the new movement. The fallacies of an older generation were evidently going to have their counterparts among the younger. Was there no law whatsoever of cumulative historical experience? In this mood I wrote from time to time the essays that compose this book.

A common theme runs through them; it is an inquiry into the so-called alienation of the intellectuals and why they have found in Marxism, with its mythology written in the language of social science, their most congenial emotional-ideological expression. In this sense the character of Karl Marx with his lifelong Promethean complex serves as the prototype of the modern intellectual. Prefigured in Marx's career we find the unique combination of the intellectual's traits—his exaltation of rebellion joined to a personal helplessness, the angry readiness for the catalytic agency of war when the more prosaic economic processes fail him, the propensity for myth united with the claim to a mastery of the law of history, the will to rule, and a drive to self-destruction. The essay "Marxism and the Hegemony of the Intellectual Class" explores the will to authoritarian rule which has been the hallmark of the socialistic systems intellectuals have fashioned from Plato to the latest Marxism.

The frustration of their will to rule has been the deepest unconscious source of the intellectual's alienation. With it have been allied their motives of altruism and self-sacrifice and their longing to merge themselves, in an alternating dominance and submission, with the physical power of the people—peasantry, proletariat, primitive peoples, colored races, or backward nations. During the thirties, the intellectuals could speak unambiguously of the "exploitation" of the worker; the depression was a palpable economic fact, and the instability of the capitalist system seemed demonstrated every day. The prosperity after the Second World War, however, brought relative contentment to the working class, but, curiously, "alienation" to the intellectuals. Many books and essays were written trying to explain what "alienation" was. The plain fact was that the intellectuals needed a vague term to characterize their own malaise precisely because they never really cared to analyze its ingredients within themselves. They were alienated as an elite because they felt they were entitled to rule, to supplant the business elite, the legal elite, the military elite, even the democratically chosen elite; the workings of history seemed to have rejected their credentials for hegemony. The intellectuals tried to project their alienation as a basic trait of all social groups in American society, and the word developed into a tedious cliché. The essay "What Is Alienation? The Career of a Concept" was written at the height of its vogue to show its myriad confusions and their uses.

Thirty to forty years earlier American intellectuals had experienced a similar "alienation" from American society though they then used other descriptive terms. They searched for an identification that would overcome their social isolation and sense of superfluousness, and they believed that they found it in the Soviet Union. Philosophers went to Russia and announced it was ruled by philosopher-kings; economists went to study Soviet planning and announced that the planners were economists like themselves; social workers beheld the Soviet Union and said it was a universal settlement house run by their colleagues; progressive teachers inspected the Soviet schools and heralded the society as a magnificent educational laboratory conducted by fellow teachers. All of them misperceived the Soviet society and the potentials of Soviet tyranny because they were stirred by the sight of a society ruled at last, they were convinced, by an intellectual elite like themselves. This story, and its influence on American ideology, I have told in "American Travelers to the Soviet Union 1917–32."

Marxism subsequently became the regnant ideology of the alienated intellectual elite. It seemed often to corrode the spirit of the idealists who felt that they could base their lives upon its doctrine. Only through the study of individuals can we hope to find the source of this corrosion. The life and suicide of Marx's talented and idealistic daughter, Eleanor, seemed to me to have foreshadowed a phenomenon that later became endemic in political lives during the twentieth century. Eleanor Marx founded her life's loyalty on her father's ideology, and at the end discovered that it foundered because it failed to recognize the autonomy of the moral sense, above and beyond economy, party, and class. The essay on Eleanor Marx entitled "Marxian Tragedians" is a philosophical biography, that is, an evaluation of an ideology as it is tested in its bearing on a person's life. In our own time Svetlana Alliluyeva has followed a similar path of self-discovery.

As a new young generation of Marxists in the early sixties exhumed the Dead Sea Scrolls of Marxism, the *Economic-Philosophic Manuscripts,* the juvenilia of Karl Marx, and, making a generational fetish of the word "alienation," undertook a largely directionless rejection of American society, I began to explore further the political significance this concept had had for Marx and Engels, and their political reasons for discarding it from their vocabulary. I found to my surprise that they had used this notion precisely at a time when Engels especially was embroiled in a project for setting up a Utopian colony in Germany on the model of the Shakers or Brook Farm. "Alienation" was the slogan-word of Marx and Engels in their Utopian phase, just as "community" was its antithesis. When they somewhat shamefacedly dropped their Utopian project, they did the same with the word "alienation." Meanwhile, having heard how the first workingmen's party in the world's history had been founded in the United States, they began to think upon the consequences of political action by the working class. The essay on American influences on the thought of Marx and Engels aims to clarify the evolution from Utopia to political action; it indicates also how the unconscious source of alienation became more manifest in the successive stages for its proposed solution; the longing for idyllic communities was transmuted into a program for a workers' political party officered by an intellectual elite. Later, however, Marx and Engels were dismayed by the vigor and therapeutic power of American society. Their most "alienated" comrades went to the "Transatlantic Republic," and shed their "alienation" shortly. An American newspaper, the *New York Tribune,* moreover, regularly published Marx's contributions, gave him the only job he ever had, and paid him relatively well. Consequently, anti-Americanism early became a Marxist theme, for America offered a social alternative that threatened to reduce Marxist modes of thought and feeling into irrelevancies and absurdities. The Alienated Intellectuals struggled to hold on to their alienation—the mark of their vocation to rule as an intellectual elite.

For a number of years, the chief spokesman of the alienated intellectuals in America was C. Wright Mills. He explicitly urged that Marxists should rid themselves of their "labor metaphysic" and overtly justify the role and rule of the intellectual elite as the sole progressive force in the world. Mills tried to bring the Marxist conception of social science with its distinctive "dialectical" standpoint up to date. To show how this Neo-Marxist ideology fails in its polemics against the notion of a general sociological theory was the aim of my essay on C. Wright Mills's *The Sociological Imagination*. It tries to show how an ideology projects itself into methodology.

Meanwhile, new varieties of Marxism have arisen in far-flung parts of the world as intellectuals from China to Ghana have undertaken to create new communist societies. The continents of Asia, Africa, and Latin America, in which these new movements arose, coincide approximately with the lands of the colored races. Their Marxism has tended to become the vehicle of a racial resentment against the white race; Marx's imagery of the exploited against the exploiters was translated by Mao Tse-tung's Minister of Defense to denote the struggle of the colored "proletariat" of Asia, Africa, and Latin America against the white capitalists of North America and Europe—a warfare in which the peoples of the countryside would encircle those of the cities. Marx himself had not known how to deal with the problem of race from the standpoint of his materialistic conception of history. Now a racial, anti-urban, and anti-Western cultural motif availed itself of the Marxist ideology. The racial "alienation" of the intellectual elites of the backward countries began to express itself in their own unique variety of Marxism. They were joined by intellectuals in secession from Western civilization who felt themselves emotionally drawn to the notion of "guerrilla warfare." I have tried to analyze the emergence of this Neo-Bakuninist, anti-intellectual Marxism—the strange mutation of a neo-primitivist Marxism among intellectuals.

In the Soviet Union, on the other hand, a new generation is chafing under the controls imposed on thought by the party dictatorship. Young thinkers in the Soviet bureaucratic society experience their own variety of "alienation." Compelled to adhere to the official dialectical materialism, they contrive, however, to express their own individual philosophical standpoints under the camouflage of skillfully chosen texts from Marx. A whole spectrum of philosophies from existentialism to positivism is concealed in Marxist guises. I had a rare opportunity to get to know this younger generation during the spring semester of 1963 which I spent as an exchange scholar at the Institute of Philosophy of the Soviet Academy of Science mostly in Moscow, but with several weeks at Tbilisi, Tashkent, and Leningrad. I found that Marxism in the Soviet Union was experiencing an unprecedented crisis; it was confronted by a philosophical-sociological problem which I called the "Great Contradiction." It arose from the efforts of the Soviet regime to provide an apologetic explanation for the pervasive, large-scale, systematic cruelties, injustices, and repressions of the Stalinist era. If they explained them along historical materialist lines, then the Soviet social system itself was at fault, as the foundation for the Stalinist superstructure. If they explained them as the outcome of Stalin's paranoid tendencies as an individual, then not only was historical materialism superseded, by the attribution of the superstructural traits of a whole era to the influence of a single individual, but the way was open for the recognizing of psychoanalytical factors in social causation. Thus either the Soviet social system or its historical materialist ideology was basically at fault. The official Marxists tried to repress the "Great Contradiction"; young Soviet philosophers, on the other hand, indicated to me that they hoped I would challenge their directors on such points, and inquire, for instance, as to why it was still virtually impossible to secure copies of Freud's works in the Soviet Union. I did raise these questions publicly, especially at my last talk to the Institute of Philosophy in Moscow. When Soviet thought resolves the "Great Contradiction" in at least an approximate way, it will be a sign that a genuine liberalization has taken place in Soviet society. Then the heritage of guilt and cowardice will begin to be expunged from the consciousness of Soviet intellectuals. There are signs indeed that a handful of courageous spirits may lead the way to such a liberation from the dead hand of official Marxist ideology. Something of this is told in the essay on my meetings with Soviet philosophers and sociologists.

At the heart of the Marxian theory lies the assumption of a technological determinism, the notion that the foreseeable development of the mode of production is the master key to the evolution of social systems. I have therefore included an earlier theoretical study, "Indeterminacy and Economic Development," in which I tried to show that within the structure of the Marxian economic theory itself, there was a basic indeterminacy that precluded any deterministic solutions. Apart from any metaphysical arguments, Marxist economic determinism was an invalid doctrine; its equations did not decree an inevitable decline of the capitalist order. Moreover, this particular theorem in economic science might be generalized into a guiding universal sociological law: for all societies, there are no economic laws that entail the development of such a degree of disequilibrium that the given society must collapse. The decisions of the human will have a far freer role in shaping their economic relations than Marx would have granted. No social revolution has ever taken place because the economic laws of the feudal or capitalist systems necessarily involved such "contradictions" that a novel economic system was required. And when totally planned socialist economies are reconstructed in the future, it will be because they suppress the human aspiration for freedom, not because of the "contradictions" of their economic laws; their systems will be abrogated because they impose a consistency against which the human spirit rebels.

I have made only a few changes from the previous published form of the essays, and these have been mostly of a stylistic kind. Occasionally I have restored pages from the original versions that were omitted from publication in journals.

The Character and Thought of Karl Marx: The Promethean Complex and Historical Materialism

Marx founded his life on a Promethean dedication to a war against the reigning gods. He thought that with the help of his materialistic conception of history he would, like Prometheus, unravel the law of man's future. At the end, however, brooding over his life's work, he was haunted by the fear that he had been enthralled by a delusion. He found a portrayal of his own state of mind in a short story by Balzac, *The Unknown Masterpiece;* it "made a deep impression on him," wrote Paul Lafargue, his son-in-law, "because it was in part a description of his own feelings."[1] In the story, a fanatical old man has worked for many years on the painting of a courtesan which, he realizes finally, "is no painting," but "a sentiment, a passion"; his research has led him "to doubt the very existence of the objects of his search"; knowledge, he then realizes, "brings you to a negation"; when he at last shows his painting to two admirers, all they perceive is a confusion of fantastical lines: "Nothing! Nothing! After ten years of work . . ." That night he commits his canvas to the flames, a last rite of "the fire of Prometheus," and dies. Thus Marx too wondered whether his Promethean fixation had distorted his perception of things. Was his own materialistic conception of history, after he had superposed all the amendments and qualifications, finally a confusion of sociological causal lines without resemblance to that picture of a transfigured working class and humanity he had set out to paint?

[1] *Karl Marx: His Life and Work, Reminiscences by Paul Lafargue and Wilhelm Liebknecht* (New York, 1943), p. 16.

The Promethean myth dominated Marx's thinking from
his adolescent years on. It brought with it an emphasis
on struggle, on defiance of the gods. "Prometheus is the
noblest of saints and martyrs in the calendar of philosophy," wrote Marx in his doctoral dissertation, and he proclaimed his life's theme in the dramatic lines from
Aeschylus' *Prometheus Bound:* "In sooth all gods I hate."
"I shall never exchange my fetters for slavish servility.
'Tis better to be chained to the rock than bound to the
service of Zeus."[2] The identification with Prometheus extended to Marx's intellectual perspective. Where Prometheus declared:

> "All is known to me
> All, all that is to be"

Marx claimed to have grasped the law of motion of capitalism. He gave himself willingly to penury and suffering,
bringing knowledge to mankind as Prometheus:

> Mine offence
> Was wilful. I avouch it willingly
> Rescuing mankind, I plunge myself in woe.[3]

With Prometheus, Marx affirmed that the technical arts
were the mainspring of man's progress, and when he was
physically tormented, his ailment was identical with that
with which Zeus afflicted Prometheus—a sickness of the
liver.

A Promethean complex came to pervade Marx's everyday deeds and attitudes; every action, even the most trivial,
was perceived under the aspect of struggle. When he urged
his friends to learn languages, Spanish, Greek, it was not by
way of extolling their beautiful literatures; rather he said:
"A foreign language is a weapon in the struggle for life."

[2] Karl Marx and Friedrich Engels, *On Religion* (Moscow, 1957),
p. 15.
[3] Aeschylus, *Prometheus Bound,* in *The Seven Plays in English
Verse,* trans. Lewis Campbell (London, 1906), pp. 238, 242.

His books, he proclaimed, were his "slaves," and must serve his will, and he gave judgment upon their authors: "I mete out historical justice, and render to each man his due." To be defeated in a game of chess plunged him into utter despondency; it was a struggle lost. And when, in exile, he took up fencing, "what he lacked in science," as Liebknecht said, "he tried to make up in aggressiveness." In a curious way, the same was true of Marx's theory of history.[4]

To Marx, with his Promethean emotional a priori, struggle was the law of existence. Contrary to the tradition that from Empedocles to Freud has perceived reality as a dual encounter between love and aggression, for Marx, aggression became all-encompassing. When an American journalist, John Swinton, interviewed him in 1880, he asked "the most ultimate question, 'What is?'" Thereupon Marx gazed "upon the roaring sea in front and the restless multitude upon the beach," and then, "in deep and solemn tone, he replied 'Struggle.'" This was his ultimate metaphysical category and indeed his highest value. A half-playful questionnaire of his daughters brought the responses: "Your idea of happiness—To fight." "The vice you detest most—Servility." Marx would have said: "I struggle; therefore I am."[5]

The Promethean complex determined a philosophy of history; as Prometheus warned Zeus of the "son more puissant than his sire" who would bring him down "from his throne of parental sovereignty," so Marx enunciated the warning to all established powers, the all-defiant generalization—all history is a history of class struggles, and the working class, growing to maturity, would end forever all class exploitation.

[4] *Reminiscences by Paul Lafargue and Wilhelm Liebknecht, op. cit.,* pp. 12, 10, 18. Wilhelm Liebknecht, Karl Marx: *Biographical Memoirs,* trans. Ernest Untermann (Chicago, 1901), pp. 119–21, 66–67, 105.

[5] *Karl Marx: Man, Thinker, and Revolutionist,* ed. D. Ryazanoff, trans. Eden and Cedar Paul (New York, 1927), p. 269. John Swinton, *John Swinton's Travels. Current views and notes of forty days in France and England* (New York, 1880).

At crucial points, Promethean emotion overcame Marx's sense of logic, of evidence, of proof. Though he was aware that Hegel's dialectical transitions often rested fragilely on "puns," on arbitrary wishes, he himself allowed his emotions rather than evidence to guide the presumable direction of the qualitative leaps of social systems. In a letter of 1852, for instance, Marx indicated what he thought his scientific achievement had been:

Long before me bourgeois historians had described the historical development of this class struggle and bourgeois economists the economic anatomy of the classes. What I did that was new was to prove: (1) that the *existence of classes* is only bound up with particular, historic phases in the development of production; (2) that the class struggle necessarily leads to the dictatorship of the proletariat; (3) that the dictatorship itself only constitutes the transition to the abolition of all classes and to a classless society.

What is astounding, of course, is that Marx thought he had proved these three propositions, that a few paragraphs in the *Communist Manifesto* and some scattered passages in his early writings sufficed to prove three propositions that embraced all past social systems and predicted the system of the future. If "Prometheus" signified literally "he who knows in advance," then Marx was being swept on by fervor to substitute prophecy for science. The forecast of proletarian dictatorship and the advent of a classless society rested on an extrapolation from the slenderest of empirical foundations, but the minimum of factual evidence was matched with a maximum of Promethean projection. History, in Marx's unconscious, was a drama of retribution and justice, and he was rendering judgment in Zeus' place on the evil and good. In 1856 Marx, responding to a toast, "The Proletarians of Europe," articulated the Promethean apocalypse.

To take vengeance for the misdeeds of the ruling class there existed in the Middle Ages in Germany a secret tribunal called the *Vehmgericht*. If a red cross was seen marked on a house, the people knew that its owner was doomed by the *Vehm*. All the houses of Europe are now marked by the mysterious red cross. History is the judge; its executioner, the proletarian.[6]

And Marx was presumably the prosecutor, or, if you will, the clerk of the court.

A life founded on myth, however, entails its repeated collisions with reality. In Marx's case, experience itself was to be the great de-mythologizer. Historical materialism was altered, recast, and supplemented with new variables; war, race, individual decision, social inertia, intellectual elitism, generational conflicts, the power of ideas, all took on a new significance as factors in social change often more important than the economic. Marx, as Liebknecht observed, was an especial victim of the "prophesying imp"; his friends ridiculed him for it, and it made him "grimly mad."[7] Insensibly, however, the myths began to recede under the cumulative pressure of events. The failure of prophecy was Marx's trauma. In 1849, in the first months of his London exile, he was absolutely certain that the social revolution would resume in a few months. In 1850, he was writing that "the revolution is imminent." Engels was reassuring him that the capitalist system was at the end of its tether: "There are no more new markets to open, . . . it is obvious that the domination of the factory-owners has reached its end. What then? . . . Social revolution and the dictatorship of the proletariat, say we."

When catastrophe was delayed, Marx scanned the sociological skies in faraway regions. The Taiping Rebellion in China moved him to write in 1853 that "the Chinese revolution will give off the sparks into the greatly charged mine of the modern industrial system and will bring about the explosion prepared long ago by the general crisis which, when it spreads abroad, will be directly followed by political revolutions on the continent." When this

[6] Karl Marx and Friedrich Engels, *Correspondence 1846–1895*, trans. Dona Torr (New York, 1935), p. 91.
[7] Liebknecht, *Karl Marx, loc. cit.*, p. 59.

breakdown failed to take place, Engels brought the comforting hope in 1856 that the Russian capital expansion would "soon lead to a crash." He wrote Marx that "when we hear of the great Irkutsk road with branches to Peking, it will be time to pack up our bags. This time there will be an unprecedented crash; all the elements are present. . . ."

Marx indeed felt in that year (1856) that a broad European crisis was at hand, and that his revolutionary vocation would be realized: "I do not think we shall be able to sit here as spectators much longer. Even the fact that I have at last got to the point of furnishing a house again and sending for my books, proves to me that the 'mobilization' of our persons is at hand." Engels responded in joyful anticipation; soon, he expected, he would be taking up arms again: "The crisis will do as much good physically as a sea-bathe, I can see that already. In 1848 we said: 'Now our time is coming'—and in a certain sense it came, but now it is coming altogether, now it will be a fight for life. This makes my military studies more practical at once."

Even as the crisis of 1857 receded, Marx feared that his economic studies would be rendered shortly unnecessary and obsolete by the quick advent of socialism. To Engels he wrote in December 1857 that he was "working like mad all through the nights putting my economic studies together so that I may at least have the outlines clear before the deluge comes. . . ." He confided to Lassalle in 1858 that he had a "presentiment" that now, "after fifteen years of study" had given him a grasp of his subject, "stormy movements from without will probably interfere." He consoled himself: "Never mind. If I get finished so late that I no longer find the world ready to pay attention to such things, the fault will obviously be my own." "On the Continent a revolution is imminent," wrote Marx in 1858, "and will also immediately assume a socialist character." But, he wondered, would it survive in view of the fact that in "a far greater territory" of the globe, presumably Asia, "the movement of bourgeois society is still on the ascendant?" He saw history in terms of tocsins and clarion calls, of harbingers and portents. The American civil war, he wrote in *Capital,* sounded the "tocsin" for the European working class. It was Promethean dramatic myth looking for its cue; the substance of history is not, however, transcribed into a dramatic script.

Invariably, Marx and Engels believed that their historical materialism had endowed them with a Promethean foreknowledge. Marx pondered the class origins of President Andrew Johnson, and was convinced he would pursue a revolutionary policy: "Johnson is stern, inflexible, revengeful and as a former poor white has a deadly hatred of the oligarchy."[8] Engels expected that after two generations the Negroes would merge with the whites. Always they looked to the mode of production to give them the key to events, and almost always the key failed to fit. David Urquhart, Marx's eccentric friend, told him that his notion of a "logic of events" was just as "senseless" as the "justice of a locomotive." Marx found this hard to accept, but he twisted the logic with each turn of events, adding his epicycles to the grand simplicity of his law of social evolution. Engels to the end of his days continued to prophesy. In 1886, he was "watching the present development of the present crisis" in America, and saw no likelihood of a resolution of the "chronic overproduction" of England, America, and Germany. Two years later, a short visit to Canada, seen through the categories of historical materialism, left him certain that "in ten years this sleepy Canada will be ripe for annexation—the farmers in Manitoba, etc., will demand it themselves."[9] Finally at the time of the Sino-Japanese War in 1894, he predicted confidently that Chinese capitalist competition would

[8] Karl Marx and Frederick Engels, *The Civil War in the United States,* 2d ed., Richard Enmale, ed. (New York, 1940), pp. 271, 275, 277.

[9] Karl Marx and Frederick Engels, *Letters to Americans: 1848–1895,* trans. L. E. Mins (New York, 1953), pp. 204, 150.

rapidly "give an impetus to the overthrow of capitalism in Europe and America."[10]

The Bible tells how Jonah was angry with God because He did not fulfill Jonah's prophecy of the destruction of Nineveh; Jonah's was the first instance of a self-nullifying prophecy, and the Book of Jonah, in effect, called for an end to prophecy as many of us have called for an end to ideology. Marx did not abandon Promethean foreknowledge when events withheld their confirmation, but he began reluctantly to revise his premises. Like Moses before him, like Trotsky after him, he realized that the Promethean role in which he cast the workers was part of a mythological drama rather than a social reality. We must say to the workers, he said in 1850: "You will have to go through fifteen or twenty or fifty years of civil wars and international wars not only in order to change extant conditions, but also in order to change yourselves and to render yourselves fit for political dominion."

But it was an ominous new note for Marx the foreseer. Angered by the frustration of history, he looked now not to the dialectical law of the decline of capitalist economy but to war as the prime mover of human history. War, not economic evolution, would transform men's characters and destroy old systems and create new ones. Every frustrated prophet finally appeals to cosmic aggression, his own anger projected as a historical force. In such a mood, Marx literally identified himself with Moses: "The present generation is like the Jews, whom Moses led through the wilderness. It has not only a new world to conquer, it must go under, in order to make room for the men who are fit for a new world."[11]

By contrast, Engels sought more prosaic explanations for their defeat; for one, chance had intervened in the form of the discovery of gold in California, which had quickened the vitality of the capitalist order; but apart from all chance, Engels acknowledged, they had simply misjudged

[10] Marx and Engels, *Correspondence 1846–1895*, p. 119.
[11] Karl Marx, *The Class Struggles in France (1848–50)*, C. P. Dutt, ed. (New York, n.d.) introduction by Friedrich Engels, p. 114.

the developmental powers of European capitalism; almost fifty years after 1848, in 1895, he recognized that the tremendous economic growth throughout the continent showed that they had been moved by revolutionary emotion rather than scientific insight: "History has proved us, and all who thought like us, wrong."[12]

As Marx watched crises subside, and the economic dialectic persisted in failing him, he turned in desperation more and more to war as the redeeming agency in history. Only some drastic dislocation could bring him and his friends to power, and he began to welcome war as the dislocating and liberating factor. In a military breakdown, a revolution might take place that ordinary economic forces were incapable of generating. It was an emotional-thought pattern typical of the finimundialist (end-of-the-world-ist) whose prognosis has been confuted. When the commercial crisis of 1857, for instance, failed to bring a universal collapse, Marx and Engels hoped in 1859 for a general European war that would bring a Russian defeat and an emergence of communist leadership. Marx welcomed the Franco-Prussian War in 1870 and wanted Bismarck to defeat Louis Napoleon; a German victory, he felt, would mean German hegemony in the international socialist movement and a setback for the French Proudhonists. Consequently Marx was angry with his follower and friend, Wilhelm Liebknecht, for refusing to vote in the Reichstag for Bismarck's war credits.

A kind of historical militarism tended to supersede historical materialism. In the spring of 1874 Marx was expecting again that the European workers' movement would be resurrected through a war: "We must go through it (a European war) before there can be any thought of the European classes having decisive influence." And Engels toward the end of his life foresaw a war in which millions of soldiers massacred each other, devastating the whole of Europe more "than any swarm of locusts," and with "one result absolutely certain: general exhaustion and

[12] *Ibid.*, p. 16.

the establishment of the conditions for the ultimate victory of the working class." This was the ultimate Promethean vision, for Prometheus' shackles would be unbound by war; and Marx made a cult of Shelley. Engels with supreme confidence declaimed: "This, my lords, princes and statesmen, is where in your wisdom you have brought old Europe. And when nothing more remains to you but to open the last great war dance—that will suit us all right."[13]

The last great war dance—and out of the catastrophe, socialism. It was an amalgam of a Promethean death-wish and transfiguration run wild, and could make no claim to science. For war, as Engels well knew in his less mythopoeic moods, had frequently in the past simply destroyed societies utterly and completely. He had noted as far back as 1853 how wars had extirpated whole Eastern societies, "the otherwise curious fact that whole stretches which were once brilliantly cultivated are now waste and bare (Palmyra, Petra, the ruins in the Yemen, districts in Egypt, Persia and Hindustan); it explains the fact that one single devastating war could depopulate a country for centuries and strip it of its whole civilisation."[14]

War, moreover, was not only the destroyer of social systems; it imposed its character on social foundations. Serfdom, for example, according to Marx and Engels in the maturity of their reflections, did not arise from any technological or economic necessity; rather it came into being as a well-nigh universal relationship of conquerors to conquered. "I am glad that on the history of serfdom we 'proceed in agreement,'" wrote Engels to Marx in 1882. "It is certain that serfdom and bondage are not a peculiarly medieval-feudal form, we find them everywhere or nearly everywhere where conquerors have the land cultivated for them by the old inhabitants. . . ." "The feudal system," Engels wrote for the *New American Cyclopaedia*, was "in its very origin a military organization. . . ." War,

[13] Marx and Engels, *Correspondence 1846–1895*, pp. 456–57.
[14] Marx and Engels, *Correspondence 1846–1895*, p. 67.

and not the mode of production, imposed aggressive social relations on the social system, or in other cases produced defensive social formations. The economic relations were a continuation of war among peoples.

Besides the question of war was that of race. Marx could never fit its facts securely into his materialistic conception of history, and the marriage of his daughter, Laura, to Paul Lafargue, a Negro by American conventions, raised it for him in a most poignant way. To begin with there was the question whether the Southern slave system was the outcome of technological requirements or whether, as Tocqueville had suggested, it arose not from any technical necessity but simply because a stronger or superior race was exploiting a weaker or inferior one. Marx at first regarded slavery as an economically necessary development, writing, for instance, in 1846 that "without slavery North America, the most progressive country, would be transformed into a patriarchal land."[15] In his more mature years, however, race took on the status of an independent, autonomous variable. He declared in a *New York Tribune* article of which Ralph Waldo Emerson took special note that in the "silent revolution" which was taking place, and which was as indifferent to human existence as an earthquake, those "races, too weak to master the new conditions of life must give way."[16]

This was a theory of racial selection and determinism of the utmost, but this view of 1853 became characteristic of Marx. Evidently he thought a great deal about the question of racial inferiority when his daughter in 1866 became engaged to Lafargue. A grandson of a Santo Domingo mulatto and a Caribbean Indian was to become his son-in-law.[17] Marx mocked at him as "cette caboche

[15] Karl Marx, *The Poverty of Philosophy* (New York, n.d.), p. 159.

[16] Lewis S. Feuer, "Ralph Waldo Emerson's Reference to Karl Marx," *New England Quarterly*, XXXIII (1960), 378–79. Karl Marx and Frederick Engels, *On Britain* (Moscow, 1953), p. 375.

[17] Georges Stolz, *Paul Lafargue: Théoricien Militant du Socialisme* (Paris, 1936), p. 5. A primitivist note entered Lafargue's conception of the socialist future: "The happy Polynesians may then

de négre," though later in introducing him to Theodor Cuno, an Internationalist who was going to America, he said: "You may do there what one of my daughters has done towards solving the color question, by marrying a nigger. . . ."[18] Yet, in the very same letter in which Marx told Engels of his daughter's betrothal, he also stated his views on racial theories and the relative inferiority of the Negro. He was especially enthusiastic over the notions of the French anthropologist Trémaux who maintained "that the common Negro type was a degeneration from a quite higher one," and that racial difference in abilities, as between the Slavic and Lithuanian, were naturally caused by differences in the earth's soil. Marx thought that Trémaux's racial anthropology was a tremendous advance over Darwin, "in the historical and practical application more important and richer than Darwin." And something of this standpoint was smuggled into historical materialism itself by the hurried statement in *Capital* that the productivity of labor is dependent not only on the social structure but also on the "constitution of man himself (race, etc.). . . ."[19]

When Marx thus recognized in racial struggles an independent factor in history, he was taking one more step in the basic transformation of historical materialism. No longer could one say with a grand generality that all history was a history of class struggles, for racial antagonisms were not reducible to those of class, and moreover, warfare rather than the mode of production could be the critical determining force; indeed, less advanced races, nomads for instance, could destroy the more advanced but sedentary ones in cities and farms.

---

love as they like without fearing the civilized Venus and the sermons of European moralists." Paul Lafargue, *The Right to Be Lazy*, trans. Charles H. Kerr (Chicago, n.d.), p. 49.

[18] Theodor Cuno, "Reminiscences," in *Reminiscences of Marx and Engels* (Moscow, n.d.), p. 212.

[19] Karl Marx and Friedrich Engels, *Historisch-Kritische Gesamtausgabe*, ed. D. Ryazanov, Band 2 (Berlin, 1930), pp. 354–56, 360–63.

With war and race upsetting the schemata of the materialistic conception of history, a third major challenge came from Russia, a backward country Marx had despised but which in the 1870s was placing revolution on its agenda. When Marx wrote *Capital*, he still believed in a universal law of social evolution; he could justify his preoccupation with Britain's industrial development on the ground that "the country that is more developed industrially only shows to the less developed, the image of its own future." To backward countries he could say in Promethean fashion: "De te fabula narratur." Hence soon after 1848 he maintained that conspirators were "the alchemists of the revolution" and that their artificially conjured crises could never accelerate the course of social development. The Russian case, however, shattered both his belief in a law of evolutionary sequence and his impersonalism, his view that individual interventions could not affect the underlying drift of events.

For Marx could not bring himself to deny to the Russian socialists of the 1870s the hope that their revolution would enable their country to skip the bourgeois stage of development and enter directly upon socialism. So Marx declared in 1877 that Russia had "the finest chance ever offered by history to a people" to avoid undergoing "all the fatal vicissitudes of the capitalist regime." What then of his Promethean warning: De te fabula narratur?

"My historical sketch of the genesis of capitalism in Western Europe," answered Marx, was not to be metamorphosed "into a historico-philosophic theory of the general path every people is fated to tread, whatever the historical circumstances in which it finds itself, in order that it may ultimately arrive at the form of economy which ensures . . . the most complete development of man."

Thus with one sentence Marx took leave of the universal evolutionary law he had once regarded as the core of historical materialism. For in 1859 he had held plainly that there was a necessary succession of "epochs in the progress of the economic formation of society," none of which ever disappeared "before all the productive forces for which there is room in it have developed." And his dialectic method, he reiterated as late as 1873, was nothing but the law of "the necessity of successive determinate orders of social conditions." The succession of social systems was now losing its necessity; Marx scrapped the dialectical law to accommodate the revolutionary will. But his social science henceforth was at odds with the Promethean myth, for he was sacrificing foreknowledge to revolutionary hope and contingency.

Marx muted his economic impersonalism before the idealistic personalism of the Russian terrorists, who revived a critical problem that the Marx of 1848 had himself never satisfactorily resolved. No practicing revolutionist wishes to bind himself to an evolutionary timetable for social change; all his instincts drive him to act, to grasp for power, and to use it for his goals. Marx's comrades of 1848 after their defeat looked askance at his withdrawal into study while he waited for history to ripen the revolutionary fruit. The job of a revolutionist was revolution, thought August Willich, and he regarded Marx's view that social classes must await their turn to rule as an absurdity; he did not propose to have the working class sit back until the bourgeoisie finally acted its assigned part. Marx, the aloof scholar whose contact with workers was limited to lecturing them, could afford to sit back admonishing them to conform their initiative to his "laws of social science." Andreas Gottschalk, the leader of the left wing, berated Marx for his "heartlessness," and as early as February 1849 scorned Marx's insistence that a bourgeois revolution must come first: "What is the purpose of such a revolution? Why should we, men of the proletariat, spill our blood for this?" Such stage-theorists, said Gottschalk, "are not in earnest about the salvation of the oppressed. The distress of the workers, the hunger of the poor have only a scientific, doctrinaire interest for them."

The activist workers no doubt remembered the sad fact that Marx and Engels in 1848 had suppressed their *Communist Manifesto* because they preferred to court the liberal bourgeoisie rather than to agitate among the workers for revolution. Marx thought getting money from the liberal establishment for his newspaper was more important than giving the *Communist Manifesto* to the workers. "If a single copy of our seventeen points were distributed here," wrote Engels, "as far as we are concerned all would be lost."[20] The proletarian revolution, Marx and Engels argued, would have to await its turn until the bourgeois stage had had its full innings. And the *Communist Manifesto* in such circumstances was, Marx and Engels felt, a sectarian document, a program prematurely born. The German revolutionary activists believed in the *Manifesto* more than did its authors.

The new generation of Russian activists, similarly unwilling to prostrate themselves and their people before an alleged law of history, deeply stirred the old Marx. Several of the Narodnaya Volya (People's Will) in 1879 and 1880 on escaping abroad were received in Marx's home. Then when Alexander II was assassinated, Marx wrote his daughter Jenny that terror was a "historically inevitable means of action," the morality of which was as useless to discuss "as the earthquake at Chios"; the Russian Terrorists, he said, were "excellent people through and through, *sans phrase* mélodramatique, simple, straightforward, heroic." Engels, broadening the framework of historical materialism to include the efficacy of conspiracy, wrote a few years later in 1885 that Russia was "one of the exceptional cases where it is possible for a handful of people to make a revolution, i.e., with one little push to cause a whole social system, which . . . is in more than labile equilibrium, to come crashing down. . . . Well now—if ever Blanquism—the fantastic idea of overturning an entire society by the action of a small conspiracy—had a certain raison d'être, that is certainly so now in Petersburg. . . ."

Thus the materialistic conception of history, with its massive, large-scale, impersonal processes, founded on the movements of the mode of production, was relaxed to include a revolution accomplished by historical idealism, by the free determination of a few individuals imposing their will on history. What was being left of the sweeping bold lines of Marx's theory as he retouched it like Balzac's painter to account for the realities of war, race, and the actions of conspirator intellectuals in backward Russia?

Meanwhile, from another intellectual source, the development of anthropological science, Marx was experiencing a singular attack on the foundation of historical materialism. The new science was bringing consciously to the fore the significance of mythology and the irrational side of man. Marx and Engels, at a loss as to how to accommodate these new findings to their standpoint, in effect decided to exempt primitive societies from the workings of historical materialism. Primitive society also raised for Marx questions of sexuality in history, in particular the status of incest. This theoretical problem coincided in his own personal life with a crisis in his relations to his beloved youngest daughter, Eleanor, whose career and love choices he opposed; Eleanor sustained several nervous breakdowns. The interpretation of primitive society became a domain for Marx's fantasy-life, in which the irrational sources of his own Promethean myth came close to the surface.

It was the Russian scholar Maxim Kovalevsky who placed in Marx's hands on his return from America a copy of Lewis Morgan's *Ancient Society*. Then Marx got hold of the writings of the American historian H. H. Bancroft, on the West Coast Indians.[21] Soon Engels was writing to Marx in 1882 that the evidence proved that "at this stage the type of production is less decisive than the degree in which the old blood bonds and the old mutual community of the sexes within the tribe have been dissolved." As Engels put it a few years later, as far as primitive society was concerned, what was primary was their false conceptions

[21] Maxim Kovalevsky, "Meetings with Marx," in *Reminiscences of Marx and Engels* (Moscow, n.d.), pp. 294–95.

of nature; he was, we might say, a Comtist in his interpretation of primitive existence: "These various false conceptions of nature, of man's own being, magic forces, etc., have for the most part only a negative economic basis; but the low economic development of the prehistoric period is supplemented and also partially conditioned and even caused by the false conceptions of nature." While still maintaining that "economic necessity was the main driving force of the progressive knowledge of nature," he felt it "would surely be pedantic to try and find economic causes for all this primitive nonsense."[22] Thus the primitive world, with its myths and magic, was consigned to an irrational realm, beyond historical materialism. The Marxist world view itself, however, was thereby almost rent asunder. For primitive men too experience "economic necessities"; withal their world-schemes are mythological. What then is signified by their "negative economic basis"? Was the primitive response to material problems irrational because their "false conceptions" had a primary determining role? And if myths and irrationality can have this status in primitive existence, why may they not have the determining role in modern history?

Marx and Engels found themselves in a further quandary as they tried to explain the Sociological Fall from primitive, communistic, stateless existence into a society of class oppression, private property, and exploitation. For if the materialistic conception were true, if the tribal communistic existence determined the tribal consciousness, how had the Fall, with its greed, avarice, and selfishness made its appearance? There had taken place, said Engels (and Marx similarly), "a fall from the simple moral greatness of the old gentile society. The lowest interests—base greed, brutal appetites, sordid avarice, selfish robbery of the common wealth—inaugurated the new, civilized class society." How such Evil could have been nurtured in the

[22] Karl Marx and Friedrich Engels, *Correspondence 1846–1895*, trans. Dona Torr (New York, 1935), p. 482.

bosom of the Good was something of a psychological *creatio ex nihilo*. There was no serpent to blame for this ouster from the Political Garden of Eden. A primitivist myth was beginning to contaminate the Promethean.

Meanwhile, Marx was especially concerned to insist that in the primitive innocence, sexual incest had been the rule. If Engels liked to dwell on the pristine free love, Marx was rather drawn to the delights of incest. When Richard Wagner doubted that brother embraced sister as bride, Marx replied in 1882: "In primitive times the sister was the wife, and *that was moral.*" When Bachofen considered punaluan marriage "lawless," Marx retorted that primitive man would likewise have regarded contemporary cousin-marriages as "incestuous." Engels was confident that among the Australian aborigines "sexual intercourse between parents and children was still not felt to be particularly horrible," though he conceded there were no such actual Australian instances.[23] It was all a bit confused but somehow incest was to be included in the primitivist fantasy.[24]

Finally, Marx's many years of residence in England brought home to him another problem for his materialistic conception of history. England was above all the country

[23] Frederick Engels, *The Origin of the Family, Private Property, and the State in the Light of the Researches of Lewis H. Morgan* (New York, 1942), pp. 32, 33, 35, 38, 44, 66–67, 73, 63, 39, 86–88, 150. Cf. Robert H. Lowie, *A History of Ethnological Theory* (New York, 1937), p. 252.

[24] Probably with his own parents in mind Engels wrote that "Protestant monogamy" at its best "is a conjugal partnership of leaden boredom, known as 'domestic bliss.'" *The Origin of the Family*, p. 63. Georg Weerth wrote in 1845 that Engels was "at terrible variance with his family; he is considered godless and impious, and the rich father will not give his son another pfennig for his keep." *Reminiscences of Marx and Engels*, pp. 194–95. Engels complained to Marx in 1845 that his communism had "roused all my father's religious fanaticism. . . . Just think of what it's like for me. . . . If I get a letter, . . . they put on such an expression of righteous indignation . . . that it nearly drives me mad. . . . I can't eat, drink, sleep or —— without that confounded look of righteous indignation before me at every turn." J. P. Mayer, *Friedrich Engels*, trans. Dora Round (Trier, 1931), p. 12.

where measures of social reform were being gradually enacted, and where "governments and parliaments appointed periodically commissions of enquiry into economic conditions," armed with "plenary powers to get at the truth," and where there was a corps of factory-inspectors, "competent, . . . free from partisanship and respect of persons. . . ." Evidently then ethical principles and conscience had a certain autonomy in determining the economic structure of society. And thus Marx found himself not quite able to deal with John Stuart Mill's challenge to historical materialism. For Mill in his *Principles of Political Economy* had above all emphasized that society's distribution of the national product depends on decisions that are not determined by the mode of production; its ethical values and choices could determine its laws of distribution. Here was a doctrine of sociological voluntarism; society, according to Mill, was not a system in which the different institutions stood in one-one relations of interdependence; rather there were alternatives from which the human will could choose. As Mill stated it, although the laws of production "partake of the character of physical truths," like the law of diminishing returns, with "nothing optional or arbitrary in them," it was quite otherwise with the laws of distribution: "Unlike the laws of Production, they are a matter of human institution solely. The things once there, mankind, individually or collectively, can do with them as they like." The distribution of wealth, wrote Mill, "is very different in different ages and countries; and might be still more different, if mankind so chose."

If mankind so chose—these words of Mill contravened Marx's historical materialism. For Marx had to hold that the mode of distribution was determined by the mode of production, in the last analysis, the technological foundation. His whole conviction that he had "proved" that the class structure of any given society was determined by its technical base was at stake.

Marx coped with Mill's problem, writing several drafts of an answer which found their way into the last pages

of the third volume of *Capital*. He clearly was at a loss
for an answer, for he fell back on a verbal dodge. He declared that the laws of distribution were just another name
for the laws of production: "The conditions of distribution
are essentially identical with these conditions of production, being their reverse side, so that both conditions share
the same historical and passing character." But then what
happened to his alleged proof "that the existence of classes
is only bound up with particular historical phases in the
development of production"? Was all this simply a matter
of words? What Marx indeed was doing was playing on
the ambiguity of "mode of production," which can refer,
on the one hand, to the given technology, and on the
other, to the socio-economic relations among people. By
smuggling the forms of distribution into the meaning of
"mode of production" as socio-economic relations, he
claimed that it was identical with the "conditions of production." But this, of course, provided no empirical argument whatsoever for the claim that the forms of distribution were determined by the technical foundation. Marx
found himself unable to answer John Stuart Mill.

Marx therefore began to move away from his own sociological determinism to something closer to sociological
voluntarism. This was shown above all by the character
and method of his last published work. To put it simply,
Marx turned from the dialectical method to survey research. Instead of trying to prove the necessary decline of
capitalist society and the necessity of revolution, he appealed to the French socialists of all schools to emulate the
example of the bourgeois British government and by helping to collect the facts concerning the workers' existence to
contribute to needed reforms. The dialectical, revolutionary phraseology was finally cast aside; one could work for
practical amelioration within the setting of the given mode
of production; the forms of distribution were not the reverse side of the mode of production; there were degrees of
freedom for intervention within and alteration of the socio-
economic relations. It was all stated by Marx in a preface

to a questionnaire of 101 items which he published in *La Revue Socialiste* in April 1881:

> The infamies of capitalist exploitation, exposed in the official investigations instituted by the British government; the legislation which these revelations compelled to be passed (limitation by law of the working day to ten hours, and the law concerning female and child labor, etc.) have made the French bourgeoisie still more fearful of the dangers which such an impartial and systematic investigation might conjure up.
> . . . we shall endeavor to launch such a questionnaire with the meagre funds at our disposal. In this we hope to receive the support of all urban and rural workers, who realise that they alone, with full knowledge of the causes, can describe the misery which they endure, that they alone, and no redeemer sent by Providence, can energetically apply the remedies to the social maladies from which they suffer. We count also on the socialists of all schools, who desiring social reforms, must know exactly and positively the conditions under which the working class . . . works. . . .
> This collection of labor data is the first task which socialist democracy must perform in order to prepare the social renovation.[25]

Evidently nothing came of Marx's attempt to bring survey research to the socialist movement. In his last years, however, his work was merging with those new currents of inquiry that by the close of the decade were to see the publication in 1889 of the first volume of Charles Booth's *Life and Labor of the People of London*. Dialectical arguments were giving way to empirical facts.

Thus Marx's Promethean complex evolved as his mythopoeic compulsion was confronted with the realities of historical defeat, with the failures of the working class to live up to the role he assigned them, and the failure of the capitalist system to fulfill his prophecies; war, race, and human irrationality thrust themselves on him. Finally he himself became tired of mythology, of ideology, and

---

[25] A. Lozovsky, *Marx and the Trade Unions* (New York, 1935), p. 117. Karl Marx, "A Worker's Inquiry," *The New International*, Vol. IV (December 1938), pp. 379–81.

turned to the prosaic inquiry of the survey researcher, with more modest aims of social reform.

Yet Marx's Promethean complex demands an understanding. He became the symbol of the intellectual joining his lot with the working class for the achievement of revolutionary goals. In a general way, Marx's Promethean complex was symbolic of the weaknesses and strengths of intellectuals. Let us therefore try to comprehend the character of this enigmatic man.

Marx was a professed fighter, a man of struggle. But no one among the nineteenth-century intellectuals seems to have been so utterly passive and incapable of taking the minimum actions to sustain himself and his family. With his children suffering and sometimes dying in his penury, with his wife rushing about desperately and borrowing money from a French refugee to pay for their child's coffin, one would have thought that this man of struggle would have tried to get a job. Perhaps he might have presented himself, as others did, as a candidate for teaching German literature or economic history at the University of London. Not so; to get a job was virtually unthinkable for Karl Marx. Only once in his life did he try to do so, when, as he wrote in December 1862, "to keep myself and my family off the streets," he finally decided "to become a 'practical man' " and applied for a position in a railway office. "Shall I call it good luck or bad? I did not get the post because of my bad handwriting."[26]

This Promethean who exalted struggle in myth and fantasy was himself the most helpless of men, relying on others to take care of him. This man who made "struggle" the center of his world system could not struggle himself. This authoritarian, would-be philosopher-king was essentially helpless in a competitive democratic system.[27] He

[26] Karl Marx, *Letters to Dr. Kugelmann* (New York, 1934), p. 24.

[27] Marx's wife wrote of him: "he who willingly and gladly helped so many others was so helpless himself." "Jenny Marx to Joseph Weydemeyer," *Reminiscences of Marx and Engels,* p. 239.

boasted in 1859 that he would not allow bourgeois society to turn him into a "money-making machine," but apart from the sacrifice he imposed on his family, there was a loss of self-respect, of manhood, in his readiness to live upon others' largess. To get *Capital* published, he went in 1861 to his Dutch uncle, the capitalist Philips, for money; ten years later he was appealing to his cousin August Philips to share in the cost of the translation.[28] Above all there was the lifelong ambiguity of his relationship with Engels. Nobody has yet calculated how much money Engels gave him, but the annual sums were occasionally near £1000.[29] Marx's wife was said to have regarded Engels as his evil genius, while Jung, an old disciple, "thought that Marx could not oppose Engels because Marx's family depended for years on the financial help they received from Engels. But this was a subject Jenny was most reluctant to talk about."[30] With good reason. For on the one occasion when relations between the two friends were strained by Marx's unfeelingness at the death of Engels' companion, Mary Burns, Marx blamed it in part on "her hysterical behavior" which "made me capable of thrusting my private needs on you. . . ."

Engels for his part led a strangely dual existence. In the daytime he was the diligent businessman in his father's Manchester firm, Ermen and Engels, working faithfully from 1850 to 1869. There is no record that he ever did anything about organizing his own workers into a trade union, no record that he ever sought to better their conditions at his factory, no record of any intervention on his part with the firm for its treatment of the proletariat.[31] In

---

[28] Franz Mehring, *Karl Marx: The Story of His Life,* trans. Edward Fitzgerald (New York, 1935), p. 324. Nicolaievsky, *op. cit.,* pp. 252, 369.

[29] C. J. S. Sprigge, *Karl Marx,* Collier edition (New York, 1962), p. 86.

[30] Rudolf Rocker, *The London Years,* trans. Joseph Leftwich (London, 1956), p. 97.

[31] Mick Jenkins, *Friedrich Engels in Manchester* (Manchester, 1951), pp. 9–10.

the evenings he fraternized with his fellow capitalists, and on weekends he rode to hounds with them, saying he was keeping fit for the military revolutionary responsibilities he would someday fulfill. His fellow capitalists never knew of his revolutionary ideas and writings, and Engels even served for four years, beginning in 1864, as president of the city's Schiller-Anstalt, helping to build its library. When Marx brought him into the General Council of the International, there were those who thought Engels' fortune was securing him his seat. At any rate, most of Marx's working years were lived in financial dependence on his friend, the Manchester textile manufacturer, a relationship of passivity toward a capitalist scarcely in keeping with the Promethean.

Was Marx indeed an activist, a committed fighter? Here too the curious passivity comes to the fore. He demanded authoritarian power, but he disliked the rough-and-tumble of politics. As Marx's wife wrote: "Karl and some of his closest friends broke completely off from the doings of the bulk of the emigrants and never took part in a single demonstration. He and his friends left the Workers' Educational Society. . . ."[32] He attended only one of the six congresses of the International Workingmen's Association. As his admiring follower Frederick Lessner described it: "The Congress at the Hague was the only one that Marx attended personally. He stayed in London, leaving to others to shine at the Congresses. When he at last resolved to go to this Congress, it was only to put an end to Bakunin's intrigues, once for all."[33] He was glad to have done with the International, to see it consigned to New York, and to return to his studies at the British Museum. Even prior to the decision to transfer the General Council to New York, Marx had decided, he said at Amsterdam, to retire from it

[32] Jenny Marx, "Short Sketch of an Eventful Life," in *Reminiscences of Marx and Engels*, p. 227.

[33] Frederick Lessner, *Sixty Years in the Social-Democratic Movement* (London, 1907), p. 56.

so that he could devote himself more fully to his scholarly researches.[34]

During the earlier years from 1850 to 1864, when he cut himself off so completely from political activities, some thought he had given up politics entirely. He and Engels took a perverse delight in being men without a party. Engels pronounced in 1851 that in exile "everyone must necessarily become a fool, an ass and a scurvy knave unless he withdraws from it completely and contents himself with being an independent writer who doesn't bother his head in the least about the so-called revolutionary party." To which Marx answered: "I very much like the public isolation in which we two find ourselves. It is quite in accordance with our attitude and our principles." Engels again responded on the joys of being free from a party: "we need no popularity and no support from any party in any country. . . ." "From now on we are responsible to ourselves alone. . . . For years we acted as though the ragtag and bobtail were our party, although we had no party. . . ." It was a remarkable confession that the *Communist Manifesto* had been a largely bogus document, speaking on behalf of a party that they regarded as a sham and for people whom they were convinced "did not understand even the elementary principles of our cause."

When Lassalle labored to have Marx's Prussian citizenship restored so that he could join with him in leading the revival of the German workers' movement, Marx showed scant enthusiasm for the project. He refused Lassalle's invitation in 1862 that they place themselves together at the head of the reviving workers' movement. He felt, apart from other reasons, that he could not interrupt his theoretical studies.

[34] Marx's daughter, Jenny, wrote in a letter of June 27, 1872: "He [Marx] is convinced that as long as he remains in the General Council, it will be impossible for him to write the second volume of *Das Kapital*, at which he has been unable to work during the last year. Consequently, he has made up his mind to give up his post as secretary immediately after the next Congress. . . ." *Archiv für Sozialgeschichte*, Band II (Hanover, 1962), p. 281.

What then was the ultimate source of Marx's Promethean complex? The explanation of the combination of traits in Marx's psyche—the exaltation of struggle joined with utter personal helplessness, the readiness to sacrifice himself for humanity joined with an utter contempt for human beings (he prefaced *Capital* with Dante's proverb, "Follow your own course, and let people talk")—still eludes us. He was a revolutionist and the most authoritarian of men, a rebel against the status quo who pictured himself as history's executioner, a political chieftain who hated to go to a political meeting and was most of his life reluctant to join any political party or group.

Unlike other famous Jewish sons, Marx hated his mother. In his innermost roots he had none of the reassurance of maternal love. If he was in Oedipal revolt against his father, it was not for love of his mother. And the curious helplessness he manifested in the midst of his struggle probably came from the lack of emotional ballast that comes with maternal rejection. At the age of fifty, he still recollected unpleasantly his mother saying in bad German, "If Karl had made capital instead of. . . ." He remembered his mother as stupid, without understanding, and suspicious of his activities. He wished she were dead, and when Mary Burns died, he wrote to Engels: "Instead of Mary, should it not have been my mother, who is full of bodily infirmities and has lived her life?"[35] His mother in 1862 would not give Marx in his desperate need a penny. And when she died in 1863, Marx's wife wrote that it would be hypocrisy to say that she had been sentimental at the news.

Marx's dislike of Henrietta Pressburg Marx reached back into his childhood, through his youth and manhood. She had evidently been the one member of the family who resisted the renunciation of Judaism; not until both her parents were dead would she consent to follow her husband's example of conversion. She complained in 1840 that Marx had become a stranger to his family, and she

[35] Nicolaievsky, *op. cit.*, p. 253.

thought his newspaper was a "fiasco." Marx in turn, com-
plaining in 1842 of "unpleasant family controversies," said
that although they were "well off" they were making difficulties that embarrassed him. The following year he wrote
bitterly that he had been engaged for seven years, and that
his fiancée had had to fight not only "the hardest battles"
with her own "aristocratic relations, whose twin objects of
worship are the 'Lord in Heaven' and the 'Lord in Berlin,'" but also with his own family. Years later Marx denied
that Jenny's relatives were actuated by anti-Semitism,
though his early letters suggest it was involved. His mother
felt that the relatives of Jenny von Westphalen humiliated
her. Probably she felt too that Karl, at the age of eighteen,
wishing to marry a girl four years older than he, was looking for a surrogate for herself. In Jenny's father, the old
Baron, who was interested in Saint-Simon, Karl Marx had
indeed found a new father, one so sympathetic to his Promethean impulses that Marx dedicated to him his doctoral
dissertation. When Marx at the age of twenty-five wrote:
"The Hebrew faith is repellent to me," he was we might
say writing down in ideological terms that he found his
mother and her ways repulsive.

The Promethean complex is basically different from the
complex associated with Napoleonic ambition. A Napoleon could venture forth, fortified by his mother's love,
with supreme self-confidence. Marx, choosing Promethean
revolt as his life's plan, a perpetual struggle against the
gods, was always to re-enact a search for self-confidence,
always seeking recognition as a god, always anticipating
rejection. His world was always to be one of struggle because he never felt secure in love. He took the eternal
Empedoclean duality of love and hatred, and suppressing
the love, warped in his relation to his mother, left only the
hatred as a motive force in history. It is indeed the rejected son who becomes the Promethean.

Marx's hatred for Judaism (otherwise inexplicable) was
the outcome of an animosity toward all that his mother signified for him. His youthful essay on the Jewish Question
was the confused argument of a man who hates his Jewish

heritage so much that he cannot bring himself to say plainly that he supports political and civil rights for the Jews. He derided Judaism; he hated the fact that the Jews, in contravention of the materialistic conception of history, had chosen to survive. "Judaism," he declared, "has been preserved, not in spite of history, but by history." Yet he knew the history of the Spanish and German Jews and their decisions to resist economic determination and to sacrifice their goods for their religious loyalties. He ridiculed the Jewish peddlers: "What is the profane basis of Judaism? Practical need, self-interest. What is the worldly cult of the Jew? Huckstering. What is his worldly God? Money." Yet his own historical knowledge should have led him to recognize what a figure of heroism the Jewish peddler was, this defenseless proto-bourgeois, this pioneer of trade, moving about through the uncertain apertures of closed, narrow, insulated feudal worlds, bringing goods, news, intelligence, himself, an itinerant rationalist, observing people's superstitions in different places, this huckster, with his pack on his back, traveling in fear of his life, in dread danger, and surviving the depredations of feudal knights and feudal mobs. This despised huckster was as noble a figure as any of the posturing actors in the revolutionary pantheon. But to Marx the Jew became the symbol for capitalist enterprise, and the Yankee by extension a Jew; the Jews were summarily informed they could be free only when capitalism was abolished. All this despite the fact that he relied on Jewish businessmen in Cologne to help finance his *Rheinische Zeitung*.[36] The Promethean rebellion against his Jewish origins became curiously united with his uprising against capitalism.

How directly Marx's anti-Semitism derived from his hatred for his mother is most remarkably evidenced by the special vindictiveness he bore for Dutch Jews. Marx's mother was, it will be recalled, a Dutch Jewess, who all her life spoke poor German. To the relatives on his moth-

---

[36] Adolf Kober, *History of Jews in Cologne*, trans. Solomon Grayzel (Philadelphia, 1940), p. 203.

er's side, the wealthy Dutch-Jewish family of Philips, Marx repeatedly turned for money. Of the Dutch Jews Marx wrote in ugly terms in one of his *New York Tribune* articles, "The Russian Loan," published on January 4, 1856:

Take Amsterdam, for instance, a city harboring many of the worst descendants of the Jews whom Ferdinand and Isabella drove out of Spain and, who, after lingering a while in Portugal, were driven thence also, and eventually found a safe place of retreat in Holland. . . . These men have their agents at Rotterdam, the Hague, Leyden, Haarlem, Nymwegen, Delft, Groningen, Antwerp, Ghent, Brussels, and various other places in the Netherlands and surrounding German and French territories. . . . Here and there and everywhere that a little capital courts investment, there is ever one of these little Jews ready to make a little suggestion or place a little bit of a loan. The smartest highwayman in the Abouzzi is not better posted up about the locale of the hard cash in a traveler's valise or pocket than these Jews about any loose capital in the hands of a trader. . . . These small Jewish agents draw their supplies from the big Jewish houses, such as that of Hollander and Lehren, Lonigswerter, Raphael, Stern, Bischoffsheim of Amsterdam, Ezekiels of Rotterdam. Hollander and Lehren are of the Portuguese sect of Jews, and practice a great ostensible devotion to the religion of their race.

Marx sank to an utter vulgarity as he described the crowds of Jewish agents in an Amsterdam office:

The language spoken smells strongly of Babel, and the perfume which otherwise pervades the place is by no means of a choice kind.

His hysterical hatred of the Jews led Marx to the verge of a conspiracy theory of history.

Thus we find every tyrant backed by a Jew, as is every Pope by a Jesuit. In truth, the cravings of oppressors would be hopeless, and the practicability of war out of the question, if there were not an army of Jesuits to smother thought and a handful of Jews to ransack pockets. . . . The fact that 1,855 years ago

Christ drove the Jewish money-changers out of the temple, and that the money-changers of our age enlisted on the side of tyranny happen again to be Jews is perhaps no more than a historic coincidence.

Thus, with heavy-handed irony, Karl Marx insinuated that it was no coincidence that "Jewish money-changers" were the villains of two thousand years of history. He was evidently going to drive them, as a new Messiah, from the modern temples. To such degraded writing and to such a distortion of history was Marx driven when the subject of the Jews was raised and his feelings of mother-rejection awakened. Here was the darkest source of the Promethean complex. Charles A. Dana, the managing editor of the *Tribune*, who got Marx's articles for publication, was ousted by his chief, Horace Greeley, in 1862. Among other reasons, Greeley said he had disliked Dana's publication of anti-Semitic articles. Marx had provided several of them.[37]

Marx's favorite metaphor for the process of social evolution, moreover, obviously reflected his mother-hatred. No other social theorist has ever spoken so much about wombs and birth pangs. "New, higher relations of production never appear before the material conditions of their existence have matured in the womb of the old society," Marx wrote in the preface of the *Contribution;* "the productive forces developing in the womb of bourgeois society create the material conditions for the solution of that antagonism." Again, in the preface to *Capital,* Marx sees the

[37] Marx wrote three such articles for the *New York Tribune.* Edmund Silberner, "Was Marx an Anti-Semite?" *Historia Judaica,* Vol. XI (April 1949), pp. 33–35. Charles J. Rosebault, *When Dana Was the Sun: A Story of Personal Journalism* (New York, 1931), p. 53. Also, cf. Frederick Engels, Paul and Laura Lafargue, *Correspondence,* trans. Yvonne Kapp (Moscow, n.d.), Vol. 3, p. 184. Marx's anti-Semitism also obtruded into *Capital:* "The capitalist knows that all commodities, however scurvy they may look, or however badly they may smell, are in faith and in truth money, inwardly circumcised Jews, . . ." Karl Marx, *Capital: A Critique of Political Economy,* trans. Samuel Moore and Edward Aveling (Chicago, 1906), p. 172.

practical contribution of social science as shortening and lessening "the birth pangs" of the new society. "In our days, everything seems pregnant with its contrary," said Marx, in a rare English speech in 1856.[38] The womb, of course, is a classical theme of imagery; psychoanalytical studies have explored the recurrent theme in myth, literature, and religion of the "return to the womb," the longing for the peaceful equilibrium of the mother's womb. But for Marx the womb became an object of constraint, of suppression; he is longing not to return to the womb but to emerge from it. Asian metaphysicians might long for the prenatal quiescence, when the individual was merged in the maternal environment, where there were no contradictions, no unsatisfied needs. Theirs, however, was a regressive dialectic rather than a "progressive" one. The rejection of the mother, the maternal womb, thus provides the most recurrent thematic imagery for Marx. It is part of the psychology of the Promethean complex, a man engaged in a mother-directed rebellion, ever uncertain of his manhood, and looking in the movement of history for a new mother to sustain him. The working class became a symbolic mother, and he hoped for himself, as he said of the Communards, that he "would be enshrined forever in the great heart of the working class."

Marx's mother-hatred, linked with his revulsion against both Judaism and capitalism, was also associated with his passivity, incapacity for personal struggle, and personal dependence upon Engels. Inevitably, it suggests an element of the fraternal sexuality which was part of the German revolutionary student culture which Marx imbibed and that persisted in his later personal habits as an eternal student. Marx's "most intimate friend" at the University of Berlin was Adolph Rutenberg, who, as a student activist a few years earlier, served several terms in Prussian prisons. It was Rutenberg who evidently introduced Marx to the exciting circle of student and university intellectuals, the

[38] Karl Marx and Friedrich Engels, *Correspondence, loc. cit.,* p. 90. Also Karl Marx, *The Civil War in France* (New York, 1933), p. 44.

Doktorklub of young Hegelians, and it was Rutenberg who, as editor in 1842 of the *Rheinische Zeitung,* brought Marx to the newspaper's staff. Marx, we might say, remained all his life fixated in the students' culture. A Prussian agent in 1853, when Marx was thirty-four years of age, described him: "Marx was leading a regular Bohemian existence. Washing and combing himself and changing his linen are rarities with him, . . . He often idles away for days on end, but when he has a great deal to do he works day and night with tireless endurance. He has not fixed times for going to bed or getting up. He often stays up for whole nights, then lies down fully clothed on the couch at midday and sleeps till evening, untroubled by people coming in or going out, for everyone has a free entrée to his house." When Marx got depressed, as he often did, he would take off several days to study, for instance, mathematics. He refused to leave the students' culture for the bourgeois world.

A personality of this kind is apt to have masochist traits, a tendency to extreme self-sacrifice by way of justifying its passivity, a self-punishment for the guilt of its own exploitation of others. Marx was aware of irrational forces within himself. His very first article on communism as editor of the *Rheinische Zeitung* in 1842 spoke of the "demons we can overcome only by submitting to them," and Engels, characterizing him in humorous verse at the same time, wrote:

> With clenched and threatening fist he rages without rest,
> As though ten thousand devils were dancing on his chest.[39]

A masochistic component indeed was evident among most of the young German Jews who became communists; Moses Hess, for instance, the "Communist Rabbi" who converted Engels to communism, married a prostitute in order to redeem her; Heinrich Heine proclaimed himself a communist even though he prophesied that after the rev-

[39] Franz Mehring, *op. cit.,* p. 121.

olution the workingmen's wives would have their groceries wrapped in the pages of his poems.[40]

Fixated in such a complex of hatred and longing, with a sensed inadequacy of his own masculinity, an intellectual like Karl Marx is especially prone to a conversionary experience; he yields himself to an identification with a lowly class endowed, he believes, with a physical power as well as a spontaneous spirit of affection and comradeship. Marx had such a conversionary experience in Paris in 1844 when he was working intensely on a history of the French Revolutionary Convention; "he was irritable and violent, particularly when he had worked himself sick and had not been to bed for three or four nights in succession," wrote his friend Arnold Ruge to Feuerbach. He was frequenting workers' meetings, deriving from them an unprecedented exhilaration, and writing that "at the communist workers' meetings brotherhood is no phrase but a reality, and a true spirit of nobility is reflected in the faces of these men hardened by labour."

Marx found himself enthralled by the workers' virtues, "their studiousness, their thirst for knowledge, their moral energy, their restless urge for development." In such a mood the Promethean spirit discovered its historic embodiment in the awakening massive physical and moral power of the proletariat. The object of Marx's science was henceforth to document and demonstrate the Promethean vision; the imperative was to transcribe the myth into reality, and for many years of his life the myth was transcendent even though with time it too was transformed, de-mythologized. Friedrich Engels meanwhile underwent a similar conversionary experience. He met in London three workingmen—a shoemaker, Bauer; a compositor, Schapper; and a watchmaker, Moll; "they were the first proletarian revolutionists I had ever met," recalled Engels. "I can never forget the profound impression these three men made upon me, a youngster at the time, just entering

---

[40] Antonina Vallentin, *Poet in Exile: The Life of Heinrich Heine*, trans. Harrison Brown (London, 1934), p. 247.

upon manhood." They were "three real men," said Engels, and he himself "had now the will to become a man." He recalled Moll and Schapper: "How often have I seen him and Schapper triumphantly defend the entrance to a hall against hundreds of assailants!"[41] To become a man! The Promethean search for manhood, revolt against the father-tyrant, prepared one's emotions for an ideological conversion. Thus Moses Hess with his "missionary zeal . . . won over a young man of twenty-two [Engels] in a single afternoon." That was how Marx described Engels' conversion; it had little to do with scientific evidence and the logic of hypotheses. Has there ever been a scientific socialist?

Marx evidently felt insecure to the end about the scientific validity of his ideas. His intellectual insecurity was such as to lead him to isolate himself from his intellectual contemporaries. All his life he was reluctant to meet men who were his intellectual equals. He could feel comfortable only as the unchallenged head of a hierarchy of admirers, but he drew back from the give-and-take of intellectual debate with trained scientists and thinkers. As Kovalevsky relates: "Many European writers of note, including Laveleye, vainly expressed the desire to be introduced to him. He kept aloof from them. . . ." Only among subordinates, among the awed artisans of the Communist League, for instance, who as Lafargue wrote, were calling him "Father Marx" even before he was thirty years old, could his Promethean unrest be stilled.

This quest for a society of subordinates to his intellectual hegemony threw a bizarre light on the unconscious goal of the Promethean rebellion. Carl Schurz, later one of Abraham Lincoln's generals and Secretary of the Interior in Grant's cabinet, saw clearly the authoritarian striving in Marx which moved his Promethean complex. He described the Marx of 1849, the editor of the *Neue Rheinische Zeitung:* "Never have I seen anyone whose

[41] Frederick Engels, *Germany: Revolution and Counter-Revolution* (New York, 1933), p. 121.

manner was more insufferably arrogant. He would not give a moment's consideration to any opinion that differed from his own. He treated with open contempt every one who contradicted him. Arguments that were not to his taste were answered either by mordant sarcasms upon the speaker's lamentable ignorance, or else by casting suspicion upon the motives of his adversary. I shall never forget the scornful tone in which he uttered the word 'bourgeois,' as if he were spewing it out of his mouth; and he stigmatized as 'bourgeois' by which he meant to imply the embodiment of profound moral degradation, every one who ventured to contradict him. It is not surprising that Marx's proposals were rejected; . . . and that, far from winning new adherents, he repelled many who might have been inclined to support him."

The sad thing was that Marx cut himself off from the European intellectual community because he could not hope to exercise the hegemony over them that he could over uneducated workingmen. Proudhon in 1846 had pleaded with him in vain: "Let us have decent and sincere polemics; let us give the world an example of learned and farsighted tolerance. But simply because we are at the head of a movement, do not let us ourselves become the leaders of a new intolerance, let us not pose as the apostles of a new religion, even though this religion be the religion of logic. . . ."[42] Marx broke with Proudhon.

He resented too the American society because its middle-class culture was exempt from the Promethean irrationality. America seemed to de-mythologize his fellow revolutionists; Willich, Weydemeyer, Heinzen, Weitling, Schurz, Jacobi—all found a new creativity in American bourgeois life, and shed their political myths as they responded to America's open possibilities and social realities. America seemed to provide a therapy for the Promethean complex. "The most advanced sons of labor fled in despair to the Transatlantic Republic," wrote Marx in 1864, and as

[42] George Woodcock, *Pierre-Joseph Proudhon* (London, 1956), pp. 92–93. J. Hampden Jackson, *Marx, Proudhon and European Socialism* (New York, 1962), reprint of 1957, pp. 52–54.

Engels observed in 1851, "the available Germans who are worth anything become easily Americanized and give up any thought of returning. . . . Those Germans who think of returning home are for the most part only demoralized individuals. . . ."

Marx himself stood in a curious relationship of gratitude and resentment to the Americans. The *New York Tribune* gave him the only long-term employment he ever had. Periodically Marx complained, as in 1857, that "it is really disgusting to be condemned to take it as a favor that such a rag admits you to its company"; he had given "these rascals," he said, "too much for their money." And Engels loyally derided the socialism of its managing editor, Charles A. Dana, as nothing but the "lousiest" petty-bourgeois cheating. The truth of the matter was that Marx was getting paid not much less than the managing editor himself, and as Engels wrote in 1853: "That Father Dana pays now 2 pounds and honors checks promptly is marvellous; . . . That Dana pays you without grumbling 2 pounds per article is the best proof of how firmly you sit in the Tribune." Such socialist disciples as Franz Mehring perpetuated the tale that Dana was a "hard-boiled Yankee business man" who "showed Marx every form of ruthlessness. . . ." Actually Dana, who had to go on strike to get his own salary raised to fourteen dollars a week, secured Marx a relatively preferential treatment. Marx lost his employment with the *Tribune* only after Dana himself was dismissed over differences stemming mostly from his more vigorous pro-Civil War stand.[43] Marx then appreciated

---

[43] The most recent Soviet version of Marx's severance is false: "One of the main reasons that impelled Marx to sever all relations with the *New York Daily Tribune* was its growing advocacy of compromising with the slave-holding South. . . ." Marx wanted to remain with the paper, but was dismissed; he never challenged Greeley's editorial policy. Cf. *The General Council of the First International 1864–1866* (Moscow, n.d.), p. 394. The details concerning Charles Dana's troubles with the *Tribune* can be found in Charles J. Rosebault, *When Dana Was the Sun*, pp. 28, 26; Candace Stone, *Dana and The Sun* (New York, 1938), pp. 7, 14; Charles A. Dana, *Recollections of the Civil War* (New York, 1902), pp. 1–2. Dana's

Dana's support, and acknowledged he missed the *Tribune* "sadly." In 1866, Marx wrote Kugelmann that he was trying without success "to re-establish my old lucrative connections with America." But the Promethean complex always required gibes at the newspaper and its managing editor because of the very fact that they did provide him with employment and a valued political forum. The Yankee newspaper became part of the feeding system, the mother, whom he repudiated. Nonetheless when Marx was being denounced as an agent of the Prussian government and was having to take time to write a book in his personal defense, it was Dana who wrote the most impressive testimonial on his behalf. Marx's Promethean complex, however, required struggle *à outrance,* and the Bourgeois Order had to be misperceived, if necessary, to justify struggle against each one of its parts. If the *New York Tribune* was growing in readership, that was *ipso facto* proof that it shared in bourgeois corruption. The Promethean complex had a compulsion for a lonely splendor of defiance.

As the years wore on, in the nightmare of personal incapacity, Marx at times recognized the hollow posture in his Promethean urge. To his daughter Laura a year before his death, he wrote that he was coming to Paris to find peace there: "By peace I mean family life, children's voices, the whole of that 'microscopic little world' which is so much more interesting than the 'macroscopic' world!" The Promethean drive became attenuated not so much because of the hatred of the gods but because of something far more corrosive—the hatred and meanness of comrades in their relation to each other, the insoluble tragedies of domestic existence.

---

testimonial on behalf of Marx, when Marx was being accused in 1860 of being an agent for the Prussian government, said: "You are not only one of the most highly valued, but one of the best paid contributors attached to the journal." Karl Marx, *Herr Vogt,* III, trans. J. Molitor (Paris, 1928), pp. 127–28. Also cf. Candace Stone, *op. cit.,* pp. 361–62, for Dana's obituary of Marx. George Ripley, as assistant editor of the *Tribune,* was receiving in 1849 about eight dollars a week. Cf. Charles Crowe, *George Ripley: Transcendentalist and Utopian Socialist* (Athens, Ga., 1967), p. 227.

A Strindbergesque shadow was cast on the Marx household. Their economic crises, physical illnesses, were only
part of the story. As Marx's wife wrote: "These were accompanied by rankling moral tortures of all kinds." Marx's
wife was beset by hysteria and nervous breakdowns. What
were the "rankling moral tortures" which weighed on
them? Probably the adultery of Marx with his wife's maid,
Helene Demuth, who served the family all her life, and the
birth to them of an illegitimate son, Frederick Demuth,
was a principal one. Marx as a young man had defended
such marital infidelity, and indeed had broken with Arnold
Ruge when the latter criticized a liaison of Georg
Herwegh. Marx's house servant, as Liebknecht describes
her, "was pretty," with "a good figure" and "pleasant and
attractive features." She evidently rejected her own suitors
to remain with the Marx family and was its dominant feminine personality. Engels wrote when she died: "It was
really due to her that Marx had peace to work for many
years, and I myself for the last seven. I don't know what
will become of me now. And I shall sadly miss her wonder-
fully tactful advice on party affairs." Engels interceded for
Marx, as he said, to protect him from a "severe domestic
conflict," and evidently supervised his illegitimate son's upbringing in a working-class home. According to Louise
Kautsky, Frederick Demuth looked "very much like Marx"
and had a "Jewish face." Other socialist comrades of Marx
knew of his existence, and the story later circulated in
socialist circles that Marx and Engels jestingly referred to
him as their "Communist Manifesto," another example of
their collaboration. But when Eleanor Marx learned the
facts from the dying Engels, who "wrote it down on a
slateboard for Tussy herself," she cried bitterly. Engels,
chagrined that Eleanor refused to credit the story and accused him of lying, had previously said that "Tussy wants
to make an idol of her father."[44]

[44] Werner Blumenberg, *Marx in Sebstzeugnissen und Bilddoku-
menten* (Hamburg, 1962), pp. 115–16. When I mentioned the fact
of Marx's illegitimate son in an article, "The Dilemma of the Soviet
Intellectual," in the *New York Times Magazine*, August 18, 1963,

At any rate, Marx, recurrently embroiled with his wife's hysteria, said in February 1862, that "a lousy life like this is not worth living." In 1858 he had wished himself a hundred fathoms deep under the earth, and then a few weeks later wrote that people with universal aspirations were stupid if they married and took on petty domestic miseries. In 1868 he complained he was "plagued like Job, though not so God-fearing." The Promethean complex provided a heroic stance for a young graduate student. But living by a myth finally entrapped one in a morass of unreality; one's revolt against the gods was a public posture belied by the helplessness of a hundred petty and sordid incidents. Marx struggled to convince himself that he was living by a higher personal ethic. He had sacrificed, he wrote in 1867, "health, happiness, and family" to finish his book: "I laugh at the so-called 'practical' men and their wisdom. If one wants to be an ox, one can easily turn one's back on human suffering and look after one's skin." But he had offered his children in sacrifice much more than himself. Prometheus never felt guilty for suffering he imposed on others. If one seeks for the psychological basis of Marx's rejection of politics at critical junctures, his destruction of both the Communist League and the International Workingmen's Association, it might lie in his periodic consciousness that the Promethean myth was hollow; August Willich and Michael Bakunin, with their respective compulsions for armed revolt, externalized the Promethean ingredient more starkly than he could, and made its incommensurability with reality too manifest for Marx himself.

The conflict with the anarchist Bakunin naturally produced a still further amendment of historical materialism. As a young communist, Marx had ridiculed any concern

---

Max Nomad wrote me: "I had heard about it in Paris in 1934 from Maria Reese (then a Trotskyist). She told me about Helene Demuth's story, and how Engels, to spare Jenny's feelings, took the responsibility for it, whereupon the child was referred to as the 'Communist Manifesto' because of their 'collaboration.' Maria Reese heard the story from Clara Zetkin whose favorite she was." (Letter of August 20, 1963).

for ethics, for moral principle. Morality, he had said in the *Communist Manifesto*, was to the proletarian "so many bourgeois prejudices." Confronted, however, with activists who practiced what he had preached, Marx, through Engels in 1872, took Bakunin to task: "It is one of his fundamental principles that keeping promises and the like are merely bourgeois prejudices, which a true revolutionary must treat with disdain. . . ." Marx, recalled Franziska Kugelmann, used to criticize Bakunin unsparingly. "He said his motto was 'everything must be ruined' and that it was absolute nonsense to destroy values, to pull down one's own and other people's houses and then run away without knowing where and how to build another one." Marx and Engels furthermore repudiated the Promethean student activists in Russia. All the latter were succeeding in doing, they said, was getting themselves sent into a useless Siberian exile; "the more serious" students, on the other hand, in their view, wisely were keeping out of secret political societies, and organizing instead practical mutual aid societies. Marx and Engels excoriated Nechayev, "the ideal type of the student," for his fraud, deceit, fanaticism, and amoralism. Twenty-five years earlier Marx had mocked at Moses Hess's ethical scruples. Now, as an old man, analyzing the Promethean complex among student activists, he found it was compounded of masochistic and sadistic ingredients.

As the Promethean motif became attenuated in Marx's last years, even his antipathy to Judaism noticeably softened. In 1877, Marx, vacationing with Eleanor at Carlsbad, met the greatest Jewish historian of his time, Heinrich Graetz, a man of the orthodox wing of Judaism. Marx liked him, sent him *Das Kapital* and *The Civil War in France* and chose him for the confidence that Eleanor was betrothed to the Frenchman Lissagaray. Graetz, on his part, told Marx his criticisms of the German Social Democratic party and sent him his book on *Koheleth* (Ecclesiastes), which he thought Marx as a secularist would like. The Preacher Solomon, wrote Graetz to Marx, was a realist who in the midst of a hypocritical world had the courage to preach the rehabilitation of the flesh (a Saint-Simonian phrase).[45] One could hardly have imagined the vindictive author of *The Jewish Question* finding the leading orthodox Jewish scholar of the era so personally and intellectually congenial; evidently some deep-seated reappraisals were going on in Marx. But Graetz was wrong when he said Marx was a secularist. When Marx's wife and an elder daughter attended the services of Charles Bradlaugh of the National Secular Society, Marx was displeased. "He had a dislike of secularism," said Eleanor Marx. He told them that if they wanted to satisfy their metaphysical needs, they should read the Jewish prophets.[46] The old Marx had come to recognize metaphysical needs in the human being. The Promethean anti-theology —"All gods I hate"—was an emotional obsolescent, a relic of restless generational striving rather than wisdom.

The Promethean myth in Marx was so de-mythologized at the end that it veered to its opposite—a myth of the decline and deterioration of humanity. A new friendship Marx formed was a symbol of this last intellectual phase. Marx's new friend was the noted biologist Edwin Ray Lankester, the first English scientist with whom he was on warm personal terms. To a Russian correspondent in 1881, Marx queried "whether Prof. Lankester's 'Chapter on Deterioration' is translated into Russian? He is a friend of mine." Lankester advised Marx on his choice of physicians during his last illness and stood among the small party at Marx's interment. His essay *Degeneration* questioned the "tacit assumption of universal progress—an unreasoning optimism." Lankester reminded both the rebels and smug Victorian England "that we are subject to the general law of evolution, and are as likely to degenerate as to progress." He challenged the Victorian ideology shared by its

[45] Salo W. Baron, *History and Jewish Historians* (Philadelphia, 1964), pp. 266, 447. Graetz's letter to Marx was published in *YIVO Studies in History*, Vol. II (1937), pp. 656–65.

[46] Max Beer, *Fifty Years of International Socialism* (London, 1935), p. 74. Also, Frederick Lessner, *Sixty Years in the Social-Democratic Movement*, p. 31.

thinkers from Herbert Spencer to Karl Marx. "Does the reason of the average man of civilized Europe stand out clearly as an evidence of progress when compared with that of men of bygone ages? Are all the inventions and figments of human superstition and folly, the self-inflicting torturing of mind, the reiterated substitution of wrong for right, and of falsehood for truth, which disfigure our modern civilization—are these evidences of progress? In such respects we have at least reason to fear that we may be degenerate." To all this Lankester appended an anxiety that "with regard to ourselves, the white races of Europe, the possibility of degeneration seems to be worth some consideration."

When Prometheus grew old, he wondered how much his rebellion had really brought liberation to humanity and how much his foreknowledge had been a bogus claim. Marx in his last years was afflicted by a "chronic mental depression," which his rising fame in Europe did little to alleviate. Engels to the end adhered to the Promethean myth, writing in October 1893, not long before his death, that "there is no great historical evil without a compensating historical progress. . . . Let fate be accomplished." It was in a spirit of historical masochism that Engels wrote: "But history is the cruellest of all goddesses, and she drives her triumphal car over heaps of corpses, not only in the war, but also in 'peaceful' economic development."[47] But Marx, observing his disciples and their quarrels, said: "All I know is that I am not a Marxist." The doubts, defeats, and reservations he had about the materialistic conception of history never left him. There were those who said his creative powers failed him in his last decade, when he failed to produce a single piece of sustained writing. But they overlook what was much more the case, that the life lived by a myth has its inward meaning shattered when the myth is de-mythologized. This was Marx's intellectual tragedy. He still had his role to play as "Father Marx" to

[47] Gustav Mayer, *Friedrich Engels,* trans. Gilbert and Helen Higlet (New York, 1936), p. 284.

visiting European socialist activists,[48] but otherwise he withdrew into his privacy, writing to his friend Kugelmann in 1874: "The more one lives, as I do, almost cut off from the outside world, the more one is caught in the emotional life of one's own circle." Not all his journeys for cures to Carlsbad could save the dissolving myth.

Marx came to recognize that mythology could be even more potent in modern times than in ancient. "Up till now it has been thought," he wrote in 1871, "that the growth of the Christian myths during the Roman Empire was possible only because printing was not yet invented. Precisely the contrary. The daily press and the telegraph, which in a moment spreads inventions over the whole earth, fabricate more myths (and the bourgeois cattle believe and enlarge upon them) in one day than could have formerly been done in a century."[49] It was his strange fate to have written the greatest mixture in modern times of myth and social science.

In a sense, Marx is the exemplar of the modern intellectual, with his noblest traits and weaknesses accentuated as in an idealized type. Marx's Promethean complex is the complex of the modern intellectual. True, only a few intellectuals have hated their mothers as much as Marx did, yet it is striking how the greatest of intellectuals, from Shaw to Einstein, have had similar traits of personal incapacity to cope with a competitive world, how often they too have found themselves possessed by the feeling of estrangement from this world, "alienated," as the fashionable phrase has it. If the eternal feminine has been strong in the character of intellectuals, they too, especially when they have found humankind wanting, have been attracted to the men of masculine determination prepared to reshape people by force to the pattern of virtue. From the Shaw of *On the Rocks* to Mao, Castro, Nkrumah, and Regis Debray, there is the continuity of a sociological world causal-line. For

[48] Lafargue noted that the members of the Communist League "called him 'Father Marx' before 1848, when he was not even thirty years of age. . . ." *Reminiscences of Marx and Engels,* p. 81.

[49] Karl Marx, *Letters to Dr. Kugelmann,* p. 128.

such reasons the culture of the intellectuals was given its impress by Karl Marx; the intellectual, with his longing for a political myth in which he could take his hero's part, found in Marx a supreme dramatic model. Weak himself, often lacking in physical power and confidence, he was strengthened by the knowledge that a powerful physical army of proletarians would march under his leadership. The new intellectuals, often displaced and misfitted in the capitalist order, compelled to work for employers they despised or to submit politically to cultural illiterates, saw themselves instated at last in the council of leadership. They would shed their femininity when they achieved, as Marx always longed to, an authoritarian power.

Thus it was that Marxism became the ideology of the emerging intellectual elite. It was indeed their "false consciousness" because they could never avow to themselves that their latent aim was to rule as philosopher-kings. They could speak with more passion and presumable sincerity when they felt they were urging the proletariat to emancipate itself. Yet the fact of the matter is that the working classes were almost always suspicious of Marxist socialism precisely because they sensed that it harbored the potential of a new dictatorship, that of the intellectuals.

A structural similarity of emotion, a psychological isomorphism, thus joins Marx with our generation of intellectuals. The New Leftist, like the Old Marxist, becomes periodically impatient with the slowness of social evolution; he then looks to wars and civil wars to hasten the process and give him his historical opportunity. A new version of Promethean mythology sees salvation emanating from a war of the countryside—Asia, Africa, Latin America—against the cities—North America and Europe. There seems to be no law of cumulative historical experience. Each modern generation seems to long to give itself self-destructively to its myths; it follows the path from Promethean grandiosity to the nothingness of Balzac's old painter. Somehow, however, one hopes that wisdom can disperse the powers of mythology; when it does, the intellectuals themselves will be liberated.

Marxism and the Hegemony
of the Intellectual Class

It is a remarkable fact that Marx and Engels provided no theory of the intellectual class. Why do intellectuals join the socialist movement? To this question, Marx and Engels had a parenthetical reply in a brief sentence in the *Communist Manifesto:* "a portion of the bourgeoisie goes over to the proletariat, and in particular a portion of the bourgeois ideologists, who have raised themselves to the level of comprehending theoretically the historical movement as a whole." This is as near as Marx and Engels came to providing a theory of the intellectual class, especially its revolutionary group. As a theory, it carries little psychological conviction, for it asserts a purely intellectual causation; it says that quite apart from any personal involvement of emotion, economic interest, or desire for power, the mere understanding of the laws of social development suffices to bring a section of the intellectuals to the proletarian side. As far as intellectuals are concerned, in other words, it affirms that existence does not determine consciousness, but that rather a purely theoretical consciousness determines existence. The revolutionary intellectual evidently then stands with Promethean exceptionalism against the whole materialist conception of history.

Whatever the underlying motivations of revolutionary intellectuals, they have not been determined primarily by the persuasion of a purely theoretical analysis. Can one say that all the personal sacrifices intellectuals have endured have been motivated by a desire to conform to a theoretical comprehension of the laws of social evolution? A profound dilemma, however, would have confronted Marx and Engels if they had tried to develop a theory of the intellectual class. They would not have been able to do so without abandoning either their materialist conception of history or their idea of the self-emancipation of the working class. In the first place, to have granted that revolutionary intellectuals are basically moved by ethical feelings, by principles of justice and equality, would have been a decisive departure from historical materialism. Marx and Engels utterly refused to acknowledge an independent role to ethical idealism in human history; they could never formally affirm that the ethical consciousness in history can transcend its material base. On the other hand, to have said instead that the revolutionary intellectuals were moved by the desire for power or economic self-interest would have meant raising a new specter to confront the proletariat—a new ruling class of intellectuals which availed itself of the workers' unrest to place itself in power. This was the dilemma that the intellectual class posed for Marx's sociology: either historical materialism was false or the advent of a new class society was likely, a problem for the Marxian system far more deep-seated in its significance than technical disputes concerning the law of the falling rate of profit. Marx and Engels met this dilemma by choosing not to discuss it.

The question of the intellectuals' hegemony, it must be remembered, was raised sharply in Marx's time. Marx's adversary, Bakunin, charged that the latent content of the Marxist program was "government by scientists (the most distressing, odious, and despicable type of government in the world)" which would constitute "notwithstanding its democratic form, a veritable dictatorship." Marx could only write the marginal note alongside Bakunin's words, *quelle rêverie*, and repeat his general view that class domination must last as long as the economic basis for classes is not destroyed.[1] But what if it were not a reverie? What if the workings of modern technology were compatible with the hegemony of a technomanagerial class?

Curiously, throughout their lives, Marx and Engels were sensitive to the authoritarian motivation of socialist intel-

[1] Henry Mayer, "Marx on Bakunin: A Neglected Text," *Études de Marxologie*, Serie S, n. 2 (1959), p. 114.

lectuals whom they characterized in probing, sardonic terms. Lassalle, the intellectuals of 1848, the German socialist students in 1879, the English Fabian intellectuals, were all, according to Marx and Engels, trying to establish themselves as dictators and managers over the workers. Lassalle's goal, said Marx, was "that of the future workers' dictator"; the people were to elect those "like himself armed with the shining sword of science into Parliament." Lassalle had indeed boasted to Bismarck that "the working class is instinctively inclined to dictatorship," and taken pride in his own dictatorial powers as president of their Association as an example of the leadership of the learned. Sixteen years later, in 1879, Marx and Engels wrote gloomily that the "educative elements," the university graduates, all believed that the working class "of itself is incapable of its own emancipation" and "must be freed from above." The later socialist student movement in Germany in 1890 similarly aroused little enthusiasm in Engels; these men were arrogant young declassed bourgeois, he said, "arriving just in time to occupy most of the editorial positions on the new journals which pullulate and, as usual, they regard the bourgeois universities as a Socialist Staff College which gives them the right to enter the ranks of the Party with an officer's, if not a general's brevet. . . ." They were evidently akin to the students, "those 'representatives of intellect,' as they liked to call themselves," who in 1848, according to Engels, "were the first to quit their standards, unless they were retained by the bestowal of officer's rank." The English Fabians finally were regarded by Engels with foreboding. They were, in his judgment, socialists who planned to establish the rule of the intellectuals over the proletariat; the Fabians, wrote Engels, "have understanding enough to realize the inevitability of the social revolution," but they are above all concerned with "making *their own* leadership secure, the leadership exercised by the 'eddicated.' "[2]

[2] Karl Marx and Friedrich Engels, *Selected Correspondence* (Moscow, 1953), pp. 388–94, 530, 537. Frederick Engels, *Germany:*

There were two components of historical inevitability as Marx and Engels conceived it, first, the economic inevitability of a planned economy, and second, the sociological inevitability that the workers emancipating themselves would achieve a social democracy. What theoretical ground could Marx and Engels provide, short of their own ethical aims and hopes, for asserting a sociological inevitability that would exclude the possible hegemony of the intellectual class? Marx and Engels, intellectuals themselves, believed that they had identified themselves wholly with "the proletarian outlook," but the intellectual authoritarians challenged the historical necessity of their identification with the working class. Then too, there was the vague, troubling doubt that even their own motives were mixed, that behind Marx's "Promethean complex" was also an authoritarian ingredient. The stormy Bakunin had not been the only one to rail against Marx's authoritarian ways. The English trade-union leaders who were delegates to the International Workingmen's Association were men accustomed to discussion, consultation, and democratic procedure. They found Marx impatient of discussion, insistent on ideological orthodoxy, and unilateral in decisions that disregarded democratic process.

Where intellectuals predominated in the Marxist movement, there authoritarianism became most pronounced. The Russian Social Democratic Labor Party, in which Lenin's authoritarian politics found its most fertile soil, was pre-eminently a party of intellectuals. "The intellectuals," wrote Lenin in 1904 in polemic with Rosa Luxemburg, "in our Party made up a much larger percentage than in the West-European parties."[3] Lenin on the face of it seemed to accept unreservedly Kautsky's theory that the intellectuals were not a class but a privileged social stratum. Kautsky like Marx had, however, continued to doubt

---

Revolution and Counter-Revolution (New York, 1933), p. 103. Frederick Engels, Paul and Laura Lafargue, *Correspondence,* Vol. 2, trans. Yvonne Kapp (London, 1960), p. 386.

[3] V. I. Lenin, *Collected Works,* Vol. 7, trans. Abraham Fineberg and Naomi Jochel (Moscow, 1961), p. 479.

the intellectuals, and advised the German Social Democrats to keep them in a subordinate position. Lenin, on the other hand, called on the intellectuals to transform themselves psychologically, to rid themselves of their liberal individualism, and to prepare themselves for the role of dictatorial, authoritarian rulers. This was indeed the most basic rupture of Lenin with classical Marxism, for he took on the character of spokesman for the hegemony of the intellectual class.

Karl Kautsky was indeed the first to use the formulation, later adopted by Stalin as well, that the intellectuals are not a class but a stratum: "the intellectual workers have this peculiarity of not having any common class interest and of having only professional interests; moreover, they are a privileged social stratum in opposition to the proletariat which wishes to put an end to all privilege." There was no hope, said Kautsky, of winning the "aristocracy of the 'intelligentsia'" to the workers' movement; many no doubt were being driven by declining economic circumstances into a situation that united them with the proletariat. Among the students, Kautsky agreed, there was an enthusiasm for socialism, but he placed little confidence in them. The student, he wrote, usually abandons his socialistic convictions as "childish ideas" when he enters "serious life." During his socialist phase, the student's superior education enables him to impose on the workers. A socialist student movement, Kautsky noted, may therefore become a danger to the movement as a whole: "where the proletarian movement is feeble and confused and where there exists alongside it a strong student socialist movement, the latter may come to dominate the former." The unreliable young intellectuals, said Kautsky, can then lead the movement into insane experiments. Fortunately, he added, such an outcome was not to be anticipated in Germany or in the greater part of the civilized world, where the student movement would remain only an "annex" to the workers.[4] With

4 Karl Kautsky, "Die Intelligenz und die Sozialdemokratie," *Die Neue Zeit,* Band II (1895), pp. 10–16, 43–49, 74–80.

unconscious prescience, however, Kautsky had stated the condition that in backward countries would assist the intellectual class to assume the hegemony of the socialist movement.

Lenin, on the contrary, explicitly called upon the intellectuals to become the bearers of bureaucracy. The word "bureaucracy" had no terrors for him; Lenin welcomed bureaucracy, and espoused it. He was the first, said the youthful Lenin, to analyze the concept of bureaucracy. "Bureaucracy *versus* democracy," he wrote, "is the same thing as centralism *versus* autonomism; it is the organizational principle of the revolutionary Social-Democrats as opposed to the organizational principle of the opportunist Social-Democrats." He ridiculed the "outcry against bureaucracy and autocracy" on the part of the Girondist-like Martov and *Iskra*. He extolled the alleged virtues of the factory-disciplined proletariat as compared to the "flabbiness and instability" of the intellectuals. The factory, said Lenin, was not only a means of exploitation; it was also a "means of organization" which inculcated discipline. Lenin had no use for the intellectuals' bemoaning of the alienation of man under modern technology: "Division of labor under the direction of a center evokes from him a tragicomical outcry against people being transformed into 'wheels and cogs.' "[5] He defended outright the authoritarian procedures of "excommunication," a "dreadful word" to the democrats. Thus, Lenin invoked a myth of proletarian discipline to impose a sense of guilt on those intellectuals who had imbibed the liberal tradition. Men like John Stuart Mill had painfully built during the nineteenth century a counterweight to authoritarian tendencies. Now Lenin, working to unleash the repressed will to authoritarianism, sanctified it by an appeal to the psychology of the proletariat. The party of the intellectuals was thus to rationalize its authoritarianism.

The authoritarianism of the intellectual class is a recur-

[5] V. I. Lenin, *One Step Forward, Two Steps Back*, reprint trans. (Moscow, 1947), pp. 52, 53, 81, 91, 94, 96, 103.

rent historical theme, yet its traits, characteristics, and sources have been little studied. When Lenin portrayed the authoritarianism of the working class, he was in large part projecting upon the workers traits peculiar to himself; the contemporary emphasis on working-class authoritarianism is perhaps similarly in large part a projection of the latent authoritarianism of intellectuals. What then are some of the evidence and sources of intellectuals' authoritarianism?

(1) There is an impressive tradition of philosophical Utopias beginning with Plato's *Republic,* going on through Campanella's *City of the Sun,* to the social diagrams in the nineteenth and twentieth centuries of Edward Bellamy's *Looking Backward* and H. G. Wells's *The Open Conspiracy.* These Utopias, a mixture of fantasy and blueprint, illumine the unconscious strivings and direction of the intellectuals. The Athenian philosopher, the Renaissance man, the American nationalist, and the English social evolutionist all shared the same vision of the rule of the scientific intellectuals. It diffused into the most distant regions as an awakener of intellectuals from social torpor. José Vasconcelos, ideologist of the Mexican Revolution of 1911, pondered Plato's *Republic,* and aspired to be the philosopher-king of Mexico. The rule of the scientist-philosophers was always to be authoritarian rule.

(2) From what psychological source does the authoritarian longing of the intellectuals arise? To answer this question, we must distinguish between the universal source of authoritarianism common to the intellectuals of all societies and those more situational roots of authoritarianism that are found in the frustrations peculiar to intellectuals in modern times. The intellectuals—in Marx's term, the "ideological class"—have in all societies felt themselves an aristocracy, an elite. Ancient Greek analogies of the state as an organism told how the head directed the hand. The intellectuals, from the time of the Pythagorean governing elite, regarded themselves as the representatives of the mind. They were indeed godlike; thought was, for instance, the unending joy and prerogative of Aristotle's God, and thought was likewise man's distinctive attribute. The intel-

lectual, the philosopher, was the representative of man at his highest. Immortality itself was made proportionate to intellectual acquirements by medieval Aristotelians; it was the lower classes who claimed eternity for the illiterate who were kind in heart.

The intellectuals conceived of themselves as meant to rule men. That was the purport of their philosophical knowledge. They were not warriors; they could not claim the right to rule by force and might. Yet in every age they have claimed that "the pen is mightier than the sword." They were often not men of property, yet they would claim, as Keynes did, that the power of ideas far exceeded that of vested interests. They were neither merchants nor artisans nor tillers of the soil, but stood somehow outside all conventional class systems. Without the laborer's skill or the rich man's wealth, they had only their intelligence and culture, but theirs was the calling to rule. The touch-stone of the rational and just society from Socrates' time on was the rule of the intellectuals.

In China, where the intellectual class ruled for two thousand years, their self-awareness as the elite most fit to govern was incorporated in the wisdom of proverbs:

"Without leaving his study, a Bachelor of Arts may understand the affairs of the empire."

"As a student—under one man; in office—over ten thousand."

"All scholars are brethren."[6]

Such was the intellectual's vocation to rule over all classes—his universal authoritarian propensity. Situational circumstances in modern times, however, ranging from his deprivation of power and employment, have bred in intellectuals a more acute authoritarianism. Situational frustrations have reinforced the role of ideas as the aggressive vehicles of dominance over others.

(3) The intellectual as a man of words has often suffered from a prolonged deprivation from action. There is a nor-

[6] Rev. W. Scarborough, *A Collection of Chinese Proverbs,* revised by Rev. C. Wilfred Allan (Shanghai, 1926), pp. 74–75.

mal biological pattern in the confrontation of problems; the problem provokes ideas, plans of action, which in the normal biological process find fulfillment in action. The rise of an intellectual class often means, however, a proliferation of thinkers who do not become doers. Thinking that does not culminate in action is, from the biological standpoint, a psychological anomaly. The very situation of the intellectual then carries with it a high degree of frustration—the outcome of a life in which important initiating stimuli to action are presented without any of the termini and consummations. The frustration of the intellectual breeds its counterpart of heightened aggressive energy. When social circumstances are most unfavorable and the hope of social action has dwindled, this aggression may be turned against one's self; the self-aggression of intellectuals is manifested in movements as diverse as monasticism and beatnikism. But where the desire for action is not subdued, it becomes imbued with the characteristics of behavior which has long been frustration-contained. The intellectual then tends to dictatorial, impatient, and ruthless modes of action. Pent-up aggressive energies tend to drive ideas to an extreme they would not have reached if those energies had been expended in action. Tocqueville said that the French intellectuals of the eighteenth century were led to the most extreme ideas because "their very way of living, . . . quite out of touch with practical politics," deprived them of the experience that would have tempered their ardor.[7] What is important, however, is not that experience confutes the schematic simplicities of a few general ideas. Rather it is that the frustration of inaction tends to make ideas into a displaced means of aggression. An extreme ideology is an idea suffused with displaced aggressive energy. The situation of the intellectual tends to make him into an ideologue.

The most eminent Fabian intellectuals thus became increasingly authoritarian as in the course of their long lives

[7] Alexis de Tocqueville, *The Old Regime and the French Revolution,* trans. Stuart Gilbert (New York, Anchor Ed., 1955), pp. 140–41.

they saw the transition of their ideas into action disrupted. Bernard Shaw in his play *On the Rocks* expressed the intellectual's self-disillusionment: "I am not a man of action, only a talker. Until the men of action clear out the talkers we who have social consciences are at the mercy of those who have none." Shaw went the gamut of an admiration for strong men which included Mussolini and Hitler, and gave way to an inner violence in which he justified the extermination of a social and political opposition. Sidney and Beatrice Webb, toward the end of their lives, had an unashamed reverence for Stalin's methods. The sundering of the thinking-action sequence made authoritarians of the most distinguished socialist intellectuals in democratic, industrial England.

(4) Movements whose membership has consisted primarily of intellectuals have tended remarkably toward an authoritarian pattern and exhibited traits of intolerance and procedures of excommunication. This has been true in science as in politics. One would have expected, for instance, that the psychoanalytical movement, born of the desire to liberate men from irrationalities, would have been characterized by a friendly exploration of differences and an overriding sense of common purpose. An intellectual movement, however, invariably centers around a strong father-figure; a scientific or philosophical school is usually defined methodologically by its adherence to a common method and basic hypotheses, but in a more basic psychological sense, it is constituted by the dominance of a particular kind of super-ego personality. Freudian psychoanalysis, for instance, was (in Erich Fromm's words) a " 'movement,' with an international organization on strictly hierarchical lines, strict rules for belonging, and for many years guided by a secret committee consisting of Freud and six other members. This movement has on occasion and in some of its representatives exhibited a fanaticism usually to be found only in religious and political bureaucracies."[8]

[8] Erich Fromm, "Freud, Friends, and Feuds: 1. Scientism or Fanaticism," *Saturday Review*, XLI (June 14, 1958), 11.

From a psychological standpoint, moreover, the intellectual can be said to have about him something of the feminine. The bookish boy growing up invariably finds himself at some odds with his less intellectual companions who regard him as "sissy" in his tastes. The young thinker later on finds that the battle of ideas has a terrible reality, and in the struggle of ideas, he finds his manhood as others did in physical conflict. Always however, as compared to "practical" men, the man of ideas is under a kind of onus to demonstrate his manhood. To do so he makes of his ideas weapons; he tries to be tough, and this indeed lends to his thought a strain of authoritarian compensational strength.[9]

(5) Political sects arise because intellectuals cannot stand differences in politics. The history of political sects is a history of intellectuals' intolerance and authoritarianism. By contrast, the large non-ideological American political parties, which embrace a variety of sections, classes, interests, and ethnic groups, and which are not led by intellectuals, have not shown a tendency to sectarian fission. In the American non-ideological parties, intellectuals have been relatively uninfluential.

Engels in 1847 noted that the socialistic sects were primarily composed of men outside the working classes, and that they looked to the "educated classes" for support.[10] During the Second Empire, when two socialist schools, the Blanquist and the Proudhonist, competed for the allegiance of Frenchmen, it was noticeable that the Blanquists, organized as an authoritarian secret society, were drawn primarily from students, while the loosely organized Proudhonists were chiefly composed of workingmen active in mutual aid, credit, and cooperative societies.[11] The law of

[9] Max Lerner, *Ideas for the Ice Age* (New York, 1941), pp. viii, 15, 98–99.

[10] Karl Marx and Friedrich Engels, *Basic Writings on Politics and Philosophy*, ed. Lewis S. Feuer (New York, 1959), pp. 4–5.

[11] Samuel Bernstein, *The Beginnings of Marxian Socialism in France* (New York, 1933), pp. 17, 28. Lucien de la Hodde, *History of Secret Societies and of the Republican Party of France from 1840 to 1848* (trans., Philadelphia, 1856), p. 110.

the extremism of the revolutionary intellectual in authoritarian sects was cogently formulated by James P. Cannon, the leader of the American Trotskyist sect, who wrote on the basis of a lifetime's experience: "It seems to be a peculiar law that the greater a party's isolation from the living labor movement, . . . all the more radical it becomes in its formulations, its program, etc. . . . You see it in the split-offs from the Trotskyist movement—our own 'lunatic fringe.' The less people listen to them, the less effect their words have on the course of human events, the more extreme and unreasonable and hysterical they become in their formulations."[12]

The revolutionary intellectual, in other words, is especially prone to sectarian behavior because he has been deprived of the continuous consummation of the transition from thought to action. An intolerant purity of principle enables him to make a virtue of his action-inhibited asceticism. His authoritarianism is the eruptive obverse of his impotence.

(6) The intellectual in the so-called backward areas tends to develop an authoritarianism proportionate to the gap between his ideas and the social environment; social reality for him is an ever present obstacle, stubborn and recalcitrant to his ideas. As an intellectual, his consciousness seeks to determine his existence; the more existence frustrates him, the more aggressive in idea becomes his consciousness. Both Mill and Marx observed that the intellectuals of materially backward countries adopted the most advanced ideas. A doctrine such as Saint-Simonianism, with its program of rule by the intellectuals, could only have arisen, wrote Mill, in a relatively underdeveloped country like France.[13] Marx remarked that the young Russian intellectuals in Germany and Paris "always

---

[12] James P. Cannon, *The History of American Trotskyism* (New York, 1944), pp. 10, 12.

[13] Richard K. P. Pankhurst, *The Saint-Simonians: Mill and Carlyle* (London, 1957), p. 15.

run after the most extreme that the West can offer";[14] his books, he observed, "had a greater sale in Russia than anywhere else. And the first foreign nation to translate *Kapital* is the Russian."

Ideas and practices that are found only among the most extreme sectarian, isolated intellectuals in the West have found a fertile transplantation among governing intellectuals in Africa and Asia. Kwame Nkrumah, Prime Minister of Ghana, tells how while associated in America with the Trotskyites, especially "one of its leading members, Mr. C. L. R. James," he learned "how an underground movement worked." A mode of organization out of place in America became the model for The Circle, a revolutionary African student group Nkrumah helped found; its members added a touch of tribal blood ritual to their dedication to an emancipated Africa. Later, when they were ministers of government, they synthesized Marxism with tribalism, and frankly expressed "the tribal impulse to destroy those who are out of step." The African intellectual elite quickly became, as K. A. Busia wrote, a ruling class.[15] In Ceylon, young intellectuals who had imbibed their doctrine from Trotskyite circles in London and from the eccentric authoritarian Scott Nearing in America emerged similarly from their underground Trotskyite movement to become members of a coalition government.[16] Debarred for years from participation in the political life of Ceylon, they had concentrated on ideology, and developed their ideological puritan intolerances. The most influential cabinet minister in 1957, Philip Gunawardena, disciple of Scott Nearing, had a simple question and answer: "Where do you find

[14] Karl Marx, *Letters to Dr. Kugelmann* (New York, 1934), pp. 77–78.

[15] Kwame Nkrumah, Ghana: *The Autobiography of Kwame Nkrumah* (New York, 1957), p. 45; K. A. Busia, "The Present Situation and Aspirations of Elites in the Gold Coast," *International Social Science Bulletin*, VIII (1956), 429; Peter Abrahams, "The Blacks," *African Treasury*, ed. Langston Hughes (New York, 1961), pp. 55–56.

[16] Calvin A. Woodward, "The Trotskyite Movement in Ceylon," *World Politics*, XIV (1962), 310–11, 315, 317.

democratic socialism? On the moon."[17] One hears much nowadays that authoritarianism is a necessary political means for the industrialization of a backward country. The facts, however, suggest that the authoritarian traits of intellectual chiefs lead them to choose that mode and speed of industrialization that is most expressive of their own authoritarian psychology.

(7) The intellectual class in modern times, furthermore, in both advanced and backward societies is most vulnerably situated with respect to the economy. England in the 1880s was already producing a surplus of intellectuals that the economy could not absorb. The "intellectual reserve army" was more articulate, resentful, and less resigned than the "industrial reserve army." William Clarke described the new "intellectual proletariat" in the first *Fabian Essays:*

Fifty years ago you could have gathered all the press writers of London into a single moderate sized room. Today all told they number ten thousand. Everybody with a pen, ink and paper and any capacity for turning out "copy" is a journalist; and you see at once that it is impossible for all these men to earn a living. They don't, and can't. . . . Now, while a workingman who has never known comfort, whose father has never known it before him, can often stand a frightful amount of poverty without getting desperate, the well-bred young man cannot; and the result is that the keenest and most dangerous discontent comes from the educated classes, who are leading the Socialist masses all over Europe.[18]

Where the intellectual experienced an economic system whose very workings deprived him of a livelihood or status, he tended to respond with a critique that was not only socialist but, in proportion to his frustration, authoritarian. Whether it was students in New York's city colleges or

[17] *New York Times,* November 23, 1957, November 25, 1957.

[18] William Clarke, "The Fabian Society," in *Fabian Essays in Socialism,* ed. G. Bernard Shaw (reprinted, Boston, 1911), pp. xxxvi–xxxix. Also Ernest Belfort Bax, *The Ethics of Socialism* (London, 4th ed., 1902), p. xi.

Kerala, India, facing the dismal prospects of a superfluous existence, or young teachers faced with insecurity, an authoritarian socialism emerged as a response.[19] The intellectual proletariat is probably the most authoritarian of all.

It would be a mistake, however, to conclude that economic resentment alone has moved intellectuals into the direction of authoritarian socialism. The few thousands of intelligentsia in Russia during the middle of the nineteenth century "could easily have been absorbed by the constantly expanding bureaucratic apparatus of the state or the growing range of the liberal professions." There were tremendous aspirations too of altruism, mixed with guilt-feelings at the people's lot, a desire to give one's self to the people almost sacrificially, combined with the longing for a free expression of one's individuality and talents. "It was a 'class' of expelled students and censored journalists, who in desperation were driven to conspiratorial extremes."[20] A psychology of "revolutionary asceticism" came to characterize the young Russian intellectuals.[21] Interwoven, however, with the ascetic self-denial was the conception of the intellectual as the historically creative individual, the one who bore the historical mission to redeem and rule.[22]

Authoritarian traits showed themselves among the Russian revolutionary intellectuals in a variety of ways. The anti-Jewish feeling, for instance, of the Narodnaya Volya in the 1880s went as far as a positive endorsement of pogroms. French socialist sects were similarly involved in anti-Semitism. Curiously the more proletarian German So-

[19] Robert W. Iversen, *The Communists and the Schools* (New York, 1959), pp. 150–52. On the Indian student, cf. *New York Times,* July 15, 1959, February 8, 1960.

[20] Martin Malia, "What is the Intelligentsia?" in *The Russian Intelligentsia,* ed. Richard Pipes, pp. 14–15. For the later period, cf. Vera Figner, *Memoirs of a Revolutionist,* trans. Camilla Chapin Daniels (New York, 1927), pp. 36–37, 76–77. I. Steinberg, *Spiridonova: Revolutionary Terrorist,* trans. Gwenda David and Eric Mosbacher (London, 1935), pp. 32–33.

[21] Nicolas Berdyaev, *Dream and Reality,* an essay in autobiography, trans. Katharine Lampert (New York, 1951), p. 113.

[22] Vera Figner, *op. cit.,* p. 63.

cial Democratic party, much less intellectual in its composition and leadership, was relatively free of anti-Semitism.
Although the academic *Kathedersozialisten* were decidedly
tinged with anti-Jewish prejudice, "there were occasions
when the Social Democratic workers made it a point of
honor to demonstrate the feelings of devotion and solidarity with leaders who were attacked twice, for being Socialists and being Jews."[23]

Lenin insisted in *What Is to Be Done?* that it was the
intellectuals who brought socialist consciousness to the
workers who otherwise would not advance beyond trade-
union consciousness. Was the conception of a socialist
society so difficult that it demanded much scientific training? In many places and many times, in Germany, for
instance, in the early 1830s, small groups of workingmen
had periodically from their own ethical and intellectual
resources sought to fashion for themselves communistic
societies.[24] What the intellectuals brought to the socialist
movement was not socialist consciousness but the notion of
their own elite authoritarianism. The socialist consciousness itself does not require any elaborate theoretical analysis but springs up indeed spontaneously from the ethical aspirations of all exploited people. What Lenin was
doing was rather to provide an ideological basis for the
hegemony of the intellectual elite.

Two impulses have always warred within the socialist
tradition, an authoritarian and a democratic, for socialism
indeed has emanated from two basically different psychological sources—one the desire of the intellectuals to be
the ruling class, the other the desire of the working class
for a society of equals. Engels called Saint-Simon an Utopian Socialist, but Saint-Simon, a child of the *philosophes,*

[23] Edmund Silberner, "Two Studies on Modern Anti-Semitism,"
Historia Judaica, XIV (1952), 104–06. Paul W. Massing, *Rehearsal
for Destruction: A Study of Political Anti-Semitism in Imperial Germany* (New York, 1949), pp. 202–03. Avrahm Yarmolinsky, *Road
to Revolution* (New York, 1959), pp. 308–09.

[24] Boris Nicolaievsky and Otto Maenchen-Helfen, *Karl Marx:
Man and Fighter,* trans. Gwenda David and Eric Mosbacher (New
York, 1936), p. 78.

plainly advocated the authoritarian rule of the intellectuals, and won numerous adherents among the engineering graduates of the Ecole Polytechnique, the new "industrial priests." Can it be that Marxism with its faith in a democratic, liberal working class, achieving its own emancipation, was daring to be far more Utopian? The authoritarian and liberal components were both present in the socialism of Marx and of Engels from their earliest writings in an unstable equilibrium. Engels indeed first claimed in 1843 that German socialism was superior to the French because of its freedom from democratic prejudices, and he envisaged the socialist society not as a workers' democracy but as ruled by a technical intelligentsia chosen "not by a majority of the community at large" but by an examination system.[25] Two years later, impressed by the reports of the American socialist communities, his socialism became more communitarian, less elitist. And Marx's socialism evolved in a more democratic spirit from the time when he wrote in 1844 in typical elitist fashion: "The head of the emancipation is philosophy, its heart is the proletariat."

But this is the eternal strife in the heart of socialism itself, the problem of the future, the strife between the authoritarian and liberal elements; it sets for the intellectual class the question how it will define its own character.

[25] Friedrich Engels, "The State of Germany," in Karl Marx, Friedrich Engels, *Historisch-Kritische Gesamtausgabe,* Erste Abteilung, Band 4 (Berlin, 1932), p. 494.

What Is Alienation?
The Career of a Concept

Every age has its key ethical concept around which it can best formulate the cluster of its basic problems. "Duty" summated for Kant the meaning of life in the Prussian bureaucratic and pietistic society; "peace" was the basic longing of Hobbes living in England's time of civil war; "happiness" defined for Bentham the aims of a middle-class England which was challenging the rule of a landed aristocracy. Twenty-five years ago, the concept of "exploitation" was the focus of most socialist and liberal political philosophy. Today many thinkers would replace it with the concept of "alienation," which has indeed become the central one for the neo-revisionist school of Marxism. By "alienation," says Erich Fromm, "is meant a mode of experience in which the person experiences himself as an alien. He has become, one might say, estranged from himself."[1] Thus, neo-revisionism introduces an unusual emphasis into the history of socialist thought. The classical revisionism of Eduard Bernstein aimed to supplant the materialist negation of ethics with a "back to Kant" movement. Where Marx and Engels looked at ethical ideas as the epiphenomenal by-products of class struggle, Bernstein and Jaurès sought a universalistic ethic with its formal expression in Kant's categorical imperative.

Neo-revisionism today returns not to Kant but to the youthful Marx who in manuscripts, sometimes unpublished, wrote down an ethical critique of capitalism. Marxism, aged, bureaucratized, and de-ethicized in the Soviet society, is being rejuvenated by young Marxists in Europe and America with the repressed and rejected ethical writings of the young Marx. In the past, the history of socialist

---

[1] Erich Fromm, *The Sane Society* (New York, 1955), pp. 110, 120.

thought has shown a certain oscillation between economics and ethics. During times of economic depression and distress, the socialist argument has tended to consist primarily of a demonstration that the economic system was beset by contradictions, disequilibria between production and consumption, which were insoluble in a capitalist society. In times of prosperity and rising living standards, on the other hand, the socialist argument has become primarily an ethical one of the disvalues of human life in capitalist society. Classical revisionism thus reflected the betterment in the life of the Western European working class at the end of the last century. Neo-revisionism today is a critique of both communist and capitalist societies, in their age of coexistent affluence, from the standpoint of the ethical aims of all human society.

In the Soviet Union itself, younger philosophers, evidently restive with the received bureaucratized version of Marxism are turning to the younger Marx, the philosopher of alienation, to express their own disaffection with the bureaucratized world. An act of publication of Marx's writings in the Soviet Union is a political decision. In this sense, the recent publication in Moscow of Russian editions and English translations of Marx's *Economic and Philosophic Manuscripts of 1844* and his and Engels' *The Holy Family* betokens an interest in the underlying ethical source of Marxism, that ethic from which Marx and the Marxists became "alienated" in later years. The recovery of ethical consciousness in Marxist circles tends naturally, as long as Marxism itself is not rejected, to proceed by way of recovery of the forgotten, repressed ethical writings of Marx. It is a devious, tradition-bound avenue to the recovery of ethical consciousness, especially since the socialist ethic emerges with greater purity in the writings of such men as William Morris. Neo-Marxism throughout the world is clearly, however, finding a temporary conceptual halfway house in "alienation."

To evaluate the significance of the revival of "alienation," let us ask the following questions:

(1) What was the meaning and use of "alienation" in Marx's thought?

(2) What accounts for the appeal of the concept "alienation" among American intellectuals?

(3) What does "alienation" signify today? Is it a useful concept for understanding societies?

The concept "alienation" has a lineage one can trace right back to Calvin who saw man alienated through all time from God by his original sin.[2] Calvin wrote with eloquence that "spiritual death is nothing else than the alienation of the soul from God, we are all born as dead men, and we live as dead men, until we are made partakers of the life of Christ."[3] Hegel imbibed the concept of alienation from pessimist Protestant theology, and the early Marx in turn, like his fellow Hegelians, regarded man's history as one of alienation. His youthful *Economic and Philosophic Manuscripts* depicted alienation as the essence of the capitalist order: "Private property is therefore the product, the necessary result of alienated labor, of the external relation of the worker to nature and to himself." Alienated man experienced himself not as an agent but as patient, not as creator but creature, not as self-determined but other-determined. The products of man's labor were transformed "into an objective power above us, growing out of our control, thwarting our expectations, bringing to naught our calculations. . . ." Because he was alienated from the product of his labor, man also became alienated from other men.[4] This estrangement from the human essence leads, in Fromm's words, to an "existential egotism," or as Marx stated it, man becomes alienated from

[2] Erich Fromm in his stimulating *Marx's Concept of Man* (New York, 1961) mistakenly says that "the thinker who coined the concept of alienation was Hegel." Cf. p. 47.

[3] John Calvin, *Commentaries on the Epistles of Paul to the Galatians and Ephesians*, trans. Rev. William Pringle (Grand Rapids, 1948), p. 219; *Commentaries on the Catholic Epistles*, trans. Rev. John Owen (Grand Rapids, 1948), p. 162.

[4] See the various passages from Marx cited in Erich Fromm, *Marx's Concept of Man*, pp. 52–53.

"his own body, external nature, his mental life, and his *human* life."

Now the evidence is strong that during the latter 1840s, Marx and Engels came to reject emphatically the use of the concept "alienation" as the foundation for their socialism. Their *Communist Manifesto* ridiculed in scathing terms the German True Socialists who refurbished the economic sense of the French socialists with their metaphysical nonsense of "alienation": "They wrote their philosophical nonsense beneath the French original. For instance, beneath the French criticism of the economic functions of money they wrote *Alienation of Humanity*. . . ."[5] For the fact of the matter is that "alienation" as first used by Marx, Engels, and their fellow young Hegelians and Feuerbachians was a romantic concept, with a preponderantly sexual connotation. It was the language of a group that made a protest of romantic individualism against the new capitalist civilization, but that soon went on to its post-adolescent peace with bourgeois society. Marx and Engels discarded a concept that became alien to their own aims.

To have developed the concept "alienation" would have meant for Marx and Engels to have taken a direction Freud later took; they would have had to study the forms of alienation, that is, neuroses, of bourgeois society, and, if "alienation" proved to be a universal concept, the modes of alienation common to all societies. "Alienation," however, was too much the catchword of the romantic intellectuals with their personal drama of temporary estrangement in an industrial civilization. Alienation moved a handful of poets and professors, who achieved their therapy with a few poems and treatises. The masses of men, on the other hand, were moved to action by exploitation.

The concept "alienation" expressed the striving of the romantic movement, the recovery of spontaneous emotional life. There was a revulsion against sexual asceticism,

---

[5] Karl Marx and Friedrich Engels, *Basic Writings on Politics and Philosophy,* ed. Lewis S. Feuer (New York, 1959), p. 33.

a rediscovery among the German intellectuals of physical pleasure. German philosophy, the product of theological seminaries, had negated the human body; the new philosophers, disciples of Ludwig Feuerbach, affirmed it. The root meaning of "alienation" for Feuerbach was, it must be emphasized, sexual; the alienated man was one who had acquired a horror of his sexual life, and whose whole way of thinking was determined by this repression of sexuality. The critique of religion was so important for Feuerbach precisely because religious dogma was the manifestation of this sexual alienation. We might cite a few passages in which Feuerbach states the primary, sexual meaning of "alienation":

The more man alienates himself from Nature . . . the greater the horror he has of Nature, or at least of those natural objects and processes which displease his imagination, which affect him disagreeably. . . . That which does not please him, which offends his transcendental, supranatural, or antinatural feelings ought not to be. . . . Thus the idea of the pure, holy Virgin pleases him; still he is also pleased with the idea of the Mother. . . . Virginity in itself is to him the highest moral idea, the *cornu copiae*, of his supranaturalistic feelings and ideas, his personified sense of honour and of shame before common nature. . . . Even the arid Protestant orthodoxy, so arbitrary in its criticism, regarded the conception of the God-producing Virgin as a great, adorable, amazing holy mystery of faith, transcending reason. . . .

Now if abstinence from the satisfaction of the sensual impulse, the negation of difference of sex and consequently of sexual love,—for what is this without the other?—is the principle of the Christian heaven and salvation; then necessarily the satisfaction of the sexual impulse, sexual love, on which marriage is founded, is the source of sin and evil. . . . The mystery of original sin is the mystery of sexual desire.[6]

Alienation in a philosophical sense, that is, the denial of the reality of the material world, was the consequence

[6] Ludwig Feuerbach, *The Essence of Christianity*, trans. George Eliot (reprinted, New York, 1957), pp. 136–38, 311. The Saint-Simonian school had previously made a central tenet of the "rehabilitation of the flesh."

of the religious alienation from sexuality. As Feuerbach stated it: "Separation from the world, from matter, from the life of the species, is therefore the essential aim of Christianity." Sexual asceticism was the source of the idealist metaphysics: "Pleasure, joy, expands man; trouble, suffering, contracts and concentrates him; in suffering man denies the reality of the world. . . ."[7]

To overcome alienation signified for Feuerbach the overcoming of the Christian heritage of masochism and the emotions and thought-ways of clerical celibacy. To Marx, writing in 1844 as a Feuerbachian, the sexual meaning of "alienation" was still central. The ultimate human relationship that provided the criterion for the evaluation of societies was for the young Marx the sexual:

> The direct, natural, and necessary relation of person to person is the *relation of man to woman*. . . . In this relationship, therefore, is *sensuously manifested,* reduced to an observable fact, the extent to which the human essence has become nature to man. From this relationship one can therefore judge man's whole level of development . . . ; the relation of man to woman is the most natural relation of human being to human being.[8]

The alienation of man from himself signified that his natural human emotions had been distorted. *Alienation signified a mode of life in which man was being compelled by social circumstances to act self-destructively,* to cooperate in his own self-mutilation, his castration, that is, the destruction of his own manhood. The economy that men had created presumably to satisfy their needs was finally warping their deepest instincts. Repeatedly the young

[7] *Ibid.,* pp. 161, 185. Feuerbach, the precursor of Freud in the psychology of religion, probed into the origin of religious dogmas in sexual asceticism. Cf. William B. Chamberlain, *Heaven Wasn't his Destination: The Philosophy of Ludwig Feuerbach* (London, 1941), pp. 60–61. Engels, in his old age, wrote energetically against Feuerbach's philosophy of "sex-love." Cf. *Basic Writings,* pp. 216 ff.

[8] Karl Marx, *Economic and Philosophic Manuscripts of 1844,* trans. Martin Milligan (Moscow, n.d.), p. 101.

Marx and Engels characterized the bourgeois society in metaphors and actualities of sexual alienation. Economic exploitation eventuated in the mutilations of sexual alienation. Thus Engels wrote in his *The Condition of the Working-Class in England* how bourgeois society "unsexes" the human being:

And yet this condition which unsexes the man and takes from the woman all womanliness, this condition, which degrades, in the most shameful way, both sexes, and through them, Humanity, is the last result of our much-praised civilization . . . ; we must admit that so total a reversal of the position of the sexes can have come to pass only because the sexes have been placed in a false position from the beginning.[9]

In these early writings, Marx and Engels, as Freudian forerunners, regarded love, not work, as the source of man's sense of reality. They wrote in *The Holy Family* against the idealistic subjectivists who could not recognize "love, which first really teaches man to believe in the objective world outside himself, which not only makes man an object, but the object a man!"[10]

The German idealistic intellectuals, whom Marx called the "Critical Critics," were estranged from reality, precisely because they repressed the natural sexual senses of love and tried with all sorts of metaphysical devices to spiritualize its reality: "Critical criticism must first seek to dispose of *love*. Love is a passion, and nothing is more dangerous for the calm of knowledge than passion." The alienated intellectuals use linguistic tricks to transform love into "a theological thing":

by making *"love"* a being apart, separate from man and as such endowed with independent being. By this simple process, by

[9] Frederick Engels, *The Condition of the Working-Class in England*, trans. Florence Kelley Wischnewetzky, in Karl Marx and Frederick Engels, *On Britain* (Moscow, 1953), p. 179.

[10] Karl Marx and Frederick Engels, *The Holy Family, or Critique of Critical Critique,* trans. R. Dixon (Moscow, 1956), p. 32.

changing the predicate into the subject, all the attributes and manifestations of human nature can be Critically transformed into their opposite and *estrangements*.[11]

Underlying the philosophers' misuse of language, according to Marx and Engels, were psychological motivations to repress the world of flesh and material reality. Socio-psychological analysis, in psychoanalytical fashion, established when a linguistic estrangement from reality was taking place. Critical Criticism eventuated in alienation because its masochistic motivation sundered man from himself and the external world: Critical Criticism was thus "a Moloch, the worship of which consists in the self-immolation and suicide of man, and in particular of his *ability to think*." "But love is an un-Critical, un-christian materialist," continued Marx and Engels. Sexual repression led to the impairment of the sense of reality, and consequently to ideological devices that substituted abstractions for things; the liberation of love led to a renewed sense of citizenship in the universe.

With heavy-handed humor, Marx and Engels satirized the critical ideologists who substituted the idealistic category of Dancing for the frank sensuality of the cancan:

The reverend parson [Szeliga] speaks here neither of the *cancan* nor of the *polka*, but of dancing in general, of the *category* Dancing, which is not performed anywhere except in his Critical cranium. If he saw a single dance at the Chaumière in Paris his Christian-German soul would be outraged by the boldness, the frankness, the graceful petulance and the music of that most sensual movement.

The dancers "give the spectator the inspiring impression of frank human sensuality"; they "can and must necessarily be frankly sensual human beings!" The anti-sensual Critic substitutes an essence for existence: "The Critic introduces us to the ball for the sake of the *essence of dancing*."[12]

---

[11] *Ibid.*, pp. 31–32.
[12] *Ibid.*, pp. 91–92.

Marx's tribute to the cancan would have outraged Khrushchev who with Bolshevik virtue railed at Hollywood for the cancan's immorality.

The idealistic metaphysicians, according to the young Marx and Engels, aim to deprive love of its bodily reality:

> As soon as there is no more nervous current and the blood in the veins is no longer hot, the *sinful body,* the seat of sensual lust becomes a *corpse* and the souls can converse unhindered about "general reason," "true love," and "pure morals." The parson debases sensuality to such an extent that he abolishes the very elements which inspire sensual love—the rush of the blood, which proves that man does not love only by insensitive phlegm; the nervous current which connects the organ that is the main seat of sensuality with the brain. He reduces true sensual love to the *mechanical secretio seminis* and lisps with an ill-renowned German theologian: "Not for the sake of sensual love, not for the lust of the flesh, but because the Lord said, increase and multiply."[13]

Eugene Sue, the author of *Les Mystères de Paris,* had similarly mystified over the sexual attraction of one of his characters, Cecily, a slave. Marx and Engels saw no point in mystifying about this attraction: "The mystery of Cecily is that she is a *half-breed.* The mystery of her sensuality is the *heat of the tropics."*[14] Behind every religious and philosophical mystery was an alienation of man's sexual nature from himself. Thus Marx and Engels rail against the "puritan sermon" which spins its unreal web of "the mystery of the mystery, the essence of the essence" of love.[15]

At this time Marx and Engels did not regard class struggle as humanity's lever for the achievement of communism. Their definition of communism omitted any reference to class struggle. Communism they defined as the

[13] *Ibid.,* pp. 88–89.
[14] *Ibid.,* p. 93.
[15] *Ibid.,* pp. 86–88.

"complete return of man to himself as a social (i.e., human) being—a return become conscious . . . it is the *genuine* resolution of the conflict between man and nature and between man and man—the true resolution of the strife between existence and essence, between objectification and self-confirmation, between freedom and necessity, between the individual and the species."[16]

Communism for Marx and Engels constituted at this time the overcoming of all alienation. The sexual overtones of "alienation" persisted as they tended to generalize the concept to signify the subjective state that accompanies any situation of emotional frustration that is the outcome of man's own misconceived social behavior and social arrangements. They expressed the hatred of commercialism common to the romantic school, which regarded bourgeois society as having alienated man from his sexuality; money, in Shakespeare's words, was the "common whore of mankind." "Money is the alienated ability of mankind," and it enables the ugly man, contrary to nature, to secure the loveliest woman: "I am ugly, but I can buy for myself the most *beautiful* of women. Therefore I am not *ugly*, for the effect of *ugliness*—its deterrent power—is nullified by money."[17] Money is an "overturning power," a destroyer of "individualities." Money makes man's love impotent: "Assume *man* to be *man* and his relationship to the world to be a human one: then you can exchange love only for love, trust for trust, etc." But, "if you love without evoking love in return . . . then your love is impotent—a misfortune."[18] In short, when love is transformed into a self-destructive experience which gives masochist traits to the character, man has been alienated, self-estranged from his essence, by the rule of money. For in bourgeois society, "you must make everything that is yours saleable"; the tyranny of the competitive market crushes "all sympathy, all trust." Political economy wars with human

[16] *Economic and Philosophic Manuscripts of 1844*, p. 102.
[17] *Economic and Philosophic Manuscripts*, pp. 136–38.
[18] *Ibid.*, pp. 138–41.

nature, "the ontological essence of human passion." Political economy castrates both capitalists and workingmen. The workingmen are asked by bourgeois economy to give up sexuality altogether. The Malthusian ideologists with their anti-sexual motivation propose that the workingmen "prove themselves continent in their sexual relations. . . . Is not this the ethics, the teaching of asceticism?"[19] Bourgeois political economy and a humanist ethics are at loggerheads. Political economy becomes the anti-human ideology of asceticism:

The science of marvellous industry is simultaneously the science of asceticism. . . . Self-denial, the denial of life and of all human needs, is its cardinal doctrine. The less you eat, drink and read books; the less you go to the theatre, the dance hall, the public-house; the less you think, love, theorize, sing, paint, fence, etc., the more you *save*—the *greater* becomes your treasure, which neither moths nor dust will devour—your *capital*. The less you *are,* the more you *have;* the less you express your own life, the greater is your alienated life—the greater is the store of your estranged being.[20]

Alienated from his own activity, the worker's life is "activity as suffering, strength as weakness, begetting as emasculating, . . ."[21] The worker is transformed, as one would say, into a masochist.

As Marx and Engels drew closer to the realities of working-class life and social struggle, they became disenchanted with the friends of their first circle, the Young Hegelians and the Feuerbachians. Their erstwhile philosophical associates seemed to them to make their preoccupation with "alienation" the basis for ridiculous gestures against society—an adolescent sowing of philosophical wild oats. The revolutionary activity of the Young Hegelians in the Society of the Free consisted of buffoonery, wild processions in the streets, "scandalous scenes in brothels

19 *Ibid.,* p. 121.
20 *Ibid.,* p. 119.
21 *Ibid.,* p. 73.

and taverns," the taunting of a clergyman at a wedding.[22]
They tended to be indifferent in 1844 to the revolt of the
Silesian weavers; not so Marx, who was stirred by their
song of protest, and saw the emergence of the proletariat
to the dignity of a self-conscious class. Arnold Ruge,
spokesman of the Young Hegelians, mocked at the "meagre
handful of artisans" in the workingmen's club, the League
of the Just, and was appalled by their communist ideas,
but this group moved Karl Marx into an intensity of
thought and action he had never experienced in the
literary-philosophical circle. The workingmen's leaders impressed Marx and Engels as "three real men," and Marx
pondered their ideas deeply.

There are scholars who maintain that Marx and Engels
came to their socialist standpoint and materialist conception of history through a study of Hegelian and Feuerbachian texts. The truth is rather that they imbibed a certain terminology from the philosophers, but the impelling
force was their own sensitivity to social movements and
their own deep sympathies for the workingmen. Engels
did not learn the significance of economic reality from an
internal criticism of Hegelian texts. Rather, he tells us,
"while living at Manchester, I was made painfully aware
that economic factors, hitherto assigned an insignificant
role or no role at all by historians, were, at least under
modern conditions, a decisive power in the world."[23]
And Marx was led to considering communist ideas by his
experiences as editor of the *Rheinische Zeitung*. He had
to write editorials in 1842 on the encroachments of rich
landowners against the peasants' common lands and the

[22] Franz Mehring, *Karl Marx,* trans. Edward Fitzgerald (New
York), 1935, p. 72. Several generations later, in the Greenwich Village of the twenties, Joseph Freeman observed, from a Marxist viewpoint, the philosophy of the Villager was that of Feuerbach, that
"sex love was the highest activity of man, ... a philosophy of life."
Alienation was conceived as having basically a sexual referent. Joseph Freeman, *An American Testament* (New York, 1936), p. 286.

[23] Frederick Engels, *Germany: Revolution and Counter-Revolution*
(New York, 1933), p. 126.

peasants' recourse to wood theft from the landowners' forests. In this pre-industrial situation, Marx undertook to plead the cause of "the unpropertied masses without political and social rights," the dispossessed peasants and pre-proletarians. In the course of this controversy, he announced that he planned to study the communist ideas of Leroux, Considérant, and Proudhon. "There was no provision in Hegel's ideological system," said Marx, for dealing with such socio-economic problems.[24] This was a journey the Young Hegelians did not make; Bruno Bauer, their leader, ridiculed the masses as in everlasting opposition to intellect, that is, the intellectuals. Logic follows on emotion, and where the social emotion was absent, the Young Hegelians wallowed in the masochistic joy of their "alienation." Marx and Engels finally discarded the vocabulary of the school, and spoke in the direct language of social realities which needed no romantic metaphor.

With their abandonment of the concept of alienation, Marx and Engels made central in their political philosophy the concept of struggle. German ethical socialists, with their humanistic talk of love, seemed indeed to Marx and Engels akin to masochist ascetics with their lack of aggressive vitality and energy. Moses Hess, who, besides introducing Marx and Engels to communist ideas, was their precursor in using "alienation" as the ground for the criticism of capitalist civilization, was a saintly figure. To Marx and Engels, however, his compulsion to undo justice which led him to marry a prostitute, must have seemed guilt-tormented and self-immolating.[25] The workingmen of the League of the Just looked with suspicion upon the "humanism" of such intellectuals.[26]

[24] Otto Rühle, *Karl Marx: His Life and Work*, trans. Eden and Cedar Paul (New York, 1929), p. 40.

[25] Isaiah Berlin, *The Life and Opinions of Moses Hess* (Cambridge, Mass., 1959), p. 10. Auguste Cornu, *The Origins of Marxian Thought* (Springfield, Ill., 1957), pp. 70–71. Edmund Silberner, "Moses Hess," *Historia Judaica* XIII (April 1951), 3–28.

[26] Boris Nicolaievsky and Otto Maenchen-Helfen, *Karl Marx: Man and Fighter* (Philadelphia, 1936), p. 76.

What emerged in Marx was a socialism founded on aggression, not on love. It must not be forgotten that force, not love, was for Marx "the midwife of every old society which is pregnant with the new," and Engels wrote eloquently of the therapy of violence, which, in Germany, "would at least have the advantage of wiping out the servility which has permeated the national consciousness. . . ." To reject violence, according to Engels, was the "parsons' mode of thought—lifeless, insipid, and impotent. . . ."[27]

This insistence on the primacy of hatred, aggression, for the socialist movement was a reiterated theme in Engels' writing. To Lavrov, the Russian Populist sociologist, Engels wrote in 1875: "In our country it is hatred rather than love that is needed—at least in the immediate future—and more than anything else a shedding of the last remnants of German idealism. . . ."[28] He and Marx feared that the entry of ethical intellectuals into the workers' movement would "castrate" the party.[29] One must avoid the mood, they said, that makes for "humble submission and confession that the punishment was deserved."[30] Not talk of " 'true love of humanity' and empty phraseology about 'justice' " but class struggle was required.[31] There was a concern always for the maintenance of the masculinity of the movement, a fear that a dwelling on concepts such as "alienation" would indeed masochize the workers' movement as it had the intellectuals.

Engels in later years regarded the writings on alienation as philosophic juvenilia which scarcely warranted the interest of the developed socialist movement. When a young Russian socialist in 1893 asked about them, "Engels was

[27] Frederick Engels, *Herr Eugen Dühring's Revolution in Science*, trans. Emile Burns (New York, n.d.), pp. 209–10.

[28] Karl Marx and Frederick Engels, *Selected Correspondence* (Moscow, ed. 1953), pp. 367–68. Also, *The German Ideology*, ed. Roy. Pascal (New York, 1939), p. 69.

[29] Karl Marx and Frederick Engels, *Selected Correspondence* (Moscow, ed. 1953), p. 395.

[30] Marx and Engels, *Selected Correspondence*, p. 392.

[31] *Ibid.*, p. 393.

embarrassed," he later recalled.[32] Both Marx and Engels still continued to entertain great hopes for a basic transformation of the character of work and the family; nevertheless, they did not make use of the concept of alienation to formulate these hopes.[33] The word "alienation" was absent from Marx's mature analysis.

Thus Marx and Engels veered to an opposite extreme as they extirpated "alienation" from their ideas and made "struggle" central. They left a tremendous gap in their theory of socialism by simply ruling out ethical ideas as "modern mythology." They made it all the easier for the Stalinist perversion of their philosophy to justify itself with appeals to technological necessity, the historical mission of hatred, and the meaninglessness of absolute justice. Whether the basis for a liberal ethic, however, can be provided by a return to the Calvinist-Hegelian concept of alienation seems doubtful. Its root-metaphor, as we shall see, is not a helpful one for the understanding of the world's problems.

Engels' reluctance to publish Marx's and his early writings has called forth contrary explanations from various scholars. A few years ago, I called the attention of Daniel Bell to these passages, and he made extensive use of them in his well-known essay "Two Roads from Marx." Then Robert Tucker in his erudite study *Philosophy and Myth in Karl Marx* tried to explain Engels' embarrassment at the mention of these early works. Marx and Engels, according to Tucker, always continued to hold to their youthful concept of alienation, but felt constrained to be "secretive" about their early writings because to publish such

[32] *Reminiscences of Marx and Engels* (Moscow, n.d.), p. 330.

[33] Frederick Engels, *Anti-Dühring,* pp. 329, 346. Karl Marx, *Capital,* Vol. I, Modern Library Edition, p. 534. The word "alienation" does occur in passing in *Capital* in a footnoted citation from Hegel, but very rarely in the text. Cf. pp. 187, 639, 827. The "estrangement" of the worker is described on pp. 471, 708. But "alienation" is hardly used as an analytical concept.

philosophical material "would confuse and disorient the always unsufficiently class-conscious workers."[34] Tucker's theory seems to me singularly unconvincing. For Marx and Engels never hesitated to follow what seemed to them the scientific course, and to publish the most technical and abstruse analyses. The proletariat had to struggle the best it could with the volumes of *Capital* and *Anti-Dühring*. No, "Engels was embarrassed," as the young Narodnik Voden put it, because he was being reminded as an old man of youthful writings which were filled with sexual and romantic language and yearnings. His paragraphs on cancan dancing, tropical love, sexual secretions, and his sexual invective against money were juvenilia which embarrassed him. Moreover, as he told his translator, Florence Kelley Wischnewetzky, in 1886, "the semi-Hegelian language of a good many passages of my old book is not only untranslatable but has lost the greater part of its meaning even in German."[35] To have put them forward seriously, and to have had them therefore taken by naïve disciples and hostile critics as the philosophical basis of the socialist movement probably seemed to him to run a needless risk of exposing Marx, himself, and the movement to considerable ridicule. So Engels classified these writings in the same category with the love lyrics Marx wrote as a student.

Let us turn now to the varieties of usage of "alienation" in contemporary social analysis.

The great problems of contemporary society have all been described as arising from different modes of alienation. We can distinguish six different principal modes in which, from the sociological standpoint, alienation is said to characterize the experience of modern people. These modes of alienation are:

[34] Robert Tucker, *Philosophy and Myth in Karl Marx* (New York, 1961), p. 173.
[35] Karl Marx, *Letters to Americans: 1848–1895* (New York, 1953), p. 151.

(1) the alienation of class society
(2) the alienation of competitive society
(3) the alienation of industrial society
(4) the alienation of mass society
(5) the alienation of race
(6) the alienation of the generations

These modes of alienation are independent of each other. A class society need not be a competitive one; there have been competitive economies that were founded on handicrafts, and mass societies, such as the Indian and Chinese, that were pre-industrial. A strict class society, carried to caste extremes, brings with it relief from competitive tension, but it aggravates the frustrations of initiative and choice of one's own work; in addition, the man of the lower class must internalize feelings of inferiority, and cultivate a degree of self-hatred and contempt. In this sense, he is internalizing feelings and attitudes toward himself of self-destruction.

A competitive system makes for a mode of alienation distinct from that in which classes are more fixed. In the United States during World War II, the men in the Air Force were found to be more discontented with their rank than were the men in the Military Police. This, despite the fact that the Air Force was full of corporals and sergeants, whereas the Military Police were mostly privates. Indeed, the very plentifulness of opportunity in the Air Force deepened the sense of disappointment, personal inadequacy, and resentment in the minds of those defeated in the competitive struggle for stripes. On the other hand, the M.P. felt less relatively deprived, since most of his friends shared his own lowly status.[36] Competition exacts this toll; from the standpoint of the deepest feelings, there is no "good loser."

Industrial society brings its characteristic mode of alien-

---

[36] Cf. Samuel A. Stouffer, "A Study of Attitudes," *Scientific American*, CLXXX (1949), 13. Samuel Stouffer, *The American Soldier* (Princeton, 1949), I, 251.

ation to the man on the assembly line. Ely Chinoy found that nearly four-fifths of his sample of automobile workers cherished the dream of leaving the factory forever. Mostly they longed for the independence of small businessmen. As he approached middle age, the worker sadly renounced his dream, and resigned himself to the assembly line.[37] This alienation of man from the machine, which stands against him, imposing its rhythm on him so that he is a satellite to its motions, is something that is common to all industrial societies, whether they be capitalist or socialist. As automobile workers told Walker and Guest:

The work isn't hard, it's the never-ending pace. . . . The guys yell "hurrah" whenever the line breaks down. . . . You can hear it all over the plant.

The job gets so sickening—day in and day out plugging in ignition wires. I get through with one motor, turn around, and there's another motor staring me in the face. It's sickening.[38]

The different segments of modern industry vary greatly in the extent to which their work processes give their respective workers a sense of alienation. Where the worker has a greater measure of control over the pace of his job, where he is relatively freer from the overseeing eye of a supervisor, where, above all, the character of the job makes possible the mutual aid, solidarity, and friendships of an on-the-job working group, to that extent job satisfaction rises.[39] Manual workers of all kinds, however, derive far less satisfaction from their work than men in the professions. Labor still remains for the bulk of mankind affected with the curse of alienation from nature that Adam and Eve sustained when they were ousted from the Garden of Eden: "Cursed is the ground for thy sake; . . .

[37] Cf. Ely Chinoy, *Automobile Workers and the American Dream* (Garden City, N.Y., 1955), pp. 82–96.

[38] Charles R. Walker and Robert H. Guest, *The Man on the Assembly Line* (Cambridge, Mass., 1952), pp. 51, 52, 55.

[39] Robert Blauner, "Work Satisfaction and Industrial Trends in Modern Society," *Institute of Industrial Relations*, Reprint No. 151 (Berkeley, Calif., 1960), pp. 346–50.

In the sweat of thy face shalt thou eat bread, . . ." No wonder that a neglected socialist classic is entitled *The Right to Be Lazy*.

The alienation of race is distinct and irreducible to the other modes. Negro writers have told of the Veil that exists between them and white men. "Within the Veil was he born, said I; and there within shall he live,—a Negro and a Negro's son," wrote W. E. B. Du Bois of his first-born.[40] This racial alienation could coexist with a planned socialized economy; it has found its place in socialist parties and labor movements. The alienation of generations appears especially in the gerontocratic societies of the Far East. The youth in the Japanese Zengakuren, for instance, find little to admire in the older generation; they must look for their inspiration to persons outside their national history or create their own ideas.

Is "alienation," however, a useful concept for the analysis of these modes of human unhappiness and frustration? Is it more than a dramatic metaphor that for reasons peculiar to intellectuals' experience has become their favorite root-metaphor for perceiving the social universe? Is it less, however, a tool for understanding than a projection of the psychology of intellectuals disenchanted with themselves?

It would be a major blunder to regard alienation as characteristically a phenomenon of modern society.[41] For what stands out from a historical and comparative standpoint is the omnipresence of alienation; it takes different guises in all societies. There are modes of alienation in small, egalitarian, cooperative, and agricultural societies. The countries of New Zealand and Sweden have achieved

[40] W. E. Burghardt Du Bois, *The Souls of Black Folk* (reprinted, New York, 1953), p. 209.

[41] Nathan Glazer once described "alienation" as "an omnibus of psychological disturbances having a similiar root cause—in this case, modern social organization." "The Alienation of Modern Man," *Commentary*, IV (1947), 380.

a high egalitarian standard of living, but qualified observers have complained of the drab and dull character of their lives. Margaret Cole, doing research on *Democratic Sweden* for the New Fabian Research Bureau, couldn't wait to leave the Scandinavian social democratic tedium, while Leslie Lipson found an oppressive "likemindedness" among the New Zealanders, a "cultural homogeneity," the offspring of equality and security, which led New Zealanders to be suspicious and intolerant of intellectuals, foreigners, and freethinkers, in short, a world "made safe for mediocrity" in a "small and culturally homogeneous milieu."[42]

The agricultural cooperative societies of Israel, the *kibbutzim,* inspire their own corresponding mode of alienation; a typical novel of kibbutz life depicts the "interminable vacuity" of its existence, and portrays characters who, becoming desperate in this collective microcosm for a sense of their own individualities, flee to their tents that shut out a world, "petty, noisy, full of shadow and darkness." "He reacted to communality by going off by himself, by standing aloof. . . . Then people show up as petty, ludicrous, selfish, malicious, cruel: You fall into an attitude of general contempt; you hate and become still further alienated from your fellows. It is a closed circle, a squirrel cage from which there is no release. . . . Pettiness and selfishness creep in, even into the midst of their community based on equality and fraternity."[43] Carol Kennicott in Sinclair Lewis' *Main Street* discovered the tyranny of the disanonymous small society, while in lonely hamlets in Vermont, farmers built their houses on hills to catch a glimpse of a neighbor; living in individualistic outposts, far from mass societies, they became ridden with

[42] Margaret Cole, *Growing Up into Revolution* (London, 1949), pp. 177–78. Leslie Lipson, *The Politics of Equality: New Zealand's Adventures in Democracy* (Chicago, 1948), pp. 491–93.

[43] Lewis S. Feuer, "Leadership and Democracy in the Collective Settlements of Israel," in *Studies in Leadership,* ed. Alvin W. Gouldner (New York, 1950), p. 375. David Maletz, *Young Hearts,* trans. Solomon N. Richards (New York, 1950), pp. 43, 46.

incest and neurosis.[44] Those who think alienation was
born with modern technology might ponder the picture of
the peasant La Bruyère gave in the French traditional society of the seventeenth century:

Certain wild animals, male and female, are scattered over the
country, dark, livid, and quite tanned to the sun, who are
chained, as it were, to the land they are always digging and
turning up and down with an unwearied stubbornness; their
voice is somewhat articulate, and when they stand erect they
discover a human face, and, indeed, are men.[45]

If alienation then is so multiform, can it be given a precise operational meaning that would be useful in social
analysis?

Able social scientists have tried in recent years to define
the dimensions of alienation, and to construct scales that
would enable one to measure statistically a person's degree of alienation. Melvin Seeman, for example, has tried
to distinguish between five variants in "alienation"—powerlessness, meaninglessness, normlessness, isolation, and
self-estrangement. Seeman wishes to remove "the critical,
polemic element in the idea of alienation," and to translate
what it has to say into the language of the psychological
theory of learning. But the will to criticize and polemicize
is precisely the essential intent behind the idea of alienation, and a multitude of alienated persons would be dis-
satisfied equally with conditions of power-possession,
meaningfulness, norm-orientedness, involvement, and self-
acknowledgment.

Alienation has a way of eluding a fixed set of dimensions
because it is as multi-potential as the varieties of human
experience. Seeman, for instance, gives an operational
definition of "meaninglessness"; it is a mode of alienation

[44] Harold Fisher Wilson, *The Hill Country of Northern New England: Its Social and Economic History, 1790–1930* (New York,
1936), pp. 146–52.
[45] *The Characters of Jean de la Bruyère,* trans. Henri van Laun
(London, 1929), p. 318.

characterized "by a low expectancy that satisfactory predictions about future outcomes of behavior can be made"; the person senses that his ability to predict behavioral outcomes is low.[46] But, contrary to Seeman's standpoint, a great deal of contemporary thought finds a state of alienation precisely in those ideologies that profess to predict with high confidence the outcome of people's behavior. What is "historicism" in modern terms if not a theory that aims to foresee the broad social resultant of the sum of individual actions? Historicism is assailed by such thinkers as Karl Popper and Isaiah Berlin exactly because they find themselves alienated in a world of social determinism; they wish for a world in which the degree of social predictability would be low. In such a world, they would feel less alienated.

Again, the alienated man is a person, according to Seeman, who finds himself at odds with popular culture. He does not read *Reader's Digest,* and like many intellectuals, attaches a low value "to goals or beliefs that are typically highly valued in the given society." Yet the plaint is often precisely in the other direction. The artist, the writer, the poet, complain how quickly they become successful, how rapidly the public now accepts them. The avant-garde cannot now long enjoy the pleasures of the vanguardian: *Holiday, Mademoiselle,* and *Esquire* compete for the most experimental poems and stories. Peter Viereck has spoken eloquently of how the artist finds quickly the accolades of popular culture, and he has protested against the very loss of loneliness and pride in isolation which was once the artist's.

Today the forces of mere prestige—the Rotarianism of the highbrows—have a more effective method than the stake. They make him chic.

Every new philosophical, literary, or religious insight (emphatically including the new conservatism) soon finds itself adopted, adulterated by the Overadjusted Man. . . . Today the

[46] Melvin Seeman, "On the Meaning of Alienation," *American Sociological Review,* XXIV (1959), 786.

lonely crowd rushes to buy an abridged pocketbook of *The Lonely Crowd* or, easier still, to read the still more abridged abridgment that appeared in a popular weekly.[47]

The avant-garde is separated now only by a few issues of a little magazine from acceptance into the big. But the artist then voices an altered mode of alienation. He dislikes acceptance even on his own terms. In retrospect, he finds values in isolation that are lacking in acceptance and identification. Whichever direction one takes on the social compass, one finds alienation.

The alienation of self-estrangement is equated by Seeman with the notion of "other-directedness" made famous by David Riesman. Yet here, too, we find that directions go awry, and that inner-directed and other-directed both share the alienated status. The child, says Riesman, is conditioned to other-directedness when it learns that whatever it does must not be valued for itself, "but only for its effect on others," and this Seeman translates as making one's behavior dependent upon anticipated future rewards; the person becomes self-estranged because he enjoys nothing for its own sake. There is a sound insight in this formulation, but it has nothing to do with other- and inner-directedness. For a Calvinist, inner-directed person, who serves his conscience and not public opinion, can be every whit as alienated as the other-directed person.

When the young John Dewey found an "inward laceration," a sense of "divisions and separations," which were "a consequence of a heritage of New England culture, divisions by way of isolation of self from the world, of soul from body, of nature from God," he was defining exactly the inner-directed mode of character from which he sought liberation.[48] The person with a strong internalized superego can feel alienated from himself, and long, as a

[47] Peter Viereck, *The Unadjusted Man: A New Hero for Americans* (Boston, 1956), pp. 16, 52.

[48] John Dewey, "From Absolutism to Experimentalism," in *Contemporary American Philosophy*, ed. G. P. Adams and W. P. Montague (New York, 1930), II, 13, 19.

matter of fact, for more "other-directedness" as a way of overcoming his inner tension. Thus Dewey looked to "shared experience," to "social" experience as the highest, as an almost mystical deliverance from alienation.

Indeed, it soon becomes evident that the categories "inner-directed" and "other-directed" are limited in clarifying the modes of alienation. For what is omitted is the quality of the feeling experienced toward the self, others, family, God, nation, or tribe. To describe an emotional vector, the kind of feeling and its intensity are dimensions as well as its direction. A man who follows the golden rule is, from one standpoint, other-directed; if he does so from dictate of conscience, he is inner-directed; but if he acts from motives of calculation, probably it would be most accurate to call him narcissistic. For whatever warm feelings he has are directed toward his self.

Dale Carnegie in *How to Win Friends and Influence People,* which sold five million copies, proposed some excellent precepts: "Be a good listener. Talk in terms of the other man's interests. Make the other person feel important." If this "other-directedness" were the outcome of a genuine affection for others, it would not signify alienation. But where it is simulated behavior, where the underlying motive is hatred and aggression toward others, then this behavior, even when successful, gives rise to alienation. For the person is then repressing his deeper feelings, and acting in ways that run contrary to what he would express. The schematic terminology of means and ends fails to state clearly the crucial significance of the underlying emotion. What matters is not that you are using others as a means but rather that your basic emotion toward others is one wishing to debase them, to use them in order to degrade them. You may treat a person as an end because of your stern conscience; you will still remain alienated because the underlying emotion remains one of hostility toward him. In any case, Riesman's terms, with their directional emphasis, do not clarify the emotional source of alienation.

In another noteworthy effort to measure alienation,

Dwight Dean has devised several scales to measure three components—powerlessness, normlessness, and social isolation.[49] Yet his attempt, too, fails as a measure of "alienation" precisely because that experience can be found in every direction of human experience—among the powerful as well as the powerless, the normful as well as the normless, the socially involved as well as the isolated. For instance, consider the item in the measurement of powerlessness:

"We are just so many cogs in the machinery of life."

The human switch or lever can, however, be as alienated as the human cog. A power-driven Stalin, aware of his own tyrannical power, but caught and haunted by never-ending anxieties, in a domain of paranoid self-aggrandizement, is an alienated man, estranged from the mankind around him and the socialist aspiration that once had partially moved him. The superpotent man is complementary in his alienation to the impotent.

Or consider again the items designed to help measure normlessness:

"The end often justifies the means."
"I often wonder what the meaning of life really is."

Leon Trotsky felt that the Bolsheviks gave meaning to their lives because they pursued an end that at least partially justified their means. By the sociologist's standards, the Bolsheviks, however, were normless.[50] Again, what of the philosophical individual who is agnostic as to norms and ultimates? Is he more an alienated man than the person who is indifferent to such questions? Many persons, however normless in an ultimate sense, find fulfillment in their human affections and their own chosen loyalty to a job. Life can provide the identification of provisional, pre-ultimate goals. "And pursue the unknown end," said

[49] Dwight G. Dean, "Meaning and Measurement of Alienation," *American Sociological Review*, 26 (1961), 753–58.

[50] Leon Trotsky, "Their Morals and Ours," *The New International*, IV (1938), 164.

Justice Holmes in his final aphorism of life, and one would hesitate to place him, therefore, among the alienated. Ignorance as to the meaning of life can be the basis for a cultivation of human experiences which become their own justification; indeed, the world of human facts may then be all the more closely sought. John Dewey, as he turned from religious metaphysics to agnosticism, found a more effective device against alienation ("dualism" and "separation" he called it) in political, social, and educational activities.

To measure the extent of social isolation, Dean proposes such items as:

"Sometimes I feel all alone in the world."

The image of "the lonely crowd" is most influential in social criticism today. The child deprived of affection or threatened with its loss finds an inner emptiness within himself, and sometimes, as he sees the world pervaded with hostility, wishes to have it all over with. At the same time, however, we have the revolt against the cult of "togetherness," against what Whyte calls the "social ethic." The right to privacy, as Brandeis named it, becomes rediscovered in a society that emphasizes collectives, committees, and cooperative achievements. If there is an alienation in loneliness or anomie, there is a corresponding alienation in togetherness and over-identification. The Hegelian philosophers reduced the individual into an adjective of the Total; there was no loneliness here, only an oppressive perpetual absorption in which the individual longed to become an independent noun.

This recovery of the sense of one's individuality, as distinct from the roles party, class, organization, or group imposes, is what lies behind what is often called "the quest for identity." Alienation lies in every direction of human experience where basic emotional desire is frustrated, every direction in which the person may be compelled by social situations to do violence to his own nature. "Alienation" is used to convey the emotional tone that accompanies any behavior in which the person is compelled to act self-destructively; that is the most general definition of alienation, and its dimensions will be as varied as human desire and need.

Why, however, should the word "alienation" be used to describe the subjective tone of self-destructive experience? The metaphor of "alienation" overlays this experience with a quality peculiar to the drama of contemporary intellectuals in their most despondent mood. The contemporary intellectual's experience of alienation is concretely one of his withdrawal from political movements; he has disavowed identifications. The existentialist's insistence on a chosen individuality which will not partake of any class, group, or party identification involves necessarily a sense of alienation. Alienation is the dramatic metaphor of the intellectual who has left the Political Garden of Eden and projects his experience as the exemplar of all human frustrations. The frustrations are immense and universal, but are they not misdescribed in this projective metaphor of a very small section of humanity?

The fondness of the contemporary intellectual for the concept "alienation" has little to do with the modes of alienation associated with mass, class, competitive, and industrial societies. The intellectual's alienation was in part a self-alienation which arose as he discovered the character of his own underlying aims. Self-discovery brought the reproaches of conscience; there was also the realization that the movement, class, or party with which he had identified himself could become as evil-ridden as the society he had hoped to help redeem. The sustaining sense of the intellectual's mission all but vanished during the last two decades; the disruption of the labor-intellectual alliance has left the intellectual, at least for a time, without the sense of a supporting identification that gives meaning to his efforts. The words meaninglessness, powerlessness, normlessness, which are used to characterize the dimensions of alienation, have a special application to the experience of the contemporary intellectual; the meaninglessness of his life is its lack of a social goal; his powerlessness reflects the intellectual's self-description: "we have no so-cial class with which to work"; his normlessness is the fact that his socialist ethic is gone, and the recognition that it's all careerism.

Every movement of social reform has been character-ized by a "back to the people" ethos; correspondingly, the end of such a movement has always been accompanied by an "away from the people" mentality. During the thirties, the American intellectual experienced an identifi-cation with the working-class movement, and regarded himself as united with labor to achieve a more just and civilized society. A few years after the Second World War, however, he was alienated from a working class which seemed to him devoid of a sense of historic mis-sion; "we disaffiliate, we disinvolve, we disengage," said the intellectuals frankly. "We were right, but they [the masses] wouldn't listen," writes Dwight Macdonald. "Noth-ing is more frustrating for an intellectual than to work out a logical solution to a problem and then find that nobody is interested."[51] Another writer described this experience of alienation in the sexual idiom of contemporary fiction:

This gentleman, and others like him, decided they'd been stood up by history for the last time. They're through with her; she seemed attractive, but has proven to be a bitch. No respectable girl would turn down clean, handsome Marxists who love her for herself, then go to bed with triflers. . . . The logic of the clean, handsome Marxists of the 1930's demands that they re-nounce such a promiscuous slut, and search for a good vir-gin. . . .[52]

Prosperity came to the generation of leftist intellectuals. Thirty years ago Walter Weyl spoke of his generation of

[51] Dwight Macdonald, *Memoirs of a Revolutionist* (New York, 1957), p. 24.

[52] Calder Willingham, "Politics and the Artist," *"New Interna-tional,"* XIII (1947), 222. Irving Howe, "Intellectuals' Flight from Politics," *Ibid.,* p. 241. By way of addendum, we might note that in 1899 the American philosopher Alfred H. Lloyd made the concept of "alienation" the basic one in his *Philosophy of History.* Lloyd was indeed the first American philosopher of man's alienation.

"tired radicals." The alienated intellectuals, however, were not tired; they were filled with creative energy and helped to research and work by the unprecedented Research Revolution in the universities and the efflorescence of magazines and television. The alienation was not weariness but a sense that they themselves were not as fine persons as once they had been, that love had left their hearts. There were those intellectuals who discovered that power, possessions and status were what they had wanted all along, but their newfound narcissism and reconciliation with their selves did not banish completely the self-reproach they call "alienation." And like a true metaphysician, the intellectual projects his "alienation" upon every facet of discontent in the social universe. A universal indictment, however, provides no lever for social action; it expresses the mood of disaffiliation. The most remarkable film of the fifties was thus a drama of high alienation, *High Noon,* in which the former leftist intellectual, speaking through the allegory of a Western story, expressed his disillusionment and ultimate rejection of every aspect of American society.

"Alienation" thus lends a distinctive emotive-dramatic metaphor to experiences of social frustration. It imposes on them the metaphor of the prophets who failed. It conveys a mood of pervasive tragedy rather than the possibility of effective action. The socialist movement proposed to eliminate economic exploitation and to abolish the class system. These were relatively definable goals. A movement cannot, however, very well propose to alienate the alienators as it did to expropriate the expropriators, for the alienated mood is so multiform in its expression, so unlocated in any specific social form, that it does not delineate the clear goals and foci for action that a political movement requires. The career of this concept, from Calvin's depiction of man, the original sinner, alienated from God for all time, to the modern notion of man alienated somehow in every form of social organization, indicates indeed that its dominant overtone is social defeat.

One sympathizes with the effort of such thinkers as Erich Fromm to restore the full ethical consciousness to the socialist philosophy. For Stalinist sadism found its theoretical apology precisely in the repression of ethics from the Marxist standpoint. The life history of the concept "alienation" suggests, however, that what it says can be better said without it; human self-destructive behavior is better dealt with without this metaphor. Some writers indeed seem to have a "will to alienation," and to revel in their perpetual alienation. An irreverent humorist indeed proposed some time ago the organization of "Alienated Anonymous."

From another standpoint, the emphasis on "alienation" is an indication of how the politics of the superstructure has in the last decade replaced the politics of the economic foundation. The advent of prosperity has meant the shelving of any mood for basic economic reconstruction. The concern shifts from the production and distribution of wealth to the question of the ends and goods to which wealth shall be devoted. Whether "alienation," however, provides an adequate basis for the definition of human good seems to me doubtful. "Alienation" remains too much a concept of political theology that bewilders rather than clarifies the direction for political action.

American Travelers to the
Soviet Union 1917–32:
The Formation of a Component
of New Deal Ideology

From its earliest days, the New Deal was characterized as "pragmatic" in philosophy, as experimental, as uniquely American. Raymond Moley, looking for its philosophic source, pondered the fact that Franklin D. Roosevelt had sat in the classroom of William James.[1] What, however, does "pragmatic" mean? It signifies not an absence of ideas but rather a readiness to try out different hypotheses. It implies a readiness to experiment with the most challenging alternatives. And by the year 1932, political pragmatism in the United States had acquired a new distinctive primary ingredient. To be a pragmatist henceforth was, according to the leaders in pragmatic thought, to regard the Soviet Union as a model of the experimental method in social practice. The whole conception of a "social experiment," the whole notion of planned human intervention into social processes to raise the welfare of the people, had become linked in the minds of America's intellectual and social leaders with the practice of the Soviet Union. This transformation in American thought was largely the work of a small number of several hundreds of travelers to the Soviet Union during the previous decade. If there was no Tocqueville among them, the reports that they published affected the American political consciousness more deeply nonetheless than any other foreign influence in its history.

Every century in modern times has had a country which

[1] Raymond Moley, *After Seven Years* (New York: Harper & Bros., 1939), pp. 174, 365.

it looked to as what we might call its "conscience-model." England was to Voltaire and the Encyclopedists in the eighteenth century the land of liberties, peace, Isaac Newton and the Quakers. France during the nineteenth century held Europe's revolutionary beacon. The Soviet Union during the fifteen years after the October Revolution became the conscience-model of the most searching of the world's intellectuals. The American travelers to the Soviet Union were part of this process; their reports, rendered in the language of American experience and pragmatism, gave to that philosophy something of the Soviet direction.

There have been several different waves of travelers to the Soviet world. The first were romantic revolutionists, journalists such as John Reed and Louise Bryant, stirred beyond themselves by a story bigger than the imagination of any city editor would have dreamed, or the aging Lincoln Steffens, cynically bored with reformers and beholding in Lenin the ultimate union of Will and Intellect, or the amateur diplomat, young William C. Bullitt, hoping to persuade statesmen to transcend their suspicions, and welcome the fledgling workers' republic into the comity of nations. There was Isadora Duncan, votary of a new art, who when she heard the first news of the Russian Revolution, danced the *Marche Slave* to an astonished American audience. She went to the reborn Russia "to dance for the people," and the three years she spent there from 1921 to 1924 she regarded as the happiest of her life. America, however, was then in no mood to listen to a dancer's Dionysiac utterances. In Boston at the end of her performance she waved her red silk scarf above her head, and cried: "This is red! So am I! It is the color of life and vigor. You were once wild here. Don't let them tame you!" Mayor James M. Curley decided she would never have a license to dance in Boston again "in view of the duty the city owes to the decent element." Isadora Duncan was, however, a prophetess of what was soon to stir a legion of intellectuals.[2]

[2] Irma Duncan and Allan Ross Macdougall, *Isadora Duncan's Russian Days* (New York: Covici-Friede, 1929), pp. 4, 152.

Meanwhile, a brief interlude of American relief person-
nel bringing food to a famine-stricken country in 1921
was followed by an evergrowing procession of social workers, artists, labor leaders, educators, social scientists, businessmen, and representatives of ethnic minorities. The decade closed with more than a thousand American engineers
in the Soviet Union building its first great modern industrial plants. For the Soviet Union was, indeed, America's
first Point Four project, without the blessing of the State
Department, to be sure, but with the support of an influential section of American industry. Thus, like modern
Magi, American travelers came seeking a new political
hope, and bringing their gifts of technology.

It is a well-attested psychological truth that what people
need shapes what they see. The travelers' needs, in large
part, conditioned their perception of Soviet reality. They
selected some segments of Soviet existence for emphasis,
while they blurred others beneath the threshold of their
perception. The idealism of American intellectuals, their
"do-gooding" impulses, were being frustrated in the era
of smugness from Harding to Hoover. The generations
that had imbibed the air of Populist, Progressive and socialist movements found themselves during the twenties in
a kind of "internal emigration." They were ready to identify
with the young Soviet republic, struggling, as they saw it,
for an ethic of human brotherhood against the hostile,
selfish capitalist world. The social worker was ready to
see the Soviet Union as a kind of Hull House on a national scale, as the land of public health and mental
hygiene; the progressive educator was ready to see the
Soviet experiment as a nationwide Laboratory School, happily freed from the surveillance of university presidents
and boards of trustees; the religious leader who saw the
Social Gospel ignored and disused in Coolidge's America
recognized witnesses to his creed in the party of dedicated political missionaries who despite their atheism were
evidently moved by a selfless emotion, unmatched in
civilization's history; the crusader for birth control and
liberal divorce laws who found himself trammeled and

sometimes jailed in his own puritan-bound and Catholic-contained America saw a land where sexual love was more nearly unfettered;[3] radical labor leaders, who bore the memory of judges' injunctions, militiamen's bayonets, and policemen's clubs, found themselves welcomed in a land whose political chief talked with them for several hours, and called them "Comrades"; the social scientists found themselves singularly at home in a society that was guided by fellow social scientists who aimed to build a rational, planned world. Such were the tidings the travelers brought from the Soviet Union to their native country. When America was beset by the depression, its emotional unconscious and inventory of ideas for confronting the crisis were imprinted with the suggestions of the Soviet model.

Probably the most influential series of articles by an American on the Soviet Union were those of John Dewey in *The New Republic* in 1928. The foremost figure in American pragmatic thought found almost the fulfillment of his philosophic hopes in the Soviet experiment. "The essence of the Revolution," he wrote, was "its release of courage, energy and confidence in life." The Soviet Union brought a new zest into the experiment of human life itself. This was a "liberation of a people to consciousness of themselves as a determining power in the shaping of their ultimate fate." This revolution, Dewey wrote, had brought "a release of human powers on such an unprecedented scale that it is of incalculable significance not only for that country, but for the world." "I lack the necessary literary skill," he said, to convey the achievement of the

[3] "Here, in the Soviet Union, the Strindbergian warfare of the sexes seems to have no meaning." Waldo Frank, *Dawn in Russia* (New York: Charles Scribner's Sons, 1932), p. 52. " 'Free love' in its proper meaning can be said to have full sway since the revolution." Theodore Dreiser, "How Russia Handles the Sex Question," *Current History*, XXIX (1929), 535. Paul Blanshard contrasted the "almost hysterical sexuality of the Berlin and Paris stage" with the "matter-of-fact robustness of Moscow." Paul Blanshard, "Sex Standards in Moscow," *The Nation*, CXXII (1926), 523. V. F. Calverton, "Red Love in Soviet Russia," *The Modern Quarterly*, IV (1927), 188–89.

Soviet schools. "I have never seen anywhere in the world such a large proportion of intelligent, happy, and intelligently occupied children." Their teachers, he continued, were "some of the wisest and most devoted men and women it has ever been my fortune to meet." The significance of the experience of the opening of the arts to the people became for him, Dewey wrote, "almost an obsession." He recognized the enormous obstacles and propagandist tendencies of Soviet cultural life, but he ventured to predict the latter would die of inanition in the degree to which the Soviet Union came to feel secure. "The main effort is nobly heroic, evincing a faith in human nature which is democratic beyond the ambitions of the democracies of the past." All his life Dewey had struggled both within himself and his social setting against separations and dualisms, the dualism of thought and action, of theory and practice. Here in the Soviet Union dualism seemed to have been overthrown by a permanent revolution. It is hard, he wrote, not to feel envious of the Soviet intellectuals. Those of other countries spend their lives in criticism, but the Russian intellectuals who have identified themselves with the new order "have a task that is total and constructive. They are organic members of an organic going movement." Here in the Soviet Union was an undertaking, "probably the first in the world to attempt scientific regulation of social growth"; the pedagogical section was an organic part of the Scientific Council that forms "plans for the social and economic development of Russia."[4]

Dewey's vision of Soviet reality was shared by such distinguished leaders of progressive education as his friends William Heard Kilpatrick and George S. Counts. The

[4] John Dewey, "Leningrad Gives the Clue," *The New Republic,* November 14, 1928; "A Country in a State of Flux," *The New Republic,* November 21, 1928; "The Great Experiment and the Future," *The New Republic,* December 19, 1928, republished in John Dewey, *Characters and Events,* ed. Joseph Ratner (New York: Henry Holt & Co., 1929), I, 378–80, 383, 388–90, 394, 426–28. Also, reprinted in John Dewey, *Impressions of Soviet Russia* (New York: New Republic, 1929), pp. 1–133.

Soviets, said Kilpatrick in 1929, had embarked on "the outstandingly ambitious enterprise that educational history has to show"; he was pleasantly surprised to find that he was well known in Russia and that his books had been translated and were being used in the training of teachers. Americans who placed their faith in the experimental method read Counts's forthright assertion: "There is one experiment, however, that dwarfs all others—so bold indeed in its ideals and its program that few can contemplate it without emotion." Counts spent a total of ten months in the Soviet Union during 1927 and 1929. As depression's gloom deepened over America, he called upon teachers to learn from the Soviet experience, and to inquire how education might promote social planning.[5]

The pragmatic philosophers and educators were not the first to discover in the Soviet experiment the full measure of the pragmatic method. They were preceded in the Soviet exploration by the pragmatic economists, or as they were once called, the institutional economists. Two of their ablest young practitioners, Rexford G. Tugwell of Columbia University and Paul Douglas of the University of Chicago, were part of the so-called Trade Union Delegation that visited the Soviet Union in 1927.[6] Only three years before, Tugwell had edited a collection of essays by his fellow pragmatic economists. His introduction to this volume aptly called *The Trend of Economics* said that "this book is a sort of a manifesto of the younger generation." Acknowledgments to Dewey's pragmatic method abounded in this manifesto which spoke of a quest for a "non-Euclidean economics."[7] Now Tugwell and Douglas

[5] Samuel Tenenbaum, *William Heard Kilpatrick* (New York: Harper & Bros., 1951), pp. 263–66. George S. Counts, *The Soviet Challenge to America* (New York: John Day, 1931), pp. ix–xi. M. Ilin, *New Russia's Primer*, trans. George S. Counts and Nucia P. Lodge (Boston: Houghton Mifflin Co., 1931), pp. viii–x.

[6] *Soviet Russia in the Second Decade*, eds. Stuart Chase, Robert Dunn, Rexford Guy Tugwell (New York: John Day, 1928).

[7] *The Trend of Economics*, ed. Rexford Guy Tugwell (New York: Alfred A. Knopf, 1924), pp. 86, 409, 422, 156 ff.

embarked on an anthropological field trip to an economic universe with Marxian geodesics and a Leninist social space; experiment merged with religious fulfillment, and the underlying motives of the pragmatic unconscious, freed from the capitalistic cultural censor, for once expressed themselves with clarity.

Doubts upon the aims of the delegation were cast by leaders of the American Federation of Labor who questioned the source of its financing and its claim to represent labor. Five officials of labor's lower echelons, however, chose to ignore their superiors' warnings; joined by a technical and advisory staff of nineteen, they made the pilgrimage to Moscow. At the Kremlin, they questioned and were cross-questioned by Joseph Stalin. Stalin called them "comrades," and the delegates indeed responded in a comradely spirit.[8] They discussed the causes of the small sympathy that American labor and its leaders had toward the Soviet Union. Paul Douglas described how American capitalists broke labor unions and sowed dissension among the different immigrant groups. The visit to the Soviet Union had a tremendous emotional impact on the social scientists of the delegation. Paul Douglas, who wrote most of the report of the American Trade Union Delegation, was like a man vouchsafed a glimpse of the world to come. "Our visit," he said, "strengthened my faith in socialism"; he was now enabled to overcome the doubts he had felt concerning the workings of socialist economy. To an America that was losing its sense of national purpose, Douglas said, "the big fact, the spiritual fact behind all this material evidence, is that there is a real community of belief, a national ideal and moral unity, which is the solid basis of the new Russia —they have really a new religion—the building up of a People's Society." He was not dismayed by the rigid dictatorship the people endured, for "their real rights, that is their economic rights," Douglas said, "are much better

[8] Joseph Stalin, *Interviews with Foreign Workers' Delegations* (New York: International, 1927), p. 38. Cf. Louis Fischer, *Men and Politics* (New York: Duell, Sloan & Pearce, 1941), pp. 89–91.

protected than in any other country."[9] Tugwell too beheld a people transfigured by Lenin's experimentalism. "There is a new life beginning there," he wrote in his report. The revolution had been harsh, but with a mixture of historicism and experimentalism, Tugwell saw this harshness as a necessary cost of progress. "The mass of peasants," he wrote, are not "to be blamed for having dimly seen that the necessities for racial advance required a drastic change, and for bringing it about—with ruthlessness if need be."[10] That period was happily past, however: "The spirit now is reconstructive; and its results seem as certain as those of most human enterprises of so vast a sort." The Soviet government was more truly concerned with the welfare of its peasants than the American government was with its farmers. Stuart Chase also contributed a chapter on the Gosplan to the report of the Trade Union Delegation. A few years later, in 1932, Stuart Chase gave currency to the expression "A New Deal" in his book with that title.[11] Still later he was to lead a popular rebellion against the tyranny of words. But in 1927, Chase was aware that Soviet reality was the newest deal for mankind as a whole. Despite its deplorably low output and conditions, he wrote, "the Russian method affects the mind of the workers particularly the younger man and woman, far more profoundly than any other I have seen in operation. It is not inconceivable that this mental stimulus may some day break the ancient working habits of the East." Above all he was amazed by the phenomenon of the Soviet manager. No "group of hungry stockholders," importunate for dividends, drove the Soviet manager. Instead, he was guided by an Argus-eyed government, "informed by battalions of statistics," and by a Communist party representative. The

[9] *Adventurous Americans,* ed. Devere Allen (New York: Farrar & Rinehart, 1932), pp. 188–90. Cf. *Russia after Ten Years: Report of the American Trade Union Delegation to the Soviet Union* (New York: International, 1927). Also, Samuel N. Harper, *The Russia I Believe In* (Chicago: University of Chicago Press, 1945), pp. 156–57.

[10] *Soviet Russia in the Second Decade,* p. 102.

[11] Stuart Chase, *A New Deal* (New York: Macmillan Co., 1932).

latter needs "no further incentive than the burning zeal to create a new heaven and a new earth which flames in the breast of every good Communist. It is something—this flame —that one has to see to appreciate. There is nothing like it anywhere in the world today. . . . Will it last? I do not know. All I can report is that after ten lean years it still scorches the face of the curious onlooker. So must the flaming sword of Allah have come over the plains of Mecca." Human nature, Stuart Chase concluded, was far more complicated than the Manchester School had believed. Meanwhile, he said, five more years were required to determine whether the Gosplan, "this courageous and unprecedented experiment," was "destined to be a landmark for the economic guidance" of the world's peoples, "or just another memorandum for the waste basket of history."[12] Five years later, the crucial experiment was evaluated by Stuart Chase as potently positive for the Soviet alternative. His book *A New Deal* ended with a summons to his depression-bewildered countrymen to learn from a society in which "the engineers and economists of the Gosplan" showed how a balance between production and distribution could be achieved. "Why," said he, "should Russians have all the fun of remaking a world?"[13]

This was a decade of crucial experiments that shattered the foundations of social and intellectual systems. The pragmatic economists, reporting on their Soviet expedi-

[12] *Soviet Russia in the Second Decade*, pp. 49–50, 54. One member of the delegation, Silas Axtell, a distinguished attorney for the International Seamen's Union, dissented vigorously from its report. He said the delegates' opinions had been "pretty well formed" before they met in Moscow. He felt "the laws of nature have been discarded" in the Soviet Union, and was not impressed by the efficiency of the industrial plants he saw. He doubted the reliability of observers who after a few weeks' visit, wrote a report on a vast country whose language they could not speak; the Soviet authorities, in his opinion, were adroit salesmen who corrupted the American delegates with free transportation, free hotel service and free barbers. Silas B. Axtell, "Russia, and her Foreign Relations," *Annals of the American Academy of Political and Social Science*, CXXXVIII (1928), 85–88.

[13] Chase, *A New Deal*, pp. 244, 252.

tion, shared the same emotion of dramatic discovery the astronomers led by Eddington had felt when one evening in 1919 before the Royal Society they reported that their observations during the sun's eclipse on an island off West Africa had confirmed Einstein's hypothesis as against the Newtonian scheme. Experimental method, pure pragmatism, was consonant with the opening up of new world systems.

No agency of the New Deal affected the lives of millions of Americans more directly than the Works Progress Administration. For many thousands of families throughout the land, the WPA, derided, condemned, ridiculed, assailed, stood nonetheless for the difference between destitution and livelihood. This massive program to put people to work on planned socially useful projects, and to avoid the respect-undermining dole, was headed by Harry Hopkins. By profession a social worker since his beginnings at the Christadora House in New York, Hopkins came to represent, for most persons, the whole underlying aim and philosophy of the New Deal. Pre-eminently the social worker in his attitudes, Hopkins was the spokesman of a standpoint that, born in the settlements of Jane Addams and Lillian D. Wald, had now matured, and was converting the national government to its philosophy of social welfare. Soviet practice became the experimental model of the leaders of social workers.

At the very outset, Jane Addams called the Russian Revolution "the greatest social experiment in history."[14] This enthusiasm became universal among her colleagues during the next years. In the new Soviet society, as they saw it, the social worker was not the "do-gooder" condescendingly tolerated by a selfish world but was rather the foremost participant and definer of the society's goals. The deepest personal influence on Hopkins was Dr. John A. Kingsbury, "a scholarly, humane and humorous man

[14] Robert Morss Lovett, *All Our Years* (New York: Viking Press, 1948), pp. 154–55.

who was General Director of the Association for Improving the Condition of the Poor." Kingsbury not only gave Hopkins his first job as a social worker but helped him obtain his first post in public service. He was a paternal figure in Hopkins' life. Hopkins chose his residence to live near Kingsbury, and made him confidant for all his marital problems. In August and September 1932, Dr. Kingsbury journeyed to the Soviet Union to appraise its public health and medical services. The Soviet system of free medical care won his unstinting admiration. "The Russian experiment," he wrote, "is a portent to the rest of the world." Would other governments be able similarly to free their people "from the haunting fear of destitution"? Dr. Kingsbury claimed that the cash nexus had "almost entirely ceased to operate in medical practice in Soviet Russia"; he reported furthermore the belief of Soviet physicians that this helped them in curative work. The vast majority of the population now had better medical care than they had ever had, and the services provided were of an astonishingly complete character. Harry Hopkins appointed his old friend as his assistant in the Works Progress Administration.[15]

Then too there was Dr. Frankwood E. Williams, to whom Harry Hopkins in his emotional difficulties turned for psychoanalytical help. Dr. Williams, editor of *The Journal of Mental Hygiene,* found the Soviet Union a mental hygienist's paradise. Here one could escape, he wrote in

[15] Robert Sherwood, *Roosevelt and Hopkins, An Intimate History* (New York: Harper & Bros., 1948), pp. 23–27, 34, 35. Sir Arthur Newsholme and John Adams Kingsbury, *Red Medicine: Socialized Health in Soviet Russia* (New York: Doubleday, Doran, 1933), p. 266. Also cf. Rexford G. Tugwell, *The Democratic Roosevelt* (New York: Doubleday & Co., 1957), p. 197. It was to Kingsbury that Franklin D. Roosevelt wrote in 1930: "There is no question in my mind that it is time for the country to become radical for at least one generation: History shows that where this occurs occasionally, nations are saved from revolution." Roosevelt, as governor of New York, frequently consulted with Kingsbury on questions of social welfare. *F.D.R.: His Personal Letters: 1928–1945,* ed. Elliott Roosevelt (New York: Duell, Sloan & Pearce, 1950), I, 118.

1932, the "atmosphere of competition and rivalry that vitiates everything from the start and at every step." Here was no patchwork of clinics and hospitals to serve as refuges from a competitive order; the whole Soviet society was a mental hygiene clinic. Squeezed in a Moscow streetcar which made the New York subway seem like a half-empty football stand, Dr. Williams had a sense of mystic communion; "for the moment we are just one body." Soviet society had accomplished the social miracle of liberating its citizens from anxieties and defensive reactions. Did Dr. Williams' mystical enthusiasm for the Soviet Union distort his perception of medical fact? Shortly thereafter, in 1932, Dr. C. P. Oberndorf, moved to skepticism by Dr. Williams' reports, went to the Soviet Union for two weeks. He found a higher percentage of young people in the Soviet hospitals with dementia praecox than in the United States, the result evidently of strains of adaptation to Soviet life. But it was the observer's reports of Dr. Williams which had the ear of Harry Hopkins and the social workers.[16]

The October Revolution was indeed a turning-point in the lives of the most distinguished social workers. Their social idealism, frustrated on the American scene, was vicariously satisfied in the Soviet achievement. The Bolshevik to them was the social worker in arms. Florence Kelley of Hull House, the revered pioneer of labor legislation who had served Governor Altgeld as his first factory inspector, dismissed the anti-Bolsheviks as persons who "waited up all night in the station for the milk train and the express whizzed by." Jane Addams and Lillian D. Wald broke their friendship with Catherine Breshkovsky, the "Little Grandmother" of the Russian Revolution, rather than condemn the Bolsheviks. Travelers' reports from Anna Louise Strong and Moissaye J. Olgin came to Lillian D. Wald "of the vast promise of the Soviet government and

[16] Frankwood E. Williams, " 'Those Crazy Russians!': A Mental-Hygiene Hunting Trip in the U.S.S.R." *The Survey*, LXVII (1932), 342–44. C. P. Oberndorf, *A History of Psychoanalysis in America* (New York: Grune & Stratton, 1953), pp. 191–93.

the strength and wisdom and social passion of Lenin."
When Olgin lectured to her House after his visit to the
Soviet Union in 1921, the audience "sat enthralled."

In 1924, Lillian D. Wald accepted an invitation to visit
the Soviet Union and discuss with Soviet leaders the problems of childhood and public health. With two coworkers
and an interpreter, she spent six weeks in Russia. She
found "the achievement of the last two or three years in
the field of public health and preventive measures . . .
extraordinary." She found the government waging a poster
campaign against swaddling clothes (Nota bene: advocates of the Gorer hypothesis). She saw the vast estates
that had been put to use for the people's recreation and
health. She was stirred by the "far-reaching plans, the desire to have the many children secure the best that science
and devotion can give." She visited the experimental
schools where she found that John Dewey's ideas were
being applied "not less than 150 per cent." She was in
Moscow when Lenin was buried in the Red Square, and
felt the tremor of the multitude as if expectant of a miracle. Lenin's image blended with Jesus in her dreams,
"for one night as I slept I watched two spirited horses
pulling a great wagon along a Russian road . . . when the
driver turned I saw the face of Christ radiant."[17]

Such was the almost religious exaltation of the social
workers. The Soviet Union was Hull House, the Educational Alliance, the Neighborhood House, projected on the
agenda for world history. Eduard C. Lindemann, professor of social philosophy at Columbia University's School
for Social Work, and a contributing editor of *The New
Republic,* saw evidence in the Soviet Union that a basic
change in human nature was under way; "acquisitive-
ness," he said, was becoming a "recessive trait."[18] This

[17] Lillian D. Wald, "Public Health in Soviet Russia," *The Survey,*
LIII (1924), 272–74; *Windows on Henry Street* (Boston: Little,
Brown & Co., 1934), pp. 255–71.
[18] Eduard C. Lindemann, "Is Human Nature Changing in Russia?"
The New Republic, LXXIV (1933), 95–98.

was the ingredient which social workers who had journeyed to Moscow imparted to the philosophy of the New Deal.

The social workers are not to be dismissed as heaven-centered idealists who had given way to wishful thinking. The greatest figure of American Progressivism in the twenties, Senator Robert M. LaFollette, progenitor of the Wisconsin Idea, and spiritual precursor of the New Deal, had a similar perception of Soviet reality. To LaFollette, the Soviet Union was in large measure Midwestern Populist Progressivism realized. The Senator with a party of seven, which included the fellow travelers Lincoln Steffens and Jo Davidson, entered the Soviet Union on August 30, 1923. His wife, Belle LaFollette, published reports on their observations in *LaFollette's Magazine;* they told with enthusiasm that the Soviet leaders were reformers just like themselves. "The Soviet government appears to me to be working with religious zeal and faith to establish what it believes to be a social and economic order that is scientific and just." They found a flourishing cooperative movement, and widespread peasant ownership of land. LaFollette had left a land that reeked of Teapot Dome and corruption in the highest places, but here in the Soviet country, graft was treason, and punished by death. The Progressive platform was evidently being realized by the Bolsheviks. "All the reforms that Florence Kelley and the Consumers' League have been working for these long years," wrote Mrs. LaFollette, have been "achieved under the Soviet Republic. And there is no danger of a Supreme Court decision setting aside the results of those years of effort." The Communists were genuinely interested in helping their farmers with scientific advice and social assistance. There was a foreshadowing of the Rural Electrification and Farm Security Administrations in Mrs. LaFollette's declaration of Soviet intent: "If the Soviets could have their way, all the land would be cultivated by tractors, all the villages lighted by electricity, each community would have a central house serving for the purpose of school, library, assembly hall, and theatre. They would have every convenience and advantage which they plan for the industrial workers in the city . . ."

Senator LaFollette, of course, unreservedly rejected dictatorship as an instrument of social change. Nonetheless, he shared a common viewpoint as to the social content of the Soviet reforms with his companions Steffens and Davidson, and indeed with his guides, Anna Louise Strong and the communist Nuorteva. The LaFollettes saw a country in which a sense of equality and cordial fellowship diffused between the workers and their chosen superintendents.[19] They were moved by the "spirit of reverence and affection" toward Lenin, then in his last illness, and reported that he was evidently worshiped by the Russian peasants.[20]

The following year Robert LaFollette was the Progressive candidate for the presidency of the United States. Behind him were grouped many of those who eight years later emerged as the intellectual leaders of the New Deal. Felix Frankfurter endorsed LaFollette's candidacy for the presidency in words that remind one of the intensity of the pragmatic disaffection with the existing political and social realities and make understandable its readiness to entertain the notion of reconstructing society in the direc-

[19] Belle Case LaFollette, "With Senator LaFollette in Russia," *LaFollette's Magazine*, XV (1923), 185–86. Belle Case LaFollette and Fola LaFollette, *Robert M. LaFollette* (New York: Macmillan Co., 1953), II, 1079–83. Jo Davidson, *Between Sittings: An Informal Autobiography* (New York: Dial Press, 1951), pp. 178–81. On Nuorteva, cf. Theodore Draper, *The Roots of American Communism* (New York: Viking Press, 1957), pp. 78, 229–32. Joseph Freeman, *An American Testament* (New York: Farrar & Rinehart, 1936), p. 546.

[20] Among the later politicians who visited the Soviet Union, we must mention Albert M. Ottinger, the Republican opponent of Franklin D. Roosevelt for the governorship of New York in 1928. Ottinger, a spokesman for a "businessmen's delegation" in 1929, delivered himself of a speech to their Soviet hosts in which he turned his eyes heavenward, and said: "And I trust, my friends, that *with God's help,* you will carry your wonderful Five Year Plan to a great success!" Eugene Lyons, *Assignment in Utopia* (New York: Harcourt, Brace & Co., 1937), pp. 229–30.

tion of planned economy: "The Republican and Democratic parties do not face the issues because there are no differences in realities cutting across the two parties. They each represent unreal cohesions, . . ." With an almost Marxist overtone, Frankfurter wrote that "both parties have an identical record of economic imperialism." He hoped for an American analogue to the British Labour party, without which, he said, "there might have been disastrous revolutionary interludes in England."[21] American pragmatists could range themselves behind LaFollette not in spite of but partially because he was the kind of man who was ready to learn from the socialist experiment of the Soviet Union.

The aspiration of the New Deal, as Samuel Lubell has emphasized, expressed in considerable part the upsurge of the ethnic minorities in the United States. Their leaders were pragmatic, but again we must recognize how much pragmatic means and ends came during the twenties to be linked to means and ends embodied in the Soviet experiment. No American philosopher had applied the spirit of William James's pragmatism more fruitfully to the problems of American democracy than had Horace M. Kallen. In a series of notable essays and books, Kallen examined with honesty and depth the dilemmas of a country whose culture was being forged by diverse immigrant groups, and his projection of a "cultural pluralism," an orchestration of diverse heritages within a common democratic setting, mitigated the harsh Americanizings of a period which knew the Palmer Raids and the Ku Klux Klan. Kallen journeyed to the Soviet Union to see with his own eyes how the Bolsheviks had met the problems of their ethnic minorities.

The Russia of the Czars had been the monstrous land of pogroms, deportations, the Pale, the *numerus clausus* and the Cossacks' knout. Kishineff and Odessa were names

[21] Felix Frankfurter, "Why I Shall Vote for LaFollette," *The New Republic*, XL (1924), 200–01.

to Jews not for civilized towns but for bestial mobs and human massacre.[22] Now Kallen found a world transformed. The Soviet Union was indeed the land of cultural pluralism. For the Jews, "more truly than for any people under the Soviets," wrote Kallen, "a new life is beginning." Jews, because of their literacy and intellectual eagerness, were welcome in numerous and important posts in the public service. This was a country in which there was no pussyfooting with anti-Semitism. The Bolshevik authority enunciated the principle: "Anti-Semitism is counter-revolutionary," and it rigorously put it into practice. Kallen, the coworker of John Dewey, observed too the miracle of Soviet education: "I came away with the feeling that the educational system itself was enough to justify the revolution."

In the United States, Kallen had been in the forefront among the small group of intellectuals that sought to awaken the American conscience against the injustices of the trial of Sacco and Vanzetti. The execution of the two Italian immigrants in 1927 seemed to many the culmination of American nativist xenophobia. The pilgrimage to the Soviet Union, however, cleansed the soul; here was a land in which the lowly and the downtrodden minorities had taken their full places in society. Horace Kallen opened his spirit to the Soviet pragmatic adventure: "All, regardless of party," he wrote, "acknowledge that the revolution has awakened the millions, that the government, 'dictatorship' though it be, has liberated their energies, animated them with an altogether unprecedented sense of personal dignity and inward worth, opened to them hitherto sealed worlds of science and art and personal advancement, . . ."[23] He was moved with respect by the austere simplicity of Stalin, living in two ascetic rooms in the Kremlin.

[22] See, for instance, Sholom Aleichem's bitter song, "Spi, Elyosha," in Melech Grafstein, *Sholom Aleichem Panorama* (London, Ontario: Jewish Observer, 1948), pp. 296–97.

[23] Horace M. Kallen, *Frontiers of Hope* (New York: H. Liveright, 1929), pp. 318–19, 326, 351–53, 381–82, 430–31; "Religion in Russia," *The New Republic*, LII (1927), 279–82.

These were Veblenite workmen who ruled Russia, not a decadent leisure class.

Very similar was the experience of Avrahm Yarmolinsky, one of the very few qualified for accurate observation of Soviet realities. Yarmolinsky, the Chief of the Slavonic Division of the New York Public Library, fluent in his native Russian tongue, educated in Russian primary and secondary schools, spent nearly a half-year in the Soviet Union during 1923–24. The Jews, he reported, "clung to the Bolsheviks as their saviors"; Jewish youth had flocked to the Red Army to fight for the ideal of Lenin's internationalism and the reality of their own lives. Yarmolinsky foretold a renaissance of Jewish culture in the free cultural pluralism of the Soviet world. And no wonder, for he found Jewish State Theaters flourishing in Kharkov, Kiev, Moscow, and Minsk; he met great Jewish poets, saw a Museum of Jewish Culture and heard Yiddish in schools as the language of instruction. Within a few years, there were upwards of a hundred Jewish soviets, with their transactions recorded in the once-despised Yiddish jargon. With faith and hope, Yarmolinsky could truthfully write: "Unless all signs fail, the future will witness the rise of a distinct Jewish culture on Russian soil."[24] The signs did fail. Yarmolinsky's gifted perception could not grasp the multiple potentialities and indeterminacies in social evolution. Who could grasp them? Meanwhile, however, the perspective for the ethnic liberalism of the New Deal was being enriched by the experience of Soviet cultural pluralism. Pragmatic experiment was showing how different peoples could be led, under Soviet guidance, to live side by side in a cooperative world.

The intellectual leaders of the American Negro likewise scanned the sociological skies, and beheld a bright star, which shone all the more in the dark despair that beclouded them in the Social Acquiescence of the twenties. W. E. B. Du Bois, spokesman for the new Negro intellec-

[24] Avrahm Yarmolinsky, *The Jews and Other Minor Nationalities under the Soviets* (New York: Vanguard Press, 1928), pp. 57, 128–36.

tual and middle class, leader of the so-called Talented Tenth, had sounded the call in 1905 for the Niagara Movement, and become the chief guide for the National Association for the Advancement of Colored People. He had almost singlehandedly created Negro sociology as a scientific study, when most American sociologists preferred to remain oblivious to racial problems. In 1926, Du Bois spent two months in the Soviet Union; his visit was financed by an American "friend of the Soviet Union." The sight of Soviet reality caused something of an emotional upheaval in Du Bois. "I am writing this in Russia," he wrote back to his readers in *The Crisis*. "I am sitting in Revolution Square . . . I stand in astonishment and wonder at the revelation of Russia that has come to me. I may be partially deceived and half-informed. But if what I have seen with my eyes and heard with my ears in Russia is Bolshevism, I am a Bolshevik." He went about observing everywhere, often with his interpreter, sometimes alone, with the same dogged persistence he had shown almost thirty years before when he interviewed family after family in the Negro slums of Philadelphia. He gathered documents and figures, plied officials and teachers with questions and gazed at "this Russia" to fathom its spirit. And now, for the first time in his life, despair left his pen. Of all the lands he had seen, "the hope" was "tensest and most flaming in Russia."[25] The Russian Dictatorship of the Proletariat was simply an instrument for imparting education and intelligence to the workingmen so that they would rule themselves. In Russia, the aim was that the Workingman would be the State. If the Bolsheviks succeeded in this noble design, said Du Bois, "the Russian Revolution will sweep the world." Du Bois noted that while the American University Travel Association accepted

[25] *The Crisis*, XXXIV (1927), 70; XXX (1926), 8, 189, 190. W. E. Burghardt Du Bois, *Dusk of Dawn: An Essay toward an Autobiography of a Race Concept* (New York: Harcourt, Brace & Co., 1940), p. 287. Also cf. Francis L. Broderick, *W. E. B. Du Bois: Negro Leader in a Time of Crisis* (Stanford, Calif.: Stanford University Press, 1959), pp. 138–40.

no Negro applicants, the Russian Student Bureau was not only inviting but urging Negro students to visit Russia.[26] When the New Deal began to grope for basic change in the philosophy of racial relations, the leaders of the Negro people could cite the report of the successful Soviet experiment in the reshaping of ethnic attitudes. The Soviet Union had enforced an equality of peoples. Its example could permeate the New Deal ideology with an indication of the evident power of governmental intervention to eradicate racial antagonisms. For the Negro leaders of the Talented Tenth had heard the Soviet story, and when they pleaded and cajoled with Washington officials, the vision of the Soviet Union as a model for racial equality was a felt presence.

From the afternoon in 1933 on which Hugh Johnson listened earnestly to the New York Jewish union leader as he expounded the clothing workers' standpoint to the National Recovery Administration, Sidney Hillman began to emerge as the labor leader who contributed most to the philosophy of the New Deal.[27] Eleven years later, campaigners of the Republican party jibed at a Democratic leadership that had decided to "clear it with Sidney." Eleven years earlier, Hillman had come to equate the meaning of pragmatic experiment in our time with the path that Lenin had opened.

Sidney Hillman, president of the Amalgamated Clothing Workers, had taken part as a youngster in the Russian Revolution of 1905. Now in 1921, saying that he hoped to visit his Orthodox parents in Lithuania, he journeyed to famine-stricken Russia. Horrified by the suffering he witnessed, he began sending cablegrams to his union asking its members to send aid at once to meet the desperate need. On a Friday morning on November 4, 1921, upon his return to New York, hundreds of clothing workers greeted him at the pier. At once, Hillman told them the upshot of

[26] *The Crisis*, XXXV (1928), 381; XXXIV (1927), 203.

[27] Hugh Johnson, *The Blue Eagle from Egg to Earth* (New York: Doubleday, Doran, 1935), p. 217.

his four weeks' journey to the Soviet Union: "The Bolshevik group is the only group with force enough and vigor enough to govern Russia." The Soviet government, Hillman later said, was "the most stable, the most efficient, and the most constructive government in Europe today."[28] He told the clothing workers: "Lenin asked me to convey to you his personal thanks and appreciation for your splendid assistance," the first and the largest shipment of aid from any labor organization; the audience responded warmly. The honesty and ability of the Soviet leaders was unquestioned, Hillman said; they had saved Russia for the Russians. Then he gave his verdict as a labor pragmatist. As to the soundness of the Soviet policies, he said, the best test is that they are getting results. They are working; the New Economic Policy especially was helping to build the economic life of the country. The Soviet leaders, Hillman continued, have not abandoned their plans for a collectivist society; they have merely changed their method of getting there. He stood by his fellow Soviet pragmatists: "My conviction is that Russia is in an era of great economic reconstruction."[29]

Probably Sidney Hillman stood closer to the thought-ways of the Bolshevik leaders than any of the other Americans who traveled to the Soviet Union. He had three conferences with Lenin at the Kremlin, and obviously felt a basic kinship with the man's ideas and methods. Lenin acknowledged that the New Economic Policy was a retreat, but reiterated that the Communist aim remained unchanged. In various ways, Hillman mispredicted the future. He expected that both the New Economic Policy and individual peasant ownership of land would persist "for years to come." But he saw clearly the pragmatic reality of a present that could be met in only one constructive way. He was indifferent to the subtleties of Menshevik and Bolshevik disputation, and had only contempt for the "brigands," the "Denikins, Kolchaks, Yudenitches, Pet-

[28] *Advance*, V (November 11, 1921), 1–2.
[29] *Advance*, V (November 18, 1921), 1–2.

luras. . . ." He felt that Lenin's party had the support of the people, that it would do the job and that the Bolshevik dictatorship was pragmatically justified. "They are the only people with a constructive program to lift the nation out of the bankruptcy and chaos it inherited from the Czar."[30]

From Hillman's experience in Russia was born an effort to organize a corporation to help its clothing manufacture. Hillman journeyed once more to the Soviet Union, signed an agreement with Lenin, which a convention of the Amalgamated Clothing Workers enthusiastically approved. As the bars of the "Internationale" sounded forth, Hillman and his fellow leaders marched to the platform, and were greeted by cablegrams of congratulation from distinguished Soviet leaders. Hillman told of Lenin, Radek, and that "other demon, Leon Trotzky." These, he said, "are the proper people to deal with." Some persons thought they were "improper." But, said Hillman sardonically: "We have even got improper people in some of the local unions of the Amalgamated Clothing Workers of America, you know, and we are nearly perfect." His conclusion was plain and unmistakable: "I have never met a group of people that is so realistic, so practical, so courageous, and so able to handle the greatest job, as the group of people who have charge of the destinies of the Russian nation today."[31] No doubt Hillman in later years revised many of his political judgments. But he never unsaid his admiration for Lenin's achievement and Soviet pragmatism. He brought to American political pragmatism the sense of a battle and direction that merged at its limit with the Soviet aspiration that had stirred him in the autumn of 1921. "In the history of the world," said Hillman, "the poets will be remembered more than the practical men, but actual life is made by the practical men, inspired at times by the writings of the dreamers. Life is made by

[30] Sidney Hillman, "How Russia Solves Her Problems," *Advance*, V (December 9, 1921), 5, 8. *Advance*, V (November 18, 1921), 2.
[31] *Advance*, VI (May 19, 1922), 1–35; (June 2, 1922), 1, 7.

the men who can take hold of life and have the power to mold it. . . ."[32]

The Soviet Union exerted its magnetic power on other spokesmen of labor who became outstanding in defining New Deal labor policy. John Brophy, who in 1935 was chosen by John L. Lewis to be the first executive director of the Committee for Industrial Organization, spoke the final words on behalf of the First American Labor Delegation to Joseph Stalin on September 9, 1927: "The presence of the American delegation in the U.S.S.R. is the best reply, and is evidence of the sympathy of a section of the American workers to the workers of the Soviet Union."[33] Men who came to the forefront of the C.I.O. during its youthful organizing days had spent years as volunteer workmen in the Soviet Union—Walter Reuther, Powers Hapgood. The president of the Pennsylvania Federation of Labor, the veteran socialist James H. Maurer, could not join right-wing social democrats in their antagonism to the Soviet Union; he had been there with the Trade Union Delegation, and he spoke of the deep impression that had been made on him by "the enthusiasm, the hope, the confidence, and the loyalty of the Russians to their government. They had something to look forward to and no sacrifice was too great for them to help it in its tremendous task. Heaven help the nation that tried to conquer it."[34] Men who fought the communists bitterly in their own unions still acknowledged the attractive power of the Soviet universe. Benjamin Schlesinger, president of the International Ladies Garment Workers' Union, came back from a visit to the Soviet Union with hopes similar to Hillman's. Schlesinger promised Lenin that he would pro-

[32] Matthew Josephson, *Sidney Hillman: Statesman of American Labor* (Garden City, Doubleday, 1952), pp. 256–67.

[33] Joseph Stalin, *Interviews with Foreign Workers' Delegations*, p. 42. Also cf. John Brophy, *A Miner's Life* (Madison: University of Wisconsin Press, 1964), pp. 220–22.

[34] James Hudson Maurer, *It Can Be Done* (New York: Rand School, 1938), pp. 291–92. Maurer and Brophy reminded critics of the Soviet Union: "After all, Russia has a workers' government." *Russia After Ten Years*, p. 96.

mote a campaign to provide sewing machines for garment factories in Russia.[35] The ensuing years, however, made communism and its methods anathema to the officers of the ILGWU. Nevertheless, when David Dubinsky, president of the union in 1931, reported to the membership on his own visit to the Soviet Union, he astonished many by his tribute to the spirit that pervaded the Russian masses. His audience was "almost spellbound" as he said that notwithstanding their terrible privations, the Soviet "workers appear to be ready to undergo all kinds of misery as a necessary sacrifice for the attainment of the ideal communistic state, which, they believe, is on the way now."[36]

Thus, as the depression deepened, and American workingmen felt that the minimal contract for social existence was being violated, the reports of a land that based itself on the united will of the workers made an ever more intense impression. That same month, garment workers read that John Dewey was calling for a special session of Congress to enact an unemployment relief program. "No one in the present crisis shall have cake until everyone is assured of bread," Dewey wrote to President Hoover. Nicholas Murray Butler echoed the opinions of senators, governors, and bankers when he said the "final test of capitalism" was upon the American people.[37] During this time, the American need shaped the perception of Soviet reality; the experiment became the practicable alternative.

It was American engineers, however, who finally brought the most convincing tidings of the Soviet experiment. An ingredient of Veblenite ideology, with its apotheosis of the role of the engineer in creating a scientific industrial civilization, went into the New Deal; the model which it invoked, the flow chart of a scientific society, was the Soviet

[35] Melech Epstein, *Jewish Labor in U.S.A.: 1914–1952* (New York: Trade Union Sponsoring Committee, 1953), p. 89.

[36] Samuel Perlmutter, "The Month in Local 10," *Justice*, XIII (October 1931), 11. Also cf. Max D. Danish, *The World of David Dubinsky* (Cleveland: World Publishing Co., 1957), pp. 66–67.

[37] Max D. Danish, "Run O' the Month," *Justice*, ibid., p. 6.

Union, as viewed by American engineers. Engineering opinion concerning the Soviet Union veered a full 180 degrees during the course of a decade. Herbert Hoover, as Secretary of Commerce in 1921, rendered the authoritative dictum that the Russian economy would never revive so long as it was fettered by a Soviet system. "Under their economic system," he said, "there can be no real return to production, and therefore, Russia will have few commodities to export, . . . The abandonment of the present economic system is essential to a restoration of production."[38] Behind Hoover's judgment, there was the rich engineering experience he had had in Russia during the six years prior to the First World War. Hoover developed in Siberia "probably the greatest and richest single body of ore known in the world," ore of such quality as "had hitherto existed only in museum specimens." He was to have received what would have been "the largest engineering fees ever known to man." He reorganized the Kyshtim mines and smelter works, which gave a livelihood to one hundred thousand workers, so that they operated on a profitable basis. He had a premonition of revolution too when he saw one day "a long line of intelligent, decent people brutally chained together" being marched toward a Siberia-bound freight car. But Hoover hated the Bolshevik Revolution. His staff of one hundred and sixty American technicians, which had once been welcomed to Russia, was deported by the communists, while many of the Russian engineers were killed. "Inherent in Communist destruction," Hoover later wrote, was a "shift from intelligence to ignorance." The once-flourishing mines and smelters became idle; "the very furies of ignorance were in the saddle."[39] Hoover knew more about Russian minerals than any man in the world. As late as 1929, the maps he made were still guiding the operations of Soviet

[38] Herbert Hoover, "Trade with Soviet Russia," *Mining and Scientific Press*, CXXII (1921), 538.

[39] *The Memoirs of Herbert Hoover: Years of Adventure, 1874–1920* (New York: Macmillan Co., 1952), pp. 102–08.

mining.[40] He was blind, however, to the latent potentialities in the Soviet idea. He saw and even understood the harshness of the revolutionary response to centuries of suppression, but he could not acknowledge that a society based on socialist premises might be able to administer the economy. His outlook was always managerial, hierarchical, and paternalist.

The recall of American engineers to Russia began seriously in 1927. That year Colonel Hugh Cooper commuted three times between New York and Moscow, and spent a total of six months in the Soviet Union in supervising the design for the dam on the Dnieper River. His reports began to confute the Hoover verdict. The Bolsheviks, said Colonel Cooper, had performed "a miracle in restoring law and order out of chaos." American engineers were especially intrigued by three themes in their perception of Soviet reality. They tended, in the first place, to be historicists; they adjusted themselves to Soviet reality by saying that the Bolshevik Revolution had been *inevitable*. Secondly, as applied scientists, they especially extolled the *experimentalism* of the Soviet rulers, their readiness to try something new; and lastly, the colossal magnitude of the Soviet effort appealed to their instinct for *bigness*, their managerial admiration of sheer size and scope. "Communism," said Colonel Cooper, "was inevitable in 1917 in Russia," just as the French Revolution had been inevitable in 1789. W. J. Austin, president of the Austin company which built the center for the manufacture of Ford cars, saw the Soviet dictatorship as historically justified because autocracy was probably required to "maintain any semblance of order in a vast country which has for centuries known only despotic government." "The rule of the Soviets," he said, "is the only sort of government that could stand between the great mass of the Russian people and chaos." T. D. Campbell, America's master agricultural engineer, found himself sympathetic to Stalin the

---

[40] Charles E. Sorensen, *My Forty Years with Ford* (New York: W. W. Norton & Co., 1956), p. 204.

disciplinarian because "any country after a war and revolution must have stern measures." Walter A. Rukeyser, consultant to the Soviet asbestos mining industry from 1929 to 1931, learned at first hand of the inefficiency and oppressiveness in Soviet existence; he observed sabotage, premeditated and frequent; he witnessed the endless red tape, and the fear of the secret police. Nevertheless, he could not help but admire the "gigantic experiment," and concluded: "Eventually, something good will come out of the sociological experiment in Russia." H. J. Freyn, after working for four years with his company to build a steel industry in the Kuznetsk Basin in Siberia, told the Taylor Society in Chicago in 1931 that the Soviets had accomplished "a remarkable technical and managerial feat, unparalleled in the world's history." T. D. Campbell used all the vocabulary of the Rotarian booster to convey his admiration of Soviet bigness; it was "the biggest farming story the world has ever heard," and the state farms were undertakings "that are simply staggering: stupendous"; he had never seen such giant farms in the United States.[41]

Above all, the work-ethic of the Soviet rulers impressed American engineers; some strain of managerial idealism found itself especially attracted by the dedication to the job which inspired the communist administrators. W. J. Austin admired the sincerity of the Soviet chiefs in their "working indefatigably on industrialization"; he paid tribute to communist leaders who would not allow communist theory to stand in the way of their fulfilling the

[41] Hugh Cooper, "Observations of Present-Day Russia," *Annals of the American Academy of Political and Social Science*, CXXXVIII (1928), 117–18. W. J. Austin, "Why Fear Russia?" as told to Frederick A. Van Fleet, *Scribner's Magazine*, XC (1931), 291–92. Thomas D. Campbell, *Russia, Market or Menace?* (New York: Longmans, Green & Co., 1932), pp. 18–19, 99, 109. H. J. Freyn, "An American Engineer Looks at the Five Year Plan," *The New Republic*, LXVI (1931), 319. Walter Arnold Rukeyser, "Do Our Engineers in Russia Damage America?" *Scribner's Magazine*, XC (1931), 523; *Working for the Soviets: An American Engineer in Russia* (New York: Covici-Friede, 1932), p. 282.

Five Year Plan. These were practical men, who knew how to teach their people to work and save. H. J. Freyn marveled at the long working hours of the Soviet leaders; an eighteen-hour day was the rule rather than the exception. T. D. Campbell was stirred by Stalin's frankness, sincerity, and capacity for leadership, and by his "strong face and piercing black eyes which concentrate on you . . . to such an extent that you hardly feel the presence of an interpreter." He was evidently impressed to such an extent as to affect his physical judgment; his estimate of Stalin as "about five feet, ten inches tall" elevated considerably the Soviet ruler's stature.[42]

Of all the travelers to the Soviet Union, the engineers were, in one sense, the most accurate observers of Soviet reality. For they were not spectators, hurried, handshaking tourists, rushing through inspections of model schools, model hospitals, and model museums. They were participant-observers; they had to work in Soviet factories and mines with Soviet managers and workingmen. They stayed for much longer periods than the usual American visitor; they would sign contracts to remain from one to three years. Everywhere they encountered the inefficiency, timidity, and obstruction of Soviet bureaucrats. The American engineers had built the plants, but, asked Walter Rukeyser, would the Russians know how to run them? "Those of us who have worked with the Soviet," he wrote, "knew only too well the inherent procrastination of the Russian temperament, the love of reports, dissertations, meetings, the cumbersome red tape which exists with every phase of communist industry. . . . There is unbelievable

[42] Stalin at this time made a great impression on Americans as a simple, straightforward man, utterly devoid of vanity. Eugene Lyons, the most critical and alienated observer in the Soviet Union, nevertheless acknowledged: "Even at moments when the behavior of his regime seemed to me most hateful, I retained that liking for Stalin as a human being. I could understand thereafter the devotion to the man held by certain writers of my acquaintance . . . in his makeup, there was nothing of make-believe, nowhere a note of falseness or affectation. His friendliness . . . rang true." Lyons, *Assignment in Utopia*, p. 340.

squandering of the blood-sweated proletarian rouble. . . ."
John Calder complained that he drew salary for three
months while the Russian engineers frustrated all he tried
to do. The Soviet coal industry was excoriated in the report
of one American technician, while the railroad experts,
headed by a Baltimore and Ohio operating man, threatened
to leave altogether. One large firm did pull out lock, stock,
and barrel. The ominous, ubiquitous presence of the Soviet
secret political police was always a generator of anxiety.
When Rukeyser encountered the chief of the Ural GPU,
he was overwhelmed by the "hatred," the "all-burning
egotism," the "sense of omnipotent power in his antagonistic
personality," and he thanked heaven that "nothing conceivable could put me in that man's power." The engineers
saw the trials and purges which were the prelude to the
culminating destruction of the old Bolshevik generation in
1936 and 1937. Rukeyser witnessed the trial and death
sentence of the ablest construction engineers in the Soviet
Union, yet he could not help justifying the secret police:
"whenever the GPU strikes, it is usually with reason.
Perhaps the accusation is trumped-up or exaggerated; . . .
yet behind these flimsy excuses, the GPU is practically
dead-certain that the accused was engaged in activities
against the state." Rukeyser was aware that engineers were
being punished for conditions beyond their power, but
historicist standards had begun to permeate the engineers'
values.[43]

The grandeur of Soviet state planning simply astounded
American engineers. Karl Marx may have ridiculed the
socialists who wrote blueprints for society, but the American engineers found themselves instinctively at home with
a government that aimed to rule by blueprints. Back home
in Montana, Thomas Campbell was running America's
largest mechanized farm—95,000 acres of soil—without a
horse or mule, and financed with two million dollars by

[43] Rukeyser, *Working for the Soviets,* pp. 219–20, 178–80, 266–
67. George A. Burrell, "Experiences of an American Engineer in
Russia," *National Petroleum News,* XXIII (September 9, 1931),
38–40.

J. P. Morgan. He used to dream of a United States Farming Corporation that would be greater than the United States Steel. Now Stalin was offering him one million acres to farm. They talked together for four hours. "I am not a Communist," insisted Campbell. ". . . Nevertheless, I am interested in your agricultural development, as I am an agricultural mechanical engineer. . . ." Stalin rose from his chair, crossed to Campbell's side of the table, took his hand in both of his, and said: "Thank you for that, Mr. Campbell. Now I know that I can believe you. Now I know that we can respect each other and perhaps we can be friends."[44] This was the fellowship of technical managerialists, and to Campbell's mind, it outweighed the peasants' resistance to collectivization, "the most smashing strike the world has ever seen," he called it, as well as the fear he found among the operators at the machine and tractor stations. The engineer felt a kinship to the planner.

Technologists of socialism and capitalism found that their sense of technological community could override their ideological differences. The collaboration of the engineers and executives of the Ford Motor Company with their Soviet counterparts was the most astonishing example of this phenomenon. An early Ford mission to the Soviet Union in 1926 had found industrial conditions too backward and unfavorable for the Ford company's initiative. The Five Year Plan, however, brought a different atmosphere. On May 31, 1929, the Ford Motor Company entered into an agreement with the Supreme Economic Council according to which it undertook to provide the complete plans for a large automobile factory, install the necessary equipment and train the working force. "No

[44] Edward Angly, "Thomas Campbell: Master Farmer," *The Forum*, LXXXVI (1931), 18, 22. Thomas D. Campbell, *Russia, Market or Menace?* pp. 15–17. Owen P. White, "Interview with Thomas D. Campbell: Wheat on the Grand Scale," *Collier's*, LXXXVI (December 20, 1930), 63, 102. Campbell was, according to John G. Winant, a friend of Franklin D. Roosevelt. Cf. John Gilbert Winant, *Letter from Grosvenor Square* (Boston: Houghton Mifflin Co., 1947), p. 189.

other American industrial firm," wrote Charles E. Sorensen, the renowned production manager of the Ford company, "ever did so much business with Communist Russia as Ford Motor Company." The Ford engineers literally created the Soviet automobile industry, as Stalin in 1933 acknowledged. A complete Ford factory called the Molotov Works arose at Gorky, and an assembly plant, the KIM Works, in Moscow. American engineers and mechanics trained Soviet technicians to do their jobs, and imparted to them the industrial common sense of keeping factories clean and free from junk, and the art of not wasting time. As New Year's Day approached in 1931, the opening day for the Molotov Works, Edsel Ford had a farewell conference with Frank Bennett and Charles Sorensen. "Mr. Bennett," said Edsel Ford, "when the first car comes off the assembly lines, would you send us a cable? It means very much to this company."[45]

The Ford company evidently sustained a financial loss in its Soviet venture of more than a half-million dollars. Nevertheless, as Nevins and Hill tell us, Henry Ford would gladly have sacrificed twice that sum to give his ideas a practical illustration on the world stage.[46] And here we have that strange phenomenon of the underlying community of technologists, transcending the divergences of social system. Charles Sorensen had no use for the bureaucratic socialism of the Soviet Union. But when he talked with the mechanical engineer, V. I. Meschlauk, chief of the Supreme Economic Council, he found they spoke a common language. He could tell him bluntly when they inspected the Putilov Steel Works that the best thing to do with them was to get a "barrel of dynamite," place it in the middle of the plant, and "blow it up." Years later, and long after the tragic death sentence of Meschlauk, Sorensen wondered if he were still alive: "I would certainly like to pay my respects. Meschlauk was the outstanding man in Rus-

[45] Sorensen, *My Forty Years with Ford*, pp. 193–94. Allan Nevins and Frank Ernest Hill, *Ford: Expansion and Challenge 1915–1933* (New York: Charles Scribner's Sons, 1957), pp. 674–80.
[46] Nevins and Hill, *Ford: Expansion and Challenge*, p. 682.

sia to carry on the developments we prepared for him."
Stalin in those days would say as he passed Sorensen's
conference table: "Allo, Sharley," the greeting to the
American Vulcan, bearer of technological know-how.

By the year 1931, the roster of firms giving "technical
aid" to the Soviet Union included General Electric, bringing its Mazda Lamps; Albert Kahn, supervising factory
construction; John Calder, directing the construction of
steel mills; McKee and Company, building the largest
iron smelting project in Europe; and Stuart, James, and
Cooke, modernizing the Soviet coal industry. That year,
however, the honeymoon period of American engineers
in the Soviet Union came to an end. By May 1931, the
reports of friction between American and Soviet engineers
began to accumulate. The tempo of the Five Year Plan
strained nerves; the Russian engineers, moreover, were
jealous of the higher salaries and better living conditions
of the Americans. Also, some American engineers were
incompetent, and others malcontent. A committee of the
American Society of Civil Engineering warned its members
about these problems, and reminded them that Russian
engineers worked under conditions of perpetual anxiety.
An error in design might be punished by death; therefore
responsibility was a burden Soviet technicians avoided.[47]

Meanwhile, however, more than one thousand American
engineers were reported working in the Soviet Union in
1931. As the depression closed opportunities to American
technologists, their eyes turned toward the society that
evidently welcomed their skills. Amtorg, the Russian commercial agency in New York, claimed that it hired ten
thousand Americans in 1931.[48] Little communal villages

[47] "Engineering Employment in Russia," *Civil Engineering,* I
(1931), 757.

[48] An American Engineer, "Industry and Engineering in the Union
of Socialist Soviet Republics," *Technology Review,* XXX (1930), 77.
Eve Garrett Grady, "American Engineers in Russia," *Saturday Eve-
ning Post,* CCIII (March 14, 1931), 42. Ruth Kennell and Milly
Bennett, "American Immigrants in Russia," *American Mercury,*
XXV (1932), 463–64.

of American engineers with their families arose in the Soviet Union. There was an awareness in the American engineering profession of a tremendous historical drama.
George M. Purver, consulting engineer, spoke and wrote
about it for the American Society of Civil Engineering in
New York:

> We are privileged to live in a time when the engineering pro-
> fession is coming into its own. . . . Before us is being opened
> a great panorama of engineering skill that the world has never
> seen before. What was formerly a backward country of over
> one hundred and fifty million population is being brought into
> contact with the most modern developments in engineering.
> . . . Many of our members will be credited with gigantic con-
> struction undertakings, crowded within a short period of time—
> "five years" in the U.S.S.R. Engineering work stands as the
> greatest monument of peaceful arts and creation; and our So-
> ciety, the great exponent of a great profession, should make
> itself felt in the land of reconstruction.[49]

Curiously, though the engineers were the best observers
of Soviet reality, they were significantly the poorest pre-
dictors of the Soviet future. Unlike the educators and social workers, they did tend to see clearly the emerging
new class hierarchy; they met daily the drab incompetence,
the creaking, ponderous sluggishness of Soviet planning,
and the dull oppressiveness of the secret police. But the
technical intellectuals tended, however, to look for the return of a variant of capitalism. Colonel Cooper felt the
Soviets would have to modify their attitude to private
capital; Walter Rukeyser doubted whether the Russian
temperament could master American technology; T. D.
Campbell thought that with general education, communism would not last another twelve years; Sorensen saw
no prospects for technological advance in a planned
economy.

[49] George M. Purver, "The Engineer and Russia," *Civil Engineering*, I (1931), 547. Also cf. Anna Louise Strong, *I Change Worlds:
The Remaking of an American* (New York: Henry Holt, 1935),
pp. 316–32.

The ideological intellectuals (writers, social scientists, social workers) were more selective in their perceptions. They wished to study education in Russia, public health, or sexual freedom, but since they scarcely worked at regular jobs in the Soviet Union, their observations had a skewness. They saw the official surface; they did not experience the inner tensions. Their own discontents, however, made them empathize with and perceive the spirit which surmounted the unimaginable technical incompetence. If the ideological intellectuals had a blind spot for the secret police, they responded to the inner liberation of Soviet energies. Almost without exception, the ideologists also went astray in their predictions; they foresaw a democratic, humanistic development; they never foresaw Stalinism.

Such was the epistemological paradox; the technical participant observed the everyday realities, but doubted that faith could move technology; the spectator idealists sensed the faith, but never grasped the potential depth of its perversion.

Meanwhile, however, the engineers' reports of the daring adventure of Soviet planned effort reached the American consciousness. "Planning" on the Soviet model became the symbol for the social intervention that would restore the social equilibrium. As George Soule wrote in 1932: "It is curious how the idea of economic planning has come to dominate all others in foreign views of the Russian revolution." The Russian economy had not conformed to Hoover's prophecy of collapse; it was speaking a language of production that was far "more comprehensible to the American consciousness than the jargon of revolutionary plotters. . . . We listened intently to what she had to say, . . ." For Russia was proposing to construct a great industrial civilization, even to surpass the American, and doing so "by an exercise of national will and a national economic plan. At once our interest in Russia was increased a hundredfold."[50]

[50] George Soule, *A Planned Society* (New York: Macmillan Co., 1932), pp. 204–06.

Eminent engineers urged the idea of planning on an American government that coped with depression. Ralph E. Flanders, then vice-president of the American Society of Mechanical Engineers, later the Senator from Vermont and bulwark against "McCarthyism," envisaged that economic planning would bring an avalanche of goods such as "no utopian dreamer in his busiest slumbers ever dreamed." The ablest engineer in the service of the New Deal, Morris Llewellyn Cooke, wrote some years later of the Soviet Union as that society which was carrying out more completely than any other the logic of large-scale production, the factory system, and the machine technique. Cooke, the foremost living exponent of scientific management in the United States, was regarded as the inspirer of "some of the New Deal's most popular programs." He wrote in praise of the directive, "teleological" approach of the Soviet Five Year Plan; he admired its conscious guidance of the use of resources to attain the national goal. The American democracy could use this approach, he said, once it cast off "such debilitating appendages as pork-barrel legislation, and monkey-gland politics."[51] The travelers' reports from the Soviet Union thus ramified themselves through the engineering consciousness of the New Deal.

The collectivist idea, fed by Soviet experience, was of course only one component in the philosophy of the New Deal. It was a "commitment," as Tugwell has written, in the formative months of its first stage. Later there was a shift "from the collectivistic First to the atomistic Second New Deal," and a standpoint more akin to that of Justice Brandeis became dominant.[52] The notion of the experimental collective reconstruction of society remained, however, as a perduring theme. The term "economic planning"

[51] Morris Llewellyn Cooke and Philip Murray, *Organized Labor and Production* (New York: Harper & Bros., 1940), pp. 30, 181–82. "Potomacus, Trouble-Shooter Extraordinary," *The New Republic*, CXII (1945), 220. Also, cf. Kenneth E. Trombley, *The Life and Times of a Happy Liberal: A Biography of Morris Llewellyn Cooke* (New York: Harper & Bros., 1954), pp. 225, 234.

[52] Tugwell, *The Democratic Roosevelt*, pp. 220, 246, 545–46.

became a basic category in American social thought. It had not appeared until 1929 among the titles of articles recorded in the *Readers' Guide to Periodical Literature,* but the depression's advent brought thirteen citations during the next three years. The example of Soviet success in planned economy in contrast to the failure of capitalist economy to surmount depression became a reiterated theme in political books and conferences.[53] By January 1933, the Soviet model had come to occupy so prominent a place in American political thinking that Colonel Edward M. House, Nestor of the Wilson Administration, could introduce a collection of travelers' essays with words of welcome.[54] The volume was edited by the fervid Pro-

[53] Paul T. Douglas, *The Coming of a New Party* (New York: McGraw-Hill Book Co., 1932), pp. 90–93. *On Economic Planning,* eds. Mary Van Kleeck and Mary L. Fleddérus (New York: Covici-Friede, 1935), pp. xiii, xiv, 239–40, 256–75, 262. Lewis L. Lorwin, *Time for Planning: A Socio-Economic Theory and Program for the Twentieth Century* (New York: Harper & Bros., 1945), pp. xx, xxi, 11, 17, 36–37. Dr. Lorwin's collaborator, A. F. Hinrichs, a director of the National Economic and Social Planning Association founded in 1934, had written after a summer in 1930 spent in the Soviet Union: "Only recently have we learned with something of a shock of the progressive development of a communistic economy." It was fitting, therefore, he said, "to develop a picture of Russian economy —the first example of a modern economic system founded and managed upon the principle of conscious planning." He was stirred as were many other economists: "A plan with a will! This is the spirit of Russian economy that distinguishes it from all others today. Elsewhere men talk of a rational organization of industry, but none of our Western discussion has yet involved the concept of purposefulness." A. Ford Hinrichs and William Adams Brown Jr., "The Planned Economy of Soviet Russia," *Political Science Quarterly,* XLVI (1931), 362, 402.

[54] *The New Russia,* ed. Jerome Davis (New York: John Day, 1933). Jerome Davis visited the Soviet Union more often than any other American. He went first as a Y.M.C.A. worker to Russia in 1915 when Czar Nicholas II still ruled. He remained for two and a half years, became fluent in Russian, witnessed the October Revolution, and was for a time in charge of all Y.M.C.A. activities in the Soviet Union. On his numerous subsequent visits, he came to know Stalin, Trotsky, and Radek. As a professor of sociology at Yale University, he had presumably the academic qualifications for accurate observation. His reports on the Stalinist era have, however, a bizarre

fessor Jerome Davis, perhaps the most uncritical of the academic admirers of Stalinism. Only a few months before, Colonel House had bestowed the blessing of Wilsonian idealism on the presidential candidate Franklin D. Roosevelt. The threads of the unsuccessful Bullitt mission of 1919 were being renewed as America pragmatically found its way toward an appreciation of Soviet experimentalism.

Thus, through its philosophers, educators, social workers, economists, engineers, and liberal spokesmen, traveling to behold the new sociological scheme of things, there was constructed in the American intellectual consciousness (or shall we say the American intellectual unconsciousness) a status for the Soviet Union as the conscience-model of social experiment.

The liberal weeklies led the way in intellectual reconstruction. Their influence on intellectual opinion, and above all, on the underlying feeling with respect to the Soviet Union, was immense. Thurman Arnold, bold New Deal attorney and admired analyst of capitalist folklore, said that by reading *The Nation* and *The New Republic* he could "tell what my liberal colleagues are going to say tomorrow . . . there have been more new notions put across by these two publications than any other two in the history of American letters. I forgot Stuart Chase. Certainly there is no small town in the country where someone is not caught by his effective illustration."[55] Liberals and New Dealers were saying in 1933 what editors of *The New Republic* taught them in the previous decade. And of the thirteen editors of *The New Republic* in 1932, five had already written their confirmatory reports of the Soviet experiment—Bruce Bliven, John Dewey, E. C. Lin-

tone when read in the light of Khrushchev's revelation of actualities at the Twentieth Party Congress in 1956. According to Professor Davis: "President Roosevelt called the moving pictures I took in Russia the best he had ever seen on the life of the common people there." Jerome Davis, *Behind Soviet Power* (New York: Readers' Press, 1946), p. 7.

[55] Malcolm Cowley, "Books That Changed Our Minds," *The New Republic*, LXXXVII (December 7, 1938), 136.

demann, Waldo Frank, and R. G. Tugwell. Bruce Bliven spoke for his magazine when he wrote that "private capitalism has never, in any country, done a job one-half so good from the standpoint of social engineering as that which is being done in the U.S.S.R. today." The building of America, he said, had been "an incredibly botched job." The significance of the Soviet experiment, he emphasized, was international; it was not merely an exhibit of what could be done in developing a backward country rapidly. This was an experiment in socialized economy with universal consequences: "if it works in Russia at all, if it succeeds even 60 or 70 per cent, . . . then there is every reason to believe that anywhere else in the Occident it would be a grand and glorious, a shining success."[56]

Oswald Garrison Villard, editor of *The Nation,* too, had already brought the full homage of American liberalism to the Soviet effort. Though the Russia he saw was almost literally "from a car window," though he spoke no Russian and never saw a Russian village or talked with any peasants, Villard was moved to write with conviction: "This, I repeat, is the most stupendous governmental feat ever undertaken—the social, moral, political, industrial, economic emancipation of a people and its reorganization upon the basis of service to the society and to the nation, with the profit-making motive suddenly removed from the individual. These Bolsheviks are playing for the greatest of stakes. . . . It suffices to say that the minority which controls the destiny of Russia is on its way with extraordinary and completely unselfish devotion, with the fiercest determination to succeed at any cost. . . ." True, the Bolshevik leaders were fanatics, but, said Villard: "Who else but fanatics would have the courage needed for the task or could be relied upon to drive through to the end without essential compromise? . . . No timid or half-way reformers could suffice for such a task." To those who found the Soviet dictatorship, violence, and repression not

[56] Bruce Bliven, "Circular Ticket," *The New Republic,* LXIX (1932), 340.

unlike Mussolini's Fascist regime, Villard replied that there was "this difference: the Bolsheviks are working for the good of the masses of the working people."[57] American liberalism at this time did not believe in Acton's metaphysical law that evil means necessarily corrupt the end.

Perhaps New Dealers learned the lesson of Soviet pragmatism too well. Thurman Arnold later saw in the Moscow trials a simple procedure by which political philosophers were being displaced by down-to-earth practical men; the Marxian theologians, he wrote, were being superseded by "the dictatorship of a practical politician." He echoed indeed the editorial of *The New Republic* which regarded the Moscow trials as evidence of the fate that awaits intellectuals who are not pragmatic enough for the historical necessities.[58] But this is a later tragic story.

To what extent finally did the reports of the American travelers to the Soviet Union affect the political philosophy of Franklin D. Roosevelt? From the first, Roosevelt had a sympathetic interest in the Soviet effort at social reconstruction, and regarded its experimentalism and social idealism as akin to his own. Many years later the pact between Stalin and Hitler brought disillusionment. Early in his administration, on October 5, 1933, President Roosevelt told his Secretary of the Interior, Harold L. Ickes, that "what we were doing in this country were some of the things that were being done in Russia and even some things that were being done under Hitler in Germany. But we were doing them in an orderly way."[59] Six years later, on a rainy afternoon on February 10, 1940, Roosevelt told a large silent crowd of students, a few of whom occasionally booed, how his attitude toward the Soviet society had evolved. He spoke from the south portico of the

[57] Oswald Garrison Villard, "Russia from a Car Window," *The Nation*, CXXIX (1929), p. 517.

[58] Thurman W. Arnold, *The Folklore of Capitalism* (New Haven; Yale University Press, 1937), pp. 92–93; "The Trial of the Trotskyites in Russia," *The New Republic*, LXXXVIII (1936), 88–89.

[59] *The Secret Diary of Harold L. Ickes: The First Thousand Days* (New York: Simon & Schuster, 1953), p. 104.

White House to several thousands of the American Youth Congress: "More than twenty years ago, while most of you were pretty young children, I had the utmost sympathy for the Russian people. In the early days of communism, I recognized that many leaders in Russia were bringing education and better health, and above all, better opportunity to millions who had been kept in ignorance and serfdom under the imperial regime." He had disliked the regimentation of communism, "abhorred the indiscriminate killings," and deprecated the banishment of religion, but had, he said, "with many of you, hoped that Russia would work out its own problems and their government would eventually become a peace-loving, popular government with free ballot, . . . That hope is today either shattered or is put away in storage against some better day. The Soviet Union, as a matter of practical fact, as everybody knows, who has got the courage to face the fact, . . . is run by a dictatorship, a dictatorship as absolute as any other dictatorship in the world."[60] With these words, Roosevelt closed the chapter of the Soviet experience in the political consciousness of the New Deal.

The American travelers did not have more than the usual share of human naïveté. They saw certain realities strongly. They did not foresee the latent evil of Stalinism. The Soviet social world turned out to be less determinate and predictable than they thought. Their perception was perspectival, as all perceptions are, distorted rather than false. And perhaps if their advice had been followed, some evils might have been spared both the Soviet Union and the rest of the world. Perhaps if the United States had earlier abandoned the Hoover thesis, if it had welcomed Soviet society into the world's councils, if it had staved off depression by progressive economic measures, perhaps if action had been taken early against Nazi Germany, then a more moderate, right-wing form of Bolshevism might have emerged dominant. We cannot say. But American liberals

[60] *New York Times*, February 11, 1940, pp. 1, 44.

must understand rather than repress the chapter of the Soviet influence from their history of the past.

Last December I asked Roger Baldwin, the leader emeritus of the American Civil Liberties Union, to tell me what he thought of his traveler's report of 1927 on the Soviet Union.[61] "We went wrong," he said, "we were starry-eyed. We didn't see the potentiality of totalitarianism." Three things moved us, he said. The stupendous change, Marx and the French Revolution rolled up into one; it was exciting, something new every day, so that an uncommitted journalist like Duranty wrote: "This is the only place in the world where the news has salt." Secondly, he said, we muckrakers and reformers had always said: "Let the people at the bottom rule, and all will be well." Now here was Soviet democracy; the people were being given their chance. And lastly, there was the communist idealism, the leap forward of the brotherhood of man. I wondered whether Mr. Baldwin's earlier perception and advocacy had been so completely the projections on history of an alienated intellectual. But the gloomy chapter of the American intellectuals was not to be gainsaid.

[61] Roger N. Baldwin, *Liberty Under the Soviets* (New York: Vanguard Press, 1928), pp. 7, 272.

Marxian Tragedians

Every movement lives on a hope; it offers its adherents a way of life, a path to happiness. And every movement likes to repress those incidents that cast doubt on its ability to bring happiness to its communicants. For a movement never lives only in the future, and its kingdom is always partially of this world. To participate in a movement here and now, to partake of its glimpse of the new world, is supposed to transmute the human character, and to alter present man into the semblance of those to come. An unregenerate, unredeemed member brings a self-doubt which the movement would prefer to forget. Such was the problem of evil that the lives of Karl Marx's daughter, Eleanor, and her lover, Edward Aveling, posed for the socialist universe. The official annals of Marxism usually pass them by.

Eleanor Marx was the youngest of her father's children. She was born to him shortly before the son, Edgar, died, and she became the supreme consolation to the sorrowing father. "Tussy," she was called, and though the household was poverty-haunted, she grew to be "a merry little thing, as round as a ball and like cream and roses." Karl Marx came to feel at one with his daughter. "Tussy is me," he said in later years. He told her never-ending fairy tales in which he projected his own character as a maker of history into that of a make-believe hero. To the listening child, the father could speak his innermost heart. One such story which "went on for months and months" was about "Hans Röckle . . . a Hoffmann-like magician, who kept a toyshop, and who was always 'hard-up.'" In short, he was Marx himself. "His shop was full of the most wonderful things—of wooden men and women, giants and dwarfs, kings and queens, workmen and masters," precisely like Marx's *Capital* and materialist conception of history. And Hans, like his progenitor, "could never meet his obligations either to the devil or the butcher, and was therefore—much against the grain—constantly obliged to sell his toys to the devil." The toys went through horrendous adventures, but finally ended happily in Hans's shop. The ordeals of history had their triumphant culmination.

Father and daughter reveled in romantic novels. Together they read Marryat, Cooper, and above all, Walter Scott. There was literally a "Scott mania" in the Marx household; the leader of the international working-class movement immersed himself in tales of feudal lords and ladies, and Scottish clans and chiefs. Eleanor was perturbed to learn that she was descended, on her mother's side, from the hated Campbells. Nonetheless, she and Karl Marx plotted to rouse the Highlanders once again in a mighty uprising. Meanwhile, Eleanor played and wrestled with the neighborhood boys in the street. For years she could not be persuaded to go to school. Her father himself taught her how to read. Eleanor would listen attentively to the grownups talking about the Civil War in America; then she would sit down and write letters of encouragement to Abraham Lincoln.

Like many an atheist father, Karl Marx found that his little daughter did not grow naturally into a simple rationalist. Eleanor, at the age of five or six, was experiencing religious longings: she had been moved by the beautiful music in a Roman Catholic church. She took her questions to her father, who put her firmly aright. "He quietly made everything clear and straight, so that from that hour to this," wrote Eleanor Marx, "no doubt would ever cross my mind again." Her father told her the Gospel in historical materialist version, the story "of the carpenter whom the rich men killed." The daughter remembered, too, his saying often: "After all, we can forgive Christianity much, because it taught us the worship of the child." Eleanor identified herself with her father's ideas and activities. She worshiped him, and she reproached herself later with his memory: "I shall never be good and unselfish as he was. I am *not good*—never shall be, though I try. . . ."[1]

But something in Eleanor remained restless and unstilled in the socialist household. There were strange tensions between the mother and daughter, between the daughter and father. "My mother and I loved each other passionately," wrote Eleanor to Olive Schreiner, "but she did not know me as Father did. One of the bitterest of many bitter sorrows of my life is that my mother died thinking, despite all our love, that I had been hard and cruel, and never guessing that to save her and Father sorrow I had sacrificed the best, freshest years of my life. But Father," she continued, "though he did not *know* till just before the end, felt he must trust me—our natures were so exactly alike!" Some darkness intervened even in Eleanor's love for her father; it left her with an abiding weakness and a craving for support. "If you had ever been in our home," she wrote, "if you had ever seen my Father and Mother, known what *he* was to me, you would understand better both my yearning for love, given and received, and my intense need of sympathy. Of my father I was so sure! For long miserable years there was a shadow between us— I must tell you the whole story some day—yet our love was always the same."[2] Her father's love, however, was of the kind that left Eleanor without confidence in herself. Despite her knowledge, zest for hard work, and vivid style,

[1] Especially illuminating on her childhood is a volume recently published by the Foreign Languages Publishing House, Moscow, entitled *Reminiscences of Marx and Engels,* which brings together much significant material, including several essays previously unavailable. The book has such articles as Eleanor Marx Aveling on "Karl Marx," and "Remarks on a Letter by the Young Marx"; Edward Aveling on "Engels at Home"; Franzisca Kugelmann, "Small Traits of Marx's Great Character"; Friedrich Lessner, "Before 1848 and After."

[2] There is an important memoir by Havelock Ellis, "Eleanor Marx," *Modern Monthly,* IX (September 1935), 283–95. Felix Barker gives valuable information in "Department of Amplification," *The New Yorker,* November 27, 1954, pp. 190–99.

she was content to serve others as a hack assistant. She had
to be urged to write her short articles for the socialist press.

Eleanor gave herself to the socialist movement as none
of Marx's other daughters did. She wrote, agitated, and
translated. She was scarcely twenty when she finished her
version of Lissagaray's *History of the Paris Commune of
1871;* her father dutifully revised and corrected her translation and made it their joint work. She translated at socialist congresses, perhaps even mistranslating when opponents of her father's doctrine spoke. She worked hard
with Will Thorne to organize the gas workers during the
wave of the New Unionism, and led the strike of the
women at Silvertown. "Tussy is the leader of the gas workers (on the sly)," wrote Engels proudly. She was among
the leaders of the epoch-making London Dockers' Strike of
1889. And in 1890 she helped organize the first International May Day demonstration in London on behalf of the
eight-hour day. A month before she died, Eleanor was
proud and joyous with a gift the Miners' Union had sent
her—a fountain pen and case, by way of thanks for her
voluntary service as translator at the International Miners'
Congress.

The theater, however, was Eleanor Marx's great love.
She wanted to become an actress, and took dramatic les-
sons, but Karl Marx begrudged his daughter's ambition.
He complained to Engels that "the child is suffering from
a mental discord which is quite undermining her health,"
that she was not frank, and was not confiding in him. "The
child" was already in her twenty-sixth year, and "burning
with eagerness" for an "independent career as an artist."
Marx, however, wished Eleanor to be more like her mother,
Jenny, who had been a model of self-effacing domestic-
ity. There had been no revolutionary women in the German
workingmen's clubs he and Engels had led. Eleanor unfortunately insisted upon applying Marx's words to the
cause of women's emancipation: she was a New Woman,
and Marx evidently was uneasy with this phenomenon.
Eleanor could at least work ardently in amateur theatri-

cals. Engels saw her act in 1881, and thought she "was very good in the emotional scenes." He gathered she was taking Ellen Terry as her model, but trusted she would soon develop her own style. Eleanor acted and recited before all sorts of workingmen's groups. She stirred one audience, gathered to help a Communard widow, with her rendition of *The Pied Piper of Hamelin*. When she lectured to the Playgoer's Club on naturalism in the modern drama, a critic said that not until he had listened to Eleanor had he realized "of what noble beauty the English language is capable."

Ibsen's plays most enraptured Eleanor Marx. When *A Doll's House* was first produced in England in 1884, it had the impact of an epochal manifesto calling on restive women to rise to end their immemorial enslavement. Outside the theater, after the first performance, a group of young women talked excitedly about the meaning of the play as harbinger to a new era: Olive Schreiner (authoress of *The Story of an African Farm*) and Eleanor Marx were among them. A generation of young women was prepared to shatter their doll's houses. Eleanor, too, was ready to live by the new gospel. Her mother, father, and a sister had all died within the last three years. Karl Marx might have stopped short this nonsense of a rival, petty-bourgeois prophet. Eleanor, living alone, embraced the new creed: was it not the corollary of all her father's writings? She left her doll's house to enter a dungeon of deceptions.

Eleanor Marx henceforth lived and breathed Ibsen. She translated *An Enemy of the People, The Lady from the Sea,* and *The Wild Duck.* The Ibsen Reading Club was a reality in 1885, and Eleanor saw a great deal of Bernard Shaw there.[3] Several years later he lampooned the young Ibsenite men and women in *The Philanderer,* but during this Ibsenite phase, Shaw joined Eleanor and Edward Aveling in drawing-room readings and performances of

[3] For details of this friendship, see Archibald Henderson, *George Bernard Shaw* (New York, 1956).

Ibsen's plays. On one such occasion, Eleanor read Nora's lines, Aveling took the husband's part, while Shaw was the blackmailer Krogstad. He even acted with Eleanor in her theatricals for workingmen's clubs. At these readings, wrote Eleanor,

we want to have only people who we know do love and understand Ibsen already, or those who will love and understand him, and who in turn will go on preaching him to others.

The young Ibsenite women tried hard, indeed, to be unwomanly. They cultivated a new standard of frankness in speaking about the details of their sexual feelings; they were done with the prudery that was the guise of women's inferiority. Olive Schreiner wrote to the inquiring Havelock Ellis in 1884 that she and Eleanor Marx both had their "most wonderful mental activity" toward the end and just after their menstrual periods. She spoke of the coextensive power of the mental-sexual and physical-sexual. The scholar A. H. Bullen was shocked by the freedom with which Eleanor discussed "the less decorous aspect" of the Elizabethan drama. Both Olive and Eleanor suffered from a variety of ailments in the stomach and chest; rebellion took its toll of the New Women in all manner of neurotic symptoms. Olive thought Eleanor might tell Ellis about her experiences so that he could use them in an article for a medical journal.[4]

The uncompromising personal rebellion in Eleanor Marx alienated a person such as Beatrice Webb (then Beatrice Potter), searching her way among London's poor and its social movements. They met one afternoon in 1883 in the British Museum's refreshment room. Beatrice was repelled by Eleanor's blunt rejection of Christianity as an "immoral illusion" and her view of Jesus as a weak-minded, unheroic individual. Beatrice was a novice in social science, and Eleanor impressed her with that fact. In her

[4] *The Letters of Olive Schreiner, 1876–1920,* edited by S. C. Cronwright-Schreiner, and the biographies of Olive Schreiner by Daisy Lucie Hobman and Vera Buchanan-Gould.

diary, Beatrice Potter wrote her impressions of this first scientific socialist she had met:

> In her person she is comely, dressed in a slovenly picturesque way, with curly black hair flying in all directions. Fine eyes full of life and sympathy, otherwise ugly features and expression, and complexion showing the signs of an unhealthy excited life, kept up with stimulants and tempered by narcotics. Lives alone, is much connected with Bradlaugh set. . . .

The young Havelock Ellis, however, found Eleanor Marx quite different. They took long walks together during a week in the country, and Ellis wrote: "I have never known a woman who on a long summer's day ramble diffused so potent an axillary fragrance." Ellis' impressions, recorded in a language of medical romanticism, are in keeping with the photograph of Eleanor, with warm lustrous eyes, and a face modeled in sincerity. Small wonder that Shaw in those days felt himself attracted to her, for Eleanor was a woman unlike the drab females he had known, a woman transfigured by a cause.[5] Eleanor was living alone, but not for long. The cause could enclose one with evil too; it tied her life to Edward Aveling.

To Eleanor Marx, agitated with the cause of women's emancipation, brooding over the death of mother, father, and sister, Edward Aveling appeared as a socialist knight in her distress. Aveling had met Karl Marx just once, but the old man had after a fashion given him his blessing. The occasion was a lecture which Aveling was giving to the children of the Orphan Working School on "Insects and Flowers." "When the lecture was over," Aveling remembered, "an old gentleman with a very leonine head,

[5] In the literature of the socialist movement, see: Eduard Bernstein, *My Years of Exile*, translated by Bernard Miall (London, 1921); H. M. Hyndman, *Further Reminiscences* (London, 1912); Max Beer, *Fifty Years of International Socialism* (London, 1935); Wilhelm Liebknecht, *Karl Marx: Biographical Memoirs*, translated by Ernest Untermann (Chicago, 1901); Beatrice Webb, *My Apprenticeship* (Penguin, 1938).

together with a lady and young girl, came up and introduced themselves to me." They were Karl Marx, his wife, and their daughter Eleanor. The gentleman gave Aveling "words of too generous appreciation and encouragement. . . ."

Edward Aveling, then barely thirty, already had an academic career behind him. He was making his living as a scientific journalist, textbook writer, and private tutor in the sciences. He had once been a professor at the London Hospital and the University of London, from which he had received a doctorate; a new career, however, opened to him when he became the tutor in science to the daughters of Charles Bradlaugh, who was battering at the doors of Parliament for admission as its first avowed atheist member. The religion of science had burst with full force on the London public. Workingmen, shopkeepers, and clerks were learning geology, chemistry, and paleontology, and watching demonstrations and experiments with all the fervor that once had gone into observing the rituals of transubstantiation. Even old Marx was captivated by the new creed, and wended his way to lectures by Huxley and Tyndall. Edward Aveling was soon called upon to teach science to Bradlaugh's coworker, the lovely Annie Besant, the most powerful woman orator in Britain, its acknowledged atheist martyr, who had had her children torn from her by a vindictive English court. Aveling taught Annie Besant science, and she led him into the ranks of Freethought. He became a prolific author of tracts for the secularist movement; among them were such titles as *A Godless Life the Happiest and Most Useful, God Dies: Nature Remains, The Wickedness of God, Irreligion of Science,* and *Why I Dare Not Be a Christian.* Soon Aveling was also writing passionate passages in rationalist journals concerning the loveliness of Annie's face, form, and mind, and announcing that "she shall be the sole mistress of my life." He wrote the creed of the secular missionary:

To us, the most intense form of affection conceivable would be between a man and a woman who both believed fully in the happier future of humanity and were both toiling to bring about that desired end.[6]

During 1882, however, Aveling began to frequent the reading room of the British Museum. Until then, as Annie Besant said, he had never uttered a word on socialism but now he "fell into company of some of the Bohemian Socialists" who gathered there, notably Eleanor Marx and Bernard Shaw. Aveling's intellectual history was written in sexual terms. He was a secularist when he was Annie Besant's lover; he became a socialist under Eleanor Marx's aegis. When Karl Marx was posthumously attacked, Aveling came to his defense in the freethinking organ *Progress*. Eleanor Marx was immensely grateful; she became Aveling's editorial assistant.

Edward Aveling was beyond doubt the most bizarre person who ever joined the socialists. His appearance was forbidding. "Nobody can be so bad as Aveling looks," it was said. Repulsive though he was, he claimed to need but a half-hour's start of the handsomest man in London to achieve his conquest. A strange evil emanated from his presence, as from a diabolical source of being. Olive Schreiner, after hearing him read *Ghosts* at the Ibsen Club, wrote: "I am beginning to have such a horror of Dr. A. . . . To say I dislike him doesn't express it all; I have a fear and horror of him when I am near. Every time I see him this shrinking grows stronger." Five years later, her horror of Aveling had grown so intense, she wrote, that it "does more to cripple my power of life and work, than all the close personal sorrows of my life."

With jealousy's agony, Annie Besant watched Edward Aveling making his transition from secularism to socialism, from herself to Eleanor Marx. She engaged Eleanor in a public controversy, allegedly over atheism, but more clearly for the claim to Edward Aveling. Annie hated Eleanor all the more as Marx's daughter gibed stridently that atheism was an outmoded bourgeois creed, and that

[6] See Gertrude Marvin Williams, *The Passionate Pilgrim: A Life of Annie Besant* (New York, 1931).

henceforth socialism was labor's philosophy. Annie read the rejection of organized atheism as the rejection of herself. She finally came to the point by publicly accusing Eleanor Marx in her weekly column in *The National Reformer* of having invented "a gross and scandalous libel on Dr. Edward Aveling," thereby bringing discord into the ranks of Freethought, and giving aid and comfort to "the Christian foe." Soon, however, the sorrowing Annie took solace in evening duets with Bernard Shaw, who had lost Eleanor as Annie had Edward. With Shaw's help, Annie Besant began her sojourn in Fabian Socialism, a brief episode in her celebrated pilgrim's progress to theosophy.

Was there any libel of which Edward Aveling was innocent? He remained cheerfully indifferent to women's rights now that Eleanor's love shone upon him. He gave to *Progress* a socialist direction, and burst into song:

> *The trill of a lark; the sound of a sea;*
> *The voice of a maid; a man's heart strife;*
> *Green grass growing on a salt-tossed lea;*
> *Strong hopes growing in a storm-tossed life.*

There was a hollow Shelleyan echo in Aveling's verse. Indeed, the two lovers thought Shelley was the poet-spokesman of the full freedom of men and women. They brought to the Shelley Society, furthermore, the endorsement of Karl Marx that Shelley was "one of the advanced guard of socialism." Freedom was both economic and sexual.

Thus it was that Eleanor Marx entered into a "free marriage" with Edward Aveling. They could not be legally united because Aveling already had a living wife. According to Aveling, she was a wealthy religious bigot who had broken with him because he was a freethinker. Eleanor was all the more moved to sympathy by the wrong her lover had sustained. From the first, however, there was sadness in this socialist union. Olive Schreiner, Eleanor's closest woman friend, wrote to Havelock Ellis in July 1884 that Eleanor Marx "is now to be called Mrs. Aveling. I was glad to see her face. I love her. But she looks so miserable." Eleanor insisted on making things difficult for herself. She formally notified the principal of the school in which she was teaching that she had entered into a free alliance, and the principal reluctantly felt obliged to dismiss her. Eleanor could take pride in her gesture for love's freedom, but her alliance brought her daily misery. Three years later, in March 1887 she wrote desperately to Havelock Ellis: "I should be glad to get any work I am capable of doing. I need work much, and find it very difficult to get. 'Respectable' people won't employ me." It was during this period that Eleanor tried without success to commit suicide by taking an overdose of opium. She was rescued. It was not known what action of Edward Aveling's had led her to this first attempt to kill herself.

Edward Aveling would have been ready to die for the Socialist Cause in some moment of supreme sacrifice; he was also ready to deceive it every day. His political life was a series of expulsions. The Executive Council of the Social Democratic Federation tried to prevent him from joining their organization. The Independent Labour party expelled him under circumstances so unpleasant that the secretary did not care to divulge them. Aveling would nonchalantly expropriate socialist funds. During the Haymarket Affair, money was collected to send a cablegram to the governor of Illinois asking him not to execute the condemned anarchists: Aveling took the money for himself. His conscience with regard to socialist women was equally easy: he seduced them wherever and whenever he could. Friedrich Engels received letters from respected women socialists saying they could not attend his social "evenings" so long as Aveling was there. Old Engels remained loyal to the daughter of his best friend and her chosen man.

Then in 1886 the Avelings made a tour of the United States on behalf of the American socialist movement. The usual troubles ensued. The Executive of the Socialist

Labour party warned their European comrades against Edward Aveling; he had cheated them with false accounts. Engels, his judgment clouded by affection, retorted vehemently that the New York Socialists were worse than the jury which had condemned the Haymarket anarchists.

I have known Aveling for four years; I know that he has twice sacrificed his social and economic position to his convictions, and might be, had he refrained from doing so, a professor, a professor in an English university and a distinguished physiologist instead of an overworked journalist with a very uncertain income.

He felt he knew Aveling's character better than his detractors because he had seen him pass through the most trying circumstances. "It will take a good deal (more than mere assertions and innuendos) before I believe what some people tell about him in New York." The crux of the matter was, however, Eleanor Marx. Could Edward Aveling be called a swindler without compromising Eleanor? Friedrich Engels could not face the thought that Eleanor was sacrificing herself for a liar and a thief; he could not bear to think that the socialist morality had led her into an impasse of unhappiness and the condonation of dishonor. If Aveling had swindled the American socialists, wrote Engels,

how could he do that during all his tour without his wife being cognisant of it? And in that case the charge included her too. And then it becomes utterly absurd, in my eyes at least. Her I have known from a child, and for the last seventeen years she has been constantly about me. And more than that, I have inherited from Marx the obligation to stand by his children as he would have done himself, and to see, as far as lies in my power, that they are not wronged. And that I shall do, in spite of fifty Executives. The daughter of Marx swindling the working class— too rich indeed![7]

[7] These citations will be found in Karl Marx and Frederick Engels, *Letters to Americans, 1845–1895*, ed. Leonard E. Mins (New York, 1953), pp. 171–72.

To defend Eleanor Marx, Engels was ready to tell off every Socialist party in the world. Under emotion's stress, he said what he really thought of the professional leaders of the proletariat: "We have seen Executives rise and fall by the dozen; we know they are as fallible as any pope, and have even known more than one that lived sumptuously on the pence of the working-men, and had swindlers and forgers of accounts in their midst." Then in 1895, Engels, ripe with years and the reverence of the growing socialist movement, died. The Avelings, with some friends, went out to the sea off Eastbourne to cast away his ashes. Eleanor was to be alone now with her socialist comrade.

For a while, thanks to Engels, the financial lot of the Avelings was easier, for he had left them a legacy of about £3000. They bought a house in Sydenham, which they called, curiously, "Jews' Den." In her loneliness, Eleanor Marx seemed to reach back for the comfort of her Jewish origin. Eduard Bernstein recalled that she took every opportunity to say with pride, "I am a Jewess." "How often," he wrote, "have I heard her shout it to the crowd, from the tribune. . . . Wherever the Jew was persecuted as a Jew, she was not misled by the proletarian class feeling deeply ingrained in her soul, but felt warmly for the oppressed without regard to their class position. So it was in the Dreyfus case. . . ." She told Max Beer that "my happiest moments are when I am in the East End amidst Jewish work-people," and she recalled that Marx had always carried around with him a photograph of his own father which he never showed to strangers; she remembered the face as "very handsome," the eyes and brow like those of the son but the features "softer about the mouth and chin," "definitely Jewish but beautifully so." Her father had harshly rejected any association with Jews, but now Eleanor seemed to be seeking in the memory of her grandfather an alternative authority to her father— one gentler, more human, which had become lost in the son's single-minded communism.

Eleanor groped with the problem of the evil in her

lover. Her father's teaching left her unprepared for the problem of life: her misery was a human triviality against the all-encompassing grandeur of the historical process. This triviality, however, was her life and it was being destroyed. H. M. Hyndman, the British socialist leader, thought that loyalty to Aveling was deteriorating Eleanor's character. Yet he acknowledged that he had never seen anyone confront this challenge of personal evil with so much individual power.

This in my opinion was the most remarkable instance I ever encountered of strength of character in a woman overcoming, and finally mastering, a pernicious influence which had gone far to wreck her life. It was wonderful to witness. Unfortunately, it did not go to the length of emancipating her from him altogether. I wish it had.

In the Marxian Decalogue, the words "good" and "justice" were myths. Eleanor had learned from childhood that the ruling class decreed the ethics that best suited its economic interest. Engels, too, had written with magisterial authority that there was no such thing as a universalistic moral sense that transcended the systems of class ethics. Eleanor had read glowing pages that foretold the era of free choice in love which would be the happy consequence of socialist revolution. Then how could Edward Aveling be morally condemned? If he expropriated all and sundry, and seduced with equal élan and extent, was he not a precursor of the man of the classless society, living his life with magnificent unconcern for "bourgeois morals"? Was he to be ostracized because he had the misfortune to be living before his time? And he was a socialist, completely and undeniably, the translator of Marx's *Capital,* the defender of his memory. She could look back to all the work she had shared with Edward on behalf of the socialist cause, innumerable lectures, committees, manifestoes, and the pages of their pioneer study *The Working-class Movement in America,* in which they had reproached American writers with ignoring the antagonism of classes, and written a remarkable chapter on the sociology of the American cowboy as the most exploited of proletarians.

No doubt Eleanor asked herself continually: why had she united herself with Edward Aveling, and why did she find that union so indissoluble? Many years before, she had had the French Communard Lissagaray as her first lover. She had regarded herself at the age of nineteen as engaged to this disinherited count and journalist. Karl Marx had refused to recognize or speak of this engagement, and had obviously wished to keep his beloved youngest by his side, though he disclaimed any intention of turning "the child" into "an old man's nurse, to be sacrificed on the family altar." Eleanor then waited till she was twenty-nine before she chose for herself Edward Aveling. Shaw thought it was sexual attraction that held Eleanor; Hyndman felt it was a hypnotic subjugation; and still others believed that some Jewish trait of reverence for the marital bond had enthralled her. Was Eleanor proving to herself that she could be just as loyal as her mother had been to her father during their many years of penuried exile? Was the socialist Aveling so much identified with her father's mission that loyalty to the one was loyalty to the other? She had acted with Edward in many plays he had written—mostly one-act curtain-raisers for amateur theatricals. Now the socialist tragedians prepared to enact their last scene; Edward Aveling wrote most of the lines.

Eleanor Marx-Aveling rarely confided in anybody, no matter how great the strain. Early in 1898, however, she was desperate. Edward, without telling her, had sold her belongings and was spending his time elsewhere; she, too, was simply an object to be used as all others. In her desperation and loneliness, she turned to Frederick Demuth, the son of her old nurse, who she had learned only three years before was her own half-brother. The circumstances of that discovery had produced a severe emotional crisis in Eleanor. Though Freddy Demuth looked very much like Marx, gossip had regarded Engels as his father. Eleanor pressed Louise Kautsky, who lived in Engels' household, to find out the truth. "Tussy pressed me so hard," wrote Louise to Bebel in 1898, "that I asked the old man directly. The General was very surprised that Tussy clung so stubbornly to her belief," and gave her the right, if it were necessary, to reveal the truth. A few days before he died, Engels confirmed in the presence of Samuel Moore, the translator of *Capital*, that Marx was, indeed, the father of Frederick Demuth. Thereupon Moore journeyed to Eleanor's house to tell her the truth of her half-brother. A terrible scene took place. "Tussy asserted that the General lies. . . ." Moore brought her words back to the dying Engels, who replied that "Tussy wants to make an idol of her father." Then the day before his death, Engels "wrote it down on a slate-board for Tussy herself, and Tussy walked out so deeply affected that she forgot all her hatred against me," write Louise, "and cried bitterly on my shoulder."[8] Now Eleanor turned to her half-brother, Frederick Demuth, whom her father had cast aside as an Ishmael. She wrote to him that she was just beginning to understand life:

There are people who lack a certain moral sense just as others are deaf or short-sighted or are in other ways afflicted. And I begin to realise the fact that one is as little justified in blaming them for the one sort of disorder as the other. We must strive to cure them, and if no cure is possible, we must do our best. I have learnt to perceive this through long suffering—suffering whose details I could not tell even to you—but I have learned it, and so I am endeavouring to bear all these trials as well as I can.

Eleanor had rejoiced that at last in her own new home she would be a housewife as other women. Jews' Den, however, brought her no peace. For Edward Aveling was evidently living in the shadow of extortionists. There was some unimaginable secret which Eleanor feared would be exposed to the world. She could not bring herself to tell it even to Freddy Demuth, her oldest, closest friend. Aveling pressed her for the bonds Engels had deposited in her name. When, during their last summer, Aveling left Eleanor, he gave her no address: she was to communicate with him only through a certain actor. Eleanor begged Demuth to seek Edward out at a socialist executive meeting:

> I cannot go there because if he's not there, I would have no excuse to give for his absence. I must bother you with all these troubles: but could you go there? . . . If he is there, you can approach him—he can't run away in front of others—and wait for him till the meeting ends. Then you can assume that he wishes to come out here; if you notice that he's simply lying, go with him to London Bridge. Then accompany him and say (you can tell him this at once) that you had told me that you wished to come, but that because of your work you would be late, and that I had replied that I would have a bed ready for you. Then he must either tell you that he's not coming, and you can take the opportunity to have a word with him—or that he is coming.

In her last bewildered days, Eleanor turned for help to the simple struggling workingman, Freddy Demuth, as once her family had to the servant girl, Lenchen Demuth. Why, asked Eleanor, had life given her these years of torment? How lucky had her sister Jenny been to die! She began to wonder whether her father had really answered all her questions. Why did evil enter people's lives? "I don't think," she wrote, "that you and I have been particularly bad people—and yet, dear Freddy, it really seems as if we were all being punished." She felt tired and isolated in the world of her brilliant socialist intellectual friends. "Dear Freddy," she said, "you are the only friend with whom I can feel completely free." Her lifetime of self-dedication to the socialist movement was summated in nullity. "You have your boy," she wrote. "I have nothing —and I see nothing to make life worth living."

Meanwhile, Edward Aveling became seriously ill, and required a dangerous operation. He was taken to Middlesex Hospital; Eleanor was always with him. "There is a French proverb," she wrote, " 'To understand is to forgive': Much suffering has taught me much understanding —and so I do not need to forgive. I can only love." But when Mrs. Hyndman walked with her in the hospital corridor, Eleanor almost broke down as she told the complete story of her humiliation. Mrs. Hyndman, aghast at what she heard, urged her to leave Aveling when he recovered, and Eleanor finally talked of doing so. When the time came, however, Eleanor took her beloved to Margate to nurse him and watch over him. "It is a hard time, for me," she wrote in her last letter, on March 1, 1898. "I fear there is little to hope for, and the pain and suffering are great. Why we go on like this I do not understand. I am ready to go and would do so with joy, but so long as he needs help I am bound to remain."

Uncertainty beclouds the last days of Eleanor Marx's life. H. M. Hyndman pieced together the sequence of events from the coroner's inquest, his own information, gossip in the socialist movement, and probably revelations from the untroubled, unhaunted Aveling himself. According to Hyndman's narrative, Eleanor Marx had finally begun to hope that her long self-sacrifice in "free marriage" was over. Aveling's legal wife had died, and Eleanor hoped that Edward would marry her. One morning the convalescent Aveling disappeared for a day. Then a letter came to Eleanor. It evidently brought the news that Edward had married anew, a young actress, Eva Frye. John Spargo, who knew both Eleanor Marx and Edward Aveling, tells me that it contained a news clipping of that marriage. Aveling later destroyed the letter before anyone else could see it.

Eleanor's world collapsed. Her island of socialist unity with a comrade was nothing more than a theme for unfeeling gossip. Edward Aveling seemed to delight in reducing her to nothingness. He persuaded Eleanor they should both commit suicide. A prescription for prussic acid and chloroform was written out, apparently in Eleanor's handwriting, but more probably by Aveling himself who had learned to imitate Eleanor's script perfectly. Probably this talent had been useful in the forgery of notes and checks. Aveling, with an executioner's calm, took the prescription to the chemist's, and got the poison. Eleanor's loyalty never faltered; she took her portion, and died. Aveling deserted her even in her dying moments; he went to the office of the Social Democratic Federation, and called the secretary's attention to the time of his arrival. He was in some confused way arranging an alibi. Eleanor left behind her a letter. It said, according to Eduard Bernstein, "How sad has life been all these years." The coroner found the letter before Aveling could destroy it. At Eleanor's funeral, Aveling indulged in a histrionic grief, then went off to a restaurant with his socialist brothers-in-law. A few months later, Aveling died.

A few years ago, however, old legal records and the tattered files of a weekly newspaper, exhumed by Felix Barker, added some facts to the story of Eleanor's death. Edward Aveling, under an assumed name, had been married to his actress friend for ten months before Eleanor killed herself. According to the coroner's interrogation, it was the Avelings' maid who went to the chemist with the prescription written on Aveling's "doctor" stationery, signed *"E.A.,"* and asking that the bearer be given poison "for the dog." The ledger for poisons delivered came back signed *"E.M.A."* Barker was inclined to exonerate Aveling from direct complicity in Eleanor's death. On the other hand, as Bernstein notes, Aveling had had several discussions with the chemist on the efficacy of different poisons. One gathers that Edward, before having left in the morning for London, allowed Eleanor to give the maid the prescription. Eleanor, moreover, signed the chemist's receipt in Aveling's presence. Then Aveling left the house. Eleanor was found dead by the maid a few hours later. She was lying on the bed dressed completely in white, and with a letter by her side:

Dear: It will soon be over now. My last word to you is the same that I have said during all the long sad years—love.

We cannot now know whether Edward Aveling made all the arrangements, the stage properties, the timings for entry and exit, for the scene of Eleanor Marx's death. Perhaps he allowed the last day to write itself in its own way, knowing what the inevitable outcome would be. Possibly he didn't know that this was the last day. The coroner's judgment was that Eleanor Marx had committed suicide while temporarily insane. Eleanor might have answered that her death was a redemptive act of sanity after years immersed in the insane. However the matter be phrased, one thing is clear: Edward Aveling had compelled the death of Eleanor Marx.

It was all hopelessly un-Marxian. For the Marxian would have said: "To understand is to act, and to forgive is craven-hearted." Self-abnegation, if it meant loving one's exploiter, was contrary to the Marxian scheme of things. But the Marxian upbringing itself had produced this apotheosis of self-immolation; the Marxian ethic in practice had negated itself. The ideological way of life left a gaping vacancy in Eleanor's existence. She longed for a fidelity purely personal, like the devotion she was prepared to give; instead, she was always asked to merge her unhappiness into the greater good of the movement to which Comrade Aveling was contributing. She endured in silence dishonesties and infamies till finally to save herself from more, she chose death. For the ideological man, she perceived, was much like the god-centered, theological one: both used the anointedness of their status to exploit. And she perceived what her father had never taught her —that exploitation is not just an economic category, not just taking the fruits of another man's work, extracting a man's surplus value. Economic exploitation was just one of a species, and there were all the forms by which one person could impoverish the life of another, all the varieties of misuses of human beings by each other. The mandate to combat exploitation in its economic form could become a license to exploit people in others.

Eleanor Marx's suicide in a blunt way refuted her father's ethic, for Marxism, defining freedom as the recognition of necessity, saw it as achieved when one worked as an appendange to the class struggle for the abolition of classes. Eleanor, in order to unite herself to the class struggle in Aveling's guise, committed surgery on her feelings and brought unreality into her life. Eleanor's surviving sister, Laura, also killed herself a few years later, presumably when she and her husband felt they had nothing more to contribute to the socialist movement.

Karl Kautsky, guardian of orthodox Marxism, wrote that Eleanor could never have chosen "freely" to desert the field of class battle. Clearly, he said, she had been overpowered by some sudden irrationality. Ethics, founded on the materialist conception of history, had finally nothing to say to the human individual but its own categorical imperative: "Act to advance the class struggle."[9]

All three of Marx's daughters were married in the political fold to active socialists. Had Marx the father somehow mangled the capacity of his children to enjoy the savor of living? Eleanor at the age of six had allowed her mind to be settled by her father; she felt no more doubts afterwards; she never questioned her father's writings; she worshiped them as sacred words. Eleanor never experienced the sense of discovering herself in conflict with her heritage. Abraham was spared the sacrifice of Isaac, but Marx's Historical Process, more like a Moloch, demanded all his sons and daughters.[10]

[9] Two important articles by Eduard Bernstein—"Eleanor Marx" and "Was Eleanor Marx in den Tod trieb?" *Die Neue Zeit*, XVI, Band II (1897–1898), 118–23, 481–91—very much confirm the story of Eleanor's death as reported by Hyndman.

[10] Five years after the publication of this essay, a full-length biography of Eleanor Marx appeared by Chushichi Tsuzuki. His interpretation generally resembled that which I had set forth in my *Encounter* article. Professor Tsuzuki, however, felt that Eleanor's materialism and Marxism had little to do with her tragedy. In that case, we might ask why he should have characterized her life, as he did in his title, "a socialist tragedy." The fact of the matter is that Marxism, with its rejection of ethics as ideological nonsense and mythology, did make for a certain moral emptiness in Eleanor's life, rendering her quite defenseless before Edward Aveling's ruthless

When George Bernard Shaw wrote his play about Eleanor Marx, he could not bring himself to leave the reality as stark as it was. He allowed the heroine of *The Doctor's Dilemma,* Jennifer Dubedat, to survive her scoundrel-husband, and to make a second, happy marriage. Eleanor was the prototype for the lovely, faithful Jennifer Dubedat, the only woman in all of Shaw's plays who loves with complete passion. Mrs. Dubedat, like Eleanor, defies the whole world to show her that her husband has done any wrong thing, and the surgeon, Ridgeon, like Shaw, cannot face-to-face tell her anything against him. Louis Dubedat, who is Edward Aveling transformed into a painter of genius reciting Shelleyan lines to the last, is an utter villain, but Shaw is of two minds about him. For Dubedat might defend his actions as simply those of a free-lancing rebel against capitalist morality. And in one passage (which the acting versions usually omit) Dubedat cites Shavian Scripture for his defense: "All your moralisings have no value for me. I don't believe in morality. I'm a disciple of Bernard Shaw . . . the most advanced man now living." Shaw was happily able to use his dramatist's liberty to make a Fabian revision of reality. The surgeon Ridgeon, asked to choose between saving the life of a working-class doctor or the artist-master, chooses the social servant. The orderly Fabian wins over the lawless rebel: "The most tragic thing in the world is a man of genius who is not also a man of honor." But in actuality, the real surgeon, Christopher Heath, saved Aveling's life, much to the dismay of Eleanor's friends. There was a suggestion left in *The Doctor's Dilemma* that with a slight turn of events, Jennifer too might be destroyed. If she lost

---

putting into practice of the Marxist critique of "bourgeois morality." Eleanor's reversion to Jewishness has a significance which, I believe, Professor Tsuzuki did not fully grasp. Here if ever was a child finding her father's materialist philosophy wanting and searching for a new way of life. Inevitably one thinks of the quest in our own time of Svetlana Alliluyeva for a religious ethic to supplant the doctrine of her father, Joseph Stalin. Cf. Chushichi Tsuzuki, *The Life of Eleanor Marx, 1855–1898: A Socialist Tragedy* (Oxford, 1967). Also, Lewis S. Feuer, "Eleanor Marx," *Encounter,* XX (April 1963), 106.

faith in Dubedat, she says, "it would mean the wreck and failure of my life," and she would show Ridgeon the very cliff from which she would jump off. Eleanor lost faith. Was the doctor's disinterested murder Shaw's own vicarious verdict in retrospect upon his rival Aveling?

The Fabian ethic was, indeed, as helpless as the Marxian, and the doctor's dilemma was Shaw's insoluble one. The Fabians wanted, like the Bolsheviks, to be the Jesuits of socialism. "Working for the cause," they believed, was the purpose of life; it would fill one's mind with divine thoughts, and one's earthly hands with things to do. The evil Aveling and the martyred Eleanor never fitted into the well-made socialist script, which tended very early to repress the recalcitrant and unsocializable. Will it some day grow wise and humane enough for both father and daughter, for both Karl and Eleanor Marx?

The Alienated Americans and Their Influence on Marx and Engels

We tend to think of Marxism as a political doctrine that emerged altogether from European experience, and that was then exported to the United States. There was an astonishing unity of experience and aspiration, however, common to America and Western Europe during the 1840s. Young men in Germany, France, and England who found themselves drawn into the new, strange, and stirring communist movement listened eagerly and avidly to the reports from the American continent that communist communities were practicable and prosperous. They drew from the American experience the evidence for their view that communism, indeed, was the next stage of human society. Friedrich Engels was the leader in expounding to his fellow Germans the significance of the American communist experience. In later years he was to ridicule "Utopian" thought and action. But as he and Marx were forming their standpoint in *The Holy Family* and the *Economic and Philosophic Manuscripts of 1844,* what the word "communism" meant for them was the kind of society that was being created by the American communist communities. The overcoming of man's alienation was then their central aim; what this signified in practical terms was the establishment of communist communities in the American style.

It was Friedrich Engels who in 1844 and 1845 brought the glad tidings of the American communities to his German comrades; later they proposed to show they were communists who could also be practical by founding a community similar to the American pattern.[1]

[1] The English edition of Gustav Mayer, *Friedrich Engels,* trans. Gilbert and Helen Highet (New York, 1936), contains no mention

During this period, when Engels spoke of communism, he meant the community system as practiced by the American colonies. The term "socialism" was usually used interchangeably with "communism," but when Engels wished to be more precise, he would use "socialism" to signify in Germany a broader, vaguer conception of social reorganization than communism: "in this country the word Socialism means nothing but the different vague, undefined, and undefinable imaginations of those who see that something must be done, and who yet cannot make up their minds to go the whole length of the Community system."[2]

On December 13, 1844, the *New Moral World,* the organ of the English Owenites published in Leeds, carried a joyful article on "Communism in Germany." Its author, who signed himself "An Old Friend of Yours in Germany," was the young Friedrich Engels. Socialism was spreading in a "quite miraculous" way, he told his English readers. Two years earlier there had been only "two solitary individuals who cared at all about Social questions"; now there were "dozens of clever writers preaching the new gospel to thousands. . . ." Every independent periodical was favorable to socialism; the liberals were courting the favor of the Socialist party, and even the German governments were feeling themselves "obliged to favor all legal movements in the direction towards Socialism."[3] The German middle class, Engels acknowledged, was the mainstay of the socialist movement; it was "far more disinterested, impartial, and intelligent" than its English counterpart; nevertheless, he was hoping soon for the support of the "working classes, who always, and everywhere must form the strength and body of the Socialist party." Mean-

---

of this phase of Engels' evolution. It receives a few lines in the original German work, Gustav Mayer, *Friedrich Engels* (Haag, 1934), Erster Band, p. 205.

[2] Karl Marx and Friedrich Engels, *Historische-Kritische Gesamtausgabe* [hereinafter cited as *MEGA*] (Berlin, 1932), Erste Abteilung, Band 4, p. 347.

[3] *Ibid.,* p. 339.

while, on every steamer, railway carriage, and mail coach in North Germany, said Engels, you met somebody who agreed with you that society must be reorganized. Then followed Engels' announcement of pending action. Socialist ideas were gaining such an allegiance among the German middle class that their next step was clear: they would found a community on the model of the American communities:

> . . . if we make as much progress during the next four or five years as we have done in the past twelve months, we shall be able to erect forthwith a Community. In fact, one of our number has been invited to draw up a plan of organization and regulations for a practical Community, with reference to the plans of Owen, Fourier, etc., and profiting of the experience gained by the American Communities and your own experiment at Harmony, which I hope goes on prosperously. The plan will be discussed by the various localities and printed with the amendments.

Then Engels listed the most active literary characters among the German socialists; Karl Marx, Moses Hess, and himself were among the six names he mentioned.[4]

As the young German socialists went about preaching their new gospel, they encountered skeptics and questioners who told them socialism was an impractical dream. Early in October 1844, Engels had written to his friend Marx in Paris that he planned to use the experience of the American and English communities to prove that communism was practicable:

> The Germans are all still unclear concerning the actual practicability of communism; to put an end to this rubbish, I shall write a small brochure to show that the project has already been realized, and to depict in a popular fashion the existing practice of communism in England and America. It will cost me three days or so, and will clear up things for the yokels very much. That I have already seen in my talks with the natives.[5]

[4] *Ibid.*, p. 341.
[5] *MEGA* (Berlin, 1929), Dritte Abteilung, Band 1, p. 3 (my translation).

A few months later, on March 8, 1845, Engels informed the readers of the *New Moral World* that a collection of communist essays had just been published "containing among the rest, an account of the American communities, as well as your own Hampshire Establishment, which has done much toward annihilating the prejudice of the impracticability of our ideas."[6] The essay on the American communities was by Engels himself. During the spring of 1845 as the antagonism between the Prussian government and the communists deepened, Engels used his studies on the American communities to good effect. At Elberfeld, for instance, the center of the manufacturing district in Rhenish Prussia, a dramatic meeting took place which Engels described in the *New Moral World* for May 10, 1845. The communists of the town were invited by its most respectable citizens to a joint discussion; forty or fifty persons attended, including the attorney general. A communist was elected chairman, then Moses Hess read a lecture on the necessity for abandoning the competitive system: "The lecture was received with much applause (the majority of the audience being Communists); after which Mr. Frederick Engels . . . spoke at some length on the practicability and the advantages of the Community system. He also gave some particulars of the American colonies and your own establishment at Harmony in proof of his assertions. After which a very animated discussion took place. . . ." The debate between the communists and the attorney general and his friends lasted from nine in the evening till one in the morning. A week later there was a second meeting at which Engels "proved" that a social revolution was imminent, and that it could be averted only by "the introduction of, and the preparation for, the Community system." At a third meeting a week later, "some particulars about the American communities were read from a printed paper." A fourth meeting saw the intervention of the mayor, the attorney general, and a troop of armed police. "Of course," wrote Engels, "under

---

[6] *MEGA*, Erste Abteilung, Band 4, p. 343.

such circumstances, no public addresses were delivered: the meeting occupied themselves with beef-steaks and wine, and gave the police no handle for interference." The audience went home, he averred, "with a greater respect for Communism," especially because "nearly every patrician member and moneyed family of the town" was represented among the communists.[7]

The public meanwhile, said Engels, was devouring every book on communism. The Puttmann collection (which contained Engels' essay on the American communities), "though prosecuted by the Prussian Government, met with a rapid sale in all quarters." Engels described its contents:

. . . an excellent paper by Dr. Hess, on the distress of modern society, and the means of redressing it; a detailed description of the distressing state of the working people of Silesia, with a history of the riots of last spring; some other articles descriptive of the state of society in Germany; and, finally, an account of the American and Harmony communities (from Mr. Finch's letters and that of 'One who has Whistled at the Plough') by F. Engels.[8]

On the very same page, Engels linked his advocacy of a society modeled on the American communities with the critique he and Marx were making of the German philosophers and ideology. "A war has been declared," wrote Engels, "against those of the German philosophers who refuse to draw from their mere theories practical inferences, and who contend that man has nothing to do but to speculate upon metaphysical questions. Messrs. Marx and Engels have published a detailed refutation of the principles advocated by B. Bauer."[9] In the press, furthermore, said Engels, were a work by Marx on politics and political economy, and his own *Condition of the Working Classes of Great Britain.* Thus, at this time,

[7] *Ibid.,* pp. 345–46.
[8] *Ibid.,* p. 347.
[9] *Loc. cit.*

when Marx and Engels wrote *The Holy Family*, devoted to a critique of the idealism of the "Bauer family," the practical bearing of their theoretical criticism was to be found in their advocacy of a society modeled on the American communities.[10] Let us therefore study the contents of the unusual essay by Engels, entitled "Description of Communist Colonies Founded in Recent Times and Still Existing."

II

The purpose of Engels' article on the communist colonies was above all to answer the objection that communism is a beautiful ideal that cannot, however, be realized. "This objection," he wrote, "is raised so frequently that it appears to the writer useful and necessary to answer it by means of some facts which are still very little known in Germany. . . ."[11] The many American communities and the one at Harmony in England had demonstrated, said Engels, that "communism, the social life and work based on the common possession of goods, is, that is to say, not only possible but has actually been realized . . . , and with the best result." The communities, in Engels' view, gave the answer to two basic objections which common sense made to socialist schemes. First, who would do "the mean and unpleasant manual work" in a communist society? Second, would not the community disintegrate as people with equal claims on common property struggled for its possession?

This was the only article in which either Engels or Marx ever considered objections to socialism as a form of social existence. In later years, they simply refused to discuss

[10] In *The Holy Family* the teachings of Robert Owen were extolled as against those of the German philosophers. Cf. Marx and Engels, *The Holy Family or Critique of Critical Critique*, trans. R. Dixon (Moscow, 1956), pp. 13, 176–77.

[11] *MEGA*, Erste Abteilung, Band 4, p. 351.

questions of that sort on the ground that all that science can do is to describe the on-going movement of social change. To discuss the operational details of a future socialist society was to their view an unscientific enterprise. They regarded themselves as the critical analysts of capitalist disintegration, not the synthetic theorists of socialist creation. They preferred to repress questions concerning the future socialist society with the argument that history itself would resolve them when the time came. But in 1845, social revolution seemed imminent. A new society was being considered to replace a bourgeois order which was itself so young that many people still alive could remember its virtual beginnings. There was no aura of immutability or inevitability about the capitalist economy. It was not hallowed by the legitimacy of a received traditional order, and it seemed to be enveloped in all the contingencies of human decision. The proponents of socialist community had to face all the queries that were posed by people who actually were making a choice between the new bourgeois society or the even newer communist direction. It was indeed an age of choice, and questions about the practicability of socialism could not be put off with references to the future deliverances of historical evolution. At the point of decision as to the unknown, no one can take refuge in historicism. So Engels therefore felt called upon to reply to the "objections" to communism.

To those who asked who would do the lowly unpleasant work in a communist society, Engels replied in a fashion typical of all communitarian thinkers:

. . . these tasks are, once they are part of the Community, no longer lowly; and then, they permit themselves to be done away with almost completely through improved contrivances, machines, and the like. Thus in New York, shoes are shined in a big hotel with steam, and in the communist colony at Harmony in England, the privies (water-closets), adapted to the convenient English style, not only clean themselves but are also provided with pipes which carry the excrement directly off to the cesspools.

This was a line of argument that later became an especial favorite with such anarchist thinkers as Kropotkin.[12] Science applied to human ends could humanize technology, and practically eliminate menial labor.

Moreover, Engels was serenely untroubled by the possibility that strife and discord would intrude into the communist colonies themselves. Communist societies, he said, tended to become so prosperous that their people had nothing to argue about: "all communistic colonies up to now have after ten or fifteen years become so enormously rich that they have more of all desirable things than they can consume, and there is scarcely any occasion for conflict."

The American communities furnished Engels with the empirical grounds for his confident assertion that communist society was not only practicable but a more successful form of social existence than competitive capitalism. Engels studied primarily the experience of several religious American communities: the Shakers at Pleasant Hill, Kentucky, and New Lebanon in New York; the Harmonizers under Rapp at Economy, Pennsylvania; and the Separatists under Pastor Bäumler at Zoar in Ohio. He referred in a more passing fashion to the colony led by Pastor Ginal in Pennsylvania; another society under a Mr. Hizby in Pittsburg, Ohio; a settlement at Skaneateles, New York, under the leadership of J. A. Collins, an English socialist; another at Minden in Massachusetts, and two at Pike County, Pennsylvania; a colony of emigrant English socialists at Equality near Milwaukee, Wisconsin, founded by Thomas Hunt; in Massachusetts, the colony at Northampton; and most notably for Americans, the "one at Brook Farm, Massachusetts, where," in Engels' words, "fifty members and thirty pupils live on about 200 acres, and have founded a distinguished school under the leadership of a Unitarian preacher, G. Ripley." Thus, Engels referred specifically by name to the experience of thirteen

---

[12] Peter Kropotkin, *The Conquest of Bread* (Vanguard ed.; New York, 1926), pp. 110 ff. *Kropotkin's Revolutionary Pamphlets,* ed. Roger N. Baldwin (New York, 1927), p. 71.

American communist colonies. There were other communities in process of formation, said Engels, concerning which details were lacking. "So much is however certain," Engels added with a cheerful ignorance and exaggeration of the facts, "that the Americans and especially the poor workers in the big cities, New York, Philadelphia, Boston, and so on, have taken the matter to heart, and have founded many societies for the establishment of similar colonies. The Americans are tired of remaining the servants of a few rich men, who live on the people's labor; and through the great activity and perseverance of this nation, it is evident that the community of goods will soon be introduced in a significant part of their land."[13]

At this time America was pre-eminently, for Engels, the land of socialist pioneering. "In those days," as G. D. H. Cole says, "men went to America in order to escape from commercialism."[14] Here, for the first time in history it had been shown that communist society was practicable. "The first people in America," Engels wrote, "and indeed in the world who brought into realization a society founded on the community of property were the so-called Shakers."[15] Engels described them at length, their strange religious opinions, their prohibition of both marriage and sexual intercourse. Their peculiarities, he said, however, were of little moment. For their ten large communities, each with three to eight hundred members, were beautiful, orderly, well-constructed towns with homes, factories, workshops, barns, meetinghouses. They had cattle and poultry of the best breeds, granaries laden with corn, storerooms stocked with clothing. Flowers and vegetable gardens were in profusion. An English traveler who visited the Shakers, Engels said, had found them so affluent that he could not understand why they worked. Evidently they did so out of pure amusement. Nobody worked unwillingly, no one was unemployed, there were no poorhouses or hospitals, to one suffering from need. Here, indeed (in

[13] *Ibid.*, pp. 360–61.
[14] G. D. H. Cole, *Robert Owen* (London, 1925), p. 181.
[15] *MEGA*, Erste Abteilung, Band 4, p. 352.

Engels' later terminology), the state had withered away: "In their ten towns there is not a single gendarme or policeman, no judge, lawyer, or soldier, no jail or penitentiary; and yet everything goes on orderly. The laws of the land mean nothing there for them, and might just as well be abolished as far as they are concerned without a cock crowing about it; for they are the quietest citizens, and have never delivered a law-breaker to prison."[16]

Scholars have usually traced the source of the communism of Marx and Engels to the grandiose and obscure writings of the metaphysician Hegel. Probably, however, the historical truth is that they were much more moved by the popular and uncritical journalistic books of such prosaic and forgotten figures as Harriet Martineau, John Melish, and James Silk Buckingham. Engels could adduce their authority as presumably qualified observers for his description of the prosperity of American communistic colonies. Almost all European travelers, he observed, visited one or other of them, and all were unanimous in praise of communist economy. True enough, they might find fault with the colonies' religious principles, but, Engels insisted, that had nothing to do with the community of goods. "I could also cite the works by Miss Martineau, by Messrs. Melish and Buckingham and many others," wrote Engels.[17] He relied most, however, on articles which John Finch had published in 1844 in the *New Moral World* under the title, "Notes of Travel in the United States."[18] He quoted in their entirety three long paragraphs from a glowing description by Finch of the economy, constitution, and quality of life in the Shaker settlement at Pleasant Hill, Kentucky, and at equal length from Finch's enthusiastic report on the Rappites at Economy. Finch was also cited for his characterization of the Separatist colony at Zoar as "the most perfectly organized community of all which live in America in community

[16] *Ibid.*, p. 353.
[17] *Ibid.*, p. 360.
[18] *Ibid.*, p. 526.

of goods," and was the source for Engels' analysis of the Separatist constitution.[19]

Who was this Finch? He was a veteran communist who had gone to the United States probably to revive a faltering faith. Finch's life had been a succession of evangelical missions. He had risen from the working class to become a successful iron merchant, and during that same time had been a disseminator of Unitarianism, temperance, and socialism. He had become known as the *King of the Teetotalers* but had lost his hegemony when they expelled him as an atheist. He revered Robert Owen, addressing him as "Social Father," and became in the forties the governor of Harmony Hall, the ill-fated Owenite community which foundered in chaos. Indeed, Finch evicted the last resident in 1846. He had interred many projects in the graveyard of revolutionary hopes. As a rationalist, he had promoted the establishment in 1839 of a Hall of Science in Liverpool. Four years later, in 1843, it had failed, and its premises were being used as a brothel. Thus, it was that in the early summer of 1843, Finch left for America to find a new light for socialism.[20] Every age has its John Reeds, and Finch's articles of 1844 were filled with the conviction that the Shakers were shaking the world.

Engels had a confirmatory witness of the Shaker success in Lawrence Pitkeithley, a prominent Chartist of the "physical force" wing, who had visited the colony at New Lebanon in New York. Pitkeithley had written his impressions in an article for the Chartist organ *Northern Star* in 1843 under the title "Emigration—Where to and how to proceed. Description of the Shaker Villages," from which Engels quoted several sentences as to how "friend-

---

[19] *Ibid.*, pp. 353–55, 356–58, 359.

[20] R. B. Rose, "John Finch, 1784–1857: A Liverpool Disciple of Robert Owen," in *Transactions of the Historic Society of Lancashire and Cheshire for the Year 1957* (Liverpool, 1958), Vol. 109, pp. 172–74, 179, 183. Frank Podmore, *Robert Owen: A Biography* (London, reprinted 1923), p. 554. Finch's name eluded mention in Max Berger's comprehensive work, *The British Traveller in America, 1836–1860* (New York, 1943).

ship and love" prevailed in their entire dwelling place.[21]

It is possible that Engels met both John Finch and Lawrence Pitkeithley, for he was in close association with the Owenites soon after his arrival in England in 1842. If he had any doubts about Finch's accuracy as a social observer, they would have been allayed, however, by the writings of Martineau, Buckingham, and Melish. It was many years later when Engels invented the expression "Utopian Socialists"; but in 1845, these self-same Utopians were impressing the world with their practical capabilities. Harriet Martineau, the respected popularizer of Ricardian economy, visited two Shaker settlements, and reported: "There is no question of their entire success, as far as wealth is concerned. A very moderate amount of labor has secured to them in perfection all the comforts of life which they know how to enjoy. . . . The earth does not show more flourishing fields, gardens, and orchards, than theirs." She raised the ultimate question as to the social import of the Shaker communist success; if such "is the result of cooperation and community of property among an ignorant, conceited, inert society like this, what might not the same principles of association achieve among a more intelligent set of people, stimulated by education and exhilarated by the enjoyment of all the blessings which Providence has placed within the reach of man?" Celibacy, in her opinion, did not contribute to the Shaker success; she believed they would have been far more wealthy without it. She found that the preoccupation with celibacy made for a "disgusting" society—pallid, spiritless, unnatural women, with a "soulless stare," who danced "like so many galvanized corpses." Celibacy avenged itself on the communists' psyche: "Their thoughts are full of the one subject of celibacy: with what effect, may be easily imagined." This was a social enclave infected with spiritual pride, insane vanity, intellectual torpor, mental grossness. Withal, she felt that the Shaker experience was

[21] *MEGA*, Erste Abteilung, Band 4, pp. 355, 526, 542. J. F. C. Harrison, "Chartism in Leeds," in *Chartist Studies*, ed. Asa Briggs (London, 1959), pp. 76, 82.

of tremendous portent for the future of the cooperative principle, "the most important dispute," she said, "that is agitating society. It will never now rest till it has been made matter of experiment. . . . There is at least every encouragement to try."[22]

In Harriet Martineau's pages, Engels also read of such a gladdening material abundance among the Rappites at Economy "that it is surprising that they work; except for want of something else to do." Human labor seemed here no longer to be alienated from itself. At the same time, the astute Englishwoman raised the basic political question which Engels never confronted. She observed that the Rappite community was a political dictatorship. "Mr. Rapp exercises an unbounded influence over his people." He did not allow the communitarians to speak with strangers; he controlled his people by keeping them ignorant and vain, preaching to them their superiority over the rest of the world. What would happen to the Rappite colony, she asked, "when it has lost its dictator. It does not appear that they can go on in their present state without a dictator."[23]

In Miss Martineau's pages, too, Engels would have read how the Rappite colony came near ruin in its encounter with crime and an evil misleader. This was a story Engels glossed over in his article. In the year 1831, he wrote, a certain Count Leon had come to the colony with a group of thirty followers. He had stirred up a large part of the membership against Pastor Rapp, and finally he and his group were expelled from the colony and indemnified with a payment of a hundred and twenty thousand dollars. Count Leon tried to found a colony himself, but it came to grief. Such was Engels' description of the evil consequences of factionalism. Actually, as Harriet Martineau told the story, Count Leon, a swindler, had, like a serpent among Eves, raised the question of allowing the joys of marriage in Economy. Seventy Rappites followed him out

[22] Harriet Martineau, *Society in America* (2d ed.; London, 1839), Vol. II, pp. 57–61.

[23] *Ibid.*, pp. 63–64.

of their Eden, but he then absconded with most of their money to Texas.[24]

Like Harriet Martineau, James Silk Buckingham, whom Engels cited, was an observer who rendered a positive verdict on the American communist experiments. Buckingham's parliamentary career had ended in 1837; he had achieved, he said, "the great object of my public life," the abolition of the East India Company's monopoly. He was a man who had traveled much in the Middle and Far East, in the most adventurous and melodramatic circumstances; when he spent three years in the United States from 1837 to 1840, he lectured (he estimated) to a million persons, and mixed with all classes; philanthropic societies especially sought him out because of his liberal reputation.[25] He, too, saw in the Shaker villages a validation of the cooperative principle. The community near the Merrimac River was, like the one near Albany, "a perfect model of neatness, order, and propriety, and every external symptom indicated a very high degree of prosperity." Not only did community in property seem to him to increase the benevolence of man, but the Shaker villages were also "an irresistible proof" that cooperation was more productive than competition. The "religious peculiarities" that were mixed in with the cooperative experiments were for Buckingham a nuisance and an excrescence; "when divested of this hindrance," he said, the principle of cooperation "will some day or other make a great change in the social arrangements of mankind."[26]

[24] A more circumstantial account by Charles Nordhoff adds still more variants to the strange story of Bernhard Muller, the self-styled Count Maximillian de Leon. See Nordhoff, *The Communistic Societies of the United States, 1875* (reprinted New York, 1961), pp. 79–80. There are additional pathetic details in William Alfred Hinds, *American Communities* (reprinted, New York, 1961), pp. 13–14.

[25] Cf., "James Silk Buckingham," *Appleton's Cyclopaedia of American Biography,* ed. James Grant Wilson and John Fiske (New York, 1887), I, 438.

[26] J. S. Buckingham, *America, Historical, Statistic, and Descriptive* (New York, 1841), Vol. 2, pp. 285, 75, Vol. 1, pp. 12–15.

John Melish, a prosperous Scottish cotton factor and noted geographer, had likewise perceived great social consequences in the American communist experiments. He had been moved in 1810 or 1811 by "the goodfellowship and material well-being" of the Rappites, then situated at the town of Harmony, near Pittsburgh. Within five years, their capital had grown more than tenfold, from $20,000 to $220,000. Their community of eight hundred persons, nine thousand acres, and one thousand sheep was inspiring for its self-sufficiency and simple contentment. This community, wrote Melish, "will, in all probability, be a model for other societies. . . . Here they have the mutual aid of each other, and are free from a thousand temptations to which mankind in general are subjected." Did communist society require, however, a religious foundation? Melish raised an issue which Engels evaded. To Melish, the cement for the Harmony community was a communal father-figure who bound together the individual consciences of its members. Their minister-founder, George Rapp, was confessor to all alike, children and adults, "who, one by one, waited upon Mr. Rapp, to make their confession."[27] Could a communist colony succeed without a religious psychological authoritarianism?[28]

Supported by this literature on the American communist colonies, Engels gave his confident judgment as a social scientist that they were not only practicable but also the next stage of history. His industry as a social researcher was astonishing. Besides the well-known travelers, his essay refers, for instance, to an article on the Zoar community which was published in the *Pittsburg Daily Advocate and*

[27] John Melish, *Travels through the United States of America in the Years 1806 and 1807, and 1809 and 1811* (Belfast, 1818), pp. 320–28, 330. Joseph Jackson, "John Melish," in *Dictionary of American Biography*, ed. Dumas Malone (New York, 1933), XII, 513.

[28] After a comprehensive survey of the history of communist colonies, Charles Gide concluded that they succeed only when led by a strong personality, and even then hardly ever except where the society "was founded upon religious discipline or even fanaticism." Charles Gide, *Communist and Co-operative Colonies*, trans. Ernest F. Row (New York, 1930), p. 214.

Advertiser for July 17, 1843. Intelligence diffused rapidly and widely among the far-flung communists of that era.

Engels could not, of course, entirely overlook the extent to which communist societies seemed to rest on a religious foundation. All the more crucial for him therefore was the existence of the Owenite colony, Harmony Hall, in Hampshire, England, a community grounded in secularism, founded indeed by the National Congress of Rational Religionists. Engels believed Harmony Hall provided the needed evidence that a secularist socialist society was possible. He devoted several pages to a report by a presumable agricultural expert which praised its "seven hundred Socialist sheep," the "socialist turnips," and the mechanized communal kitchen.[29] Harmony Hall's children, receiving a secular socialist education, were spared "religious and theological squabbling," and were not tormented with Latin and Greek. Their school was often held under the free sky, and work was part of their education. Moral teaching was limited to one precept: what you do not wish others to do to you, do not do to them.[30]

Even as his article was being published, Engels' high hopes for Harmony Hall were being confuted by its disharmonies. The balance sheet for the year ending March 31, 1844, had shown a heavy loss, and by the summer of 1845 the colony was virtually dead.[31] Engels had written with supreme confidence that "the survival of the colony is secure" and that "the opponents of Community would not experience the triumph of seeing it destroyed."[32] The communists, however, proved themselves inept agriculturists; the farms were mismanaged and the buildings were extravagantly costly. Many of the colonists were vegetarians, but as their experiment gradually failed, they were reduced to suppers of bread and water. The quarrels among the members were such that in the course of five

---

[29] A large part of the letter from "One who has Whistled at the Plough" is quoted in Frank Podmore, *Robert Owen*, pp. 547–60.

[30] *MEGA*, Erste Abteilung, Band 4, p. 364.

[31] Podmore, *op. cit.*, pp. 558–65.

[32] *MEGA*, Erste Abteilung, Band 4, p. 365.

years there were "two or three processes of purgation."[33] Of such facts, Engels' essay preserved a cheerful ignorance. What he professed to see in the efforts of the English socialists was the demonstration that a socialist community could flourish without any religion whatsoever. Irrational religion, he wrote, was a hindrance to community, and without it communities would prosper all the more.[34]

Meanwhile, society had been given, Engels wrote, "a view of an independent, secure and anxiety-free (*sorgenfreie*) existence, . . ." He called upon the German workers to take it to heart, but he also at this time looked to the human understanding and sympathy of the upper classes: "There is also a large section of well-to-do and cultured people in every part of Germany," he wrote, "who have openly declared themselves on behalf of the Community of goods, and who defend the demands of the people for the goods of this earth which the wealthy class has expropriated."[35] The socialist hope still expressed the common consciousness of the community; it was not yet tied to the notion of one class struggling for dictatorial political power over others.

Thus, to Engels in 1845, America was the proving ground of communism. The facts of this stage in his and Marx's evolution have important bearings for our understanding of the history and theory of socialism.

III

There has been considerable discussion concerning the meaning of "alienation" in the thought of Marx and Engels. It now becomes clear what the political significance of this concept was for them. At this stage in their intellectual development, when the overcoming of human alienation and estrangement was their centrally defined aim,

---

[33] Podmore, *op. cit.*, pp. 552–53, 556.
[34] *MEGA*, Erste Abteilung, Band 4, p. 352.
[35] *Ibid.*, p. 366.

the political program of Marx and Engels was the establishment of socialist communities. Community was precisely the means for the end of man's alienation. When Engels and Marx discarded the concept of "alienation" as the basis for their political philosophy, they were discarding as well the program of founding communist colonies. The affinity between the theory of "alienation" and the practice of "community" is one which has persisted in socialist thinking. Martin Buber, for instance, in *Paths in Utopia* has virtually returned to the philosophy of Engels and Marx in their communitarian, pre-Manifesto days. Buber has reached back into the positive content of that movement which Engels and Marx later assailed as "Utopian"; he has seen in the village communes in Israel the most outstanding contemporary example of the overcoming of "collective loneliness."[36] He has unwittingly retraced a path to the Engels of the essay on the American communist colonies, the Engels who was rejoicing that Ludwig Feuerbach, the philosopher of alienation, had perceived that communities were the political consequence of his critique of alienation. Feuerbach was especially enthusiastic over a new book by Wilhelm Weitling, a self-taught journeyman tailor, in which the author set forth a comprehensive scheme for the founding of cooperative handicraft societies; thus, said Engels, was being accomplished the union between the philosophers and the workingmen, "a union which, a year ago had been predicted by Dr. Marx."[37]

[36] Martin Buber, *Paths in Utopia*, trans. R. F. C. Hull (Boston, 1958), pp. 14, 140–41.

[37] In the same article of February 22, 1845, in which Engels informed the *New Moral World* of his work on American communities, he announced proudly: "Dr. Feuerbach, the most eminent philosophical genius in Germany at the present time, has declared himself a Communist." Feuerbach, he continued, had declared "his full conviction that Communism was only a necessary consequence of the principles he had proclaimed, and that Communism was, in fact, only the *practice* of what he had proclaimed long before theoretically." *MEGA*, Erste Abteilung, Band 4, p. 344. Marx indeed, in August 1844, had also greeted the publication of Wilhelm Weitling's *Guarantees of Harmony and Freedom* as "the unmeasured and brilliant literary debut of the German workers." "A philosophical na-

For Weitling, however, the union with philosophy was to be short and ill-fated. Driven from the European movement by Marx's invective, he became anti-intellectual, and tried, in 1853, to found a colony *Communia* in Iowa. It came to grief amidst charges of dictatorship. Weitling sadly concluded that communism was "an impossibility in our present society, and not even appealing for the future, and therefore, impractical."[38]

In the years 1844 and 1845, indeed, "Utopian" socialism seemed to many not Utopian, but realizable. Able, capable men were concerned with the practical possibilities of communist colonies. They seemed to pose a viable alternative to the new capitalistic society, comparable to Israel's present-day *kibbutzim,* to which visitors from Burma and Africa come to study whether these communal villages represent a social form more congenial for their own peoples than competitive economy. John Stuart Mill, beginning his *Principles of Political Economy* in the autumn of 1845, shared a hope in workingmen's associations not unlike that of Engels and Marx: "There exist, or existed a short time ago," he wrote, "upwards of a hundred successful, and many eminently prosperous, associations of operatives in Paris alone. . . ." The practical experience and success of these associations, said Mill, had taken them out of the realm of fancy: "So long as this idea remained in a state of theory, in the writings of Owen or of Louis Blanc, it may have appeared, to the common modes of judgment, incapable of being realized, and not likely to be tried unless by seizing on the existing capital. . . ." But now the democratic associations of la-

---

tion can only find its corresponding practice in socialism," he wrote, and by "socialism" he meant the kinds of communities which Weitling advocated. Weitling, himself a student of Fourier and Owen, had already published articles on the "Rappist colony of Harmonie, near Pittsburgh." He hoped in 1841 to use the profits of the Geneva co-operative taverns to finance a colony in America. Carl Wittke, *The Utopian Communist: A Biography of Wilhelm Weitling* (Baton Rouge, 1950), pp. 42, 48. Karl Marx and Friedrich Engels, *Correspondence 1846–1895,* trans. Dona Torr (New York, 1935), p. 351.

[38] Wittke, *op. cit.,* p. 275.

borers would reveal the "capacity of exertion and self-denial in the masses of mankind."[39] Mill shared the same enthusiasm for Fourier as did the German Marx and Engels and the American George Ripley. Fourier's was "the most skillfully combined, and with the greatest foresight of objections, of all the forms of Socialism." Only his skeptical empiricism kept Mill from an unqualified endorsement; he wondered how liberty would fare under socialism, and on what basis it would assign unpleasant labor. And Charles A. Dana, correspondent and city editor of the *New York Tribune,* observing the European social ferment at first hand, wrote home in December 1848: "the principle of co-operation is surely, I believe, supplanting that of competition. Here in Paris there are now in operation some fifty associations of workmen, and they are springing up in other places also. . . . In five years the greater part of the labor done in Paris will be so done that the workman will be his own master, and receive the full fruit of his toil. This will settle the question for the whole of Europe."[40]

This was an era indeed in which socialism was receiving an earnest hearing from all ranks of society. Socialism was not yet linked with class struggle and political revolution; it was a scheme of communist colonization which commended itself to all classes, and which relied on voluntary action for its realization; it needed no parliamentary parties. There was more socialist sentiment in the United States at this time than in any other period of its history. Robert Owen, newly arrived in America in 1825, en route to New Harmony, Indiana, was actually invited to give two lectures in the Hall of the Congress of the United States on his schemes for reorganizing society.

[39] John Stuart Mill, *Principles of Political Economy,* new ed., W. J. Ashley (London, 1909), pp. 773–74, 213–15. Engels in 1845 translated a fragment of Fourier on trade, and wrote an enthusiastic introduction. Cf. *MEGA,* Erste Abteilung, Band 4, pp. 406–53. Also, Karl Marx and Friedrich Engels, *The German Ideology,* ed. R. Pascal (New York, 1939), pp. 152–58.

[40] James Harrison Wilson, *The Life of Charles A. Dana* (New York, 1907), p. 91.

John Quincy Adams took time out from working on his inaugural address as President to listen to Owen on February 13, 1825, and then went again to the Capitol a few days after his inaugural to hear the second lecture, "which," he wrote in his diary, "was nearly three hours long. He [Robert Owen] read a great part of it from a printed book. President Monroe was there. . . ." Almost twenty years later, on December 30, 1844, the indefatigable Owen once more called on Adams with a scheme for organizing a community in the Washington neighborhood "to revolutionize the world." Adams, though dubious, was prepared to help to the extent of moving on January 7, 1845, in Congress that Robert Owen be allowed to deliver four lectures "upon his projects of reformation in human society." At first, the majority of Congress was evidently willing, but subsequently opposition developed from the side of "the Southern slave-mongers" (as Adams called them) and the conservative Whigs, and the matter was tabled by a vote of 91 to 63. This was the highest point of socialism in the history of the United States.[41] The tolerant John Quincy Adams, nonetheless, as a realist, regarded Owen personally as "a speculative, scheming, mischievous man," trumpeting his Utopia, and mesmerizing individuals with his humbug for abolishing poverty. Albeit, he and almost half the Congress were prepared in the America of the Industrial Revolution in 1845 to listen to Owen's theories.[42]

[41] James Madison, the venerable former President, also had a long serious discussion with Owen. He posed powerful questions: what of the pressure of increasing population under socialism? He got no real answer. Owen made a variety of sanguine assumptions, Madison thought, concerning human nature. Nevertheless, Madison, an American experimentalist, preserved an open mind concerning Owen's project: "His enterprise is nevertheless an interesting one. It will throw light on the maximum to which the force of education and habit can be carried." *Letters and Other Writings of James Madison* (Philadelphia, 1876), III, 576–78.

[42] *Memoirs of John Quincy Adams*, ed. Charles Francis Adams (Philadelphia, 1875), VI, 512, 514, 522, 524, 527; (1877), XII, 133, 142–43, 155, 157. Podmore, *op. cit.*, pp. 289–91. Cole, *op. cit.*, p. 182.

Engels and Marx soon dropped both their communitarian program and their vision of a total overcoming of alienation. From a psychological standpoint, probably both Engels and Marx, after their first warm glow of communitarian idealism, must have realized how utterly unfitted both of them were for communitarian life. Marx was a complete individualist, contemptuous alike of party committees, editorial boards, and the opinion of the masses. He was absolutely without any technical knack and was helpless before the most elementary machine, although he could write a classical chapter in *Capital* on the historical role of machinery.[43] He could write as a Utopian in *The German Ideology* that with the advent of communist society, it would be "possible for me to do one thing today and another tomorrow, to hunt in the morning, fish in the afternoon, rear cattle in the evening, criticize after dinner, just as I have a mind, without ever becoming hunter, fisherman, shepherd or critic."[44]

But in a more critical mood, Marx must have known that his experience would have been the kind that Nathaniel Hawthorne, plowman at Brook Farm, had when after five months of communitarian existence he wrote, in 1841, to his fiancée of his soon-anticipated liberation from community: "And—joyful thought—in a little more than a fortnight, thy husband will free from his bondage— . . . free to think and feel! . . . Even my Custom House experience was not such a thraldom and weariness; my mind and heart were freer. Oh, belovedest, labor is the curse of this world, . . . Dost thou think it a praiseworthy matter, that I spent five golden months in providing food for cows and horses?" On a brief vacation from Community, Hawthorne voiced his intense feeling about what we would call today the alienation of man under Community: "I should judge it to be twenty years since I left Brook Farm; and I take this to be one proof that my life

---

[43] "The simplest technical reality demanding perception is harder to me than to the biggest blockheads," wrote Marx to Engels in 1863. Marx and Engels, *Correspondence 1846–1875*, p. 141.

[44] Marx and Engels, *The German Ideology*, p. 22.

there was an unnatural and unsuitable, and therefore an unreal one. It already looks like a dream behind me. The real Me was never an associate of the community; there has been a spectral appearance there. . . ."[45] His election as chairman of the finance committee did not alter Hawthorne's opinions.

This theme of the estrangement of man under communism was one Engels and Marx could not bring themselves to face. As social scientists, they could not help but note how almost all the successful communities owed their cohesion to some aberrant religious separatism, how they were all at war with what the Shakers called "the World's people," and how often they required sexual celibacy or austerity. The liberal Brook Farm, with only its four married couples, was untouched by any insinuation of sexual scandal.[46] Could the libertine Engels, however, have conformed his ways to communitarian sexual austerity? A man like Moses Hess, the exemplar of the "true socialist," a man of self-denying character who had chosen to marry a prostitute,[47] was perhaps fitted for community. Engels, in tawdry fashion, spread gossip in July 1846 about Sibylle Hess. Then he availed himself of Moses Hess's confidence in order to seduce his wife. Hess was torn with anger when he learned what had happened. Engels thereupon wrote to Marx in the language of sexual cynicism: "The business with Mosi has amused me, amazingly, although it is very annoying to me that it came out. . . . Moses threatened to show off his horns with pistols before all of Brussels, . . . He is perfectly free to take his revenge on all my present, past and future mistresses and I recommend to him for this purpose 1. the Flemish

---

[45] *Autobiography of Brook Farm,* ed. Henry W. Sams (Englewood Cliffs, N.J., 1958), pp. 19, 30, 34.

[46] One observer, however, Charles Lane, noted that "the slight allusion in all the writers of the 'Phalansterian' class, to the subject of marriage, is rather remarkable." *Ibid.,* p. 92.

[47] The correspondence between Karl Marx and Moses Hess has evidently not been fully published. Probably it would illumine the Utopian phase of Marx and Engels. Cf. Edmund Silberner, "Moses Hess," *Historia Judaica,* XIII (1951), 7.

Riesin, who lived at first in my previous residence at 87 chaussée d' Ixelles and is called Mademoiselle Felice, who arrives in Brussels on Sunday, . . . It would be terribly annoying if he should succeed with neither of them. I impart this information to him, if you please, so that he can recognize my uprightness. *I will give him fair play.* [In English]."[48]

By way of self-extenuation, Engels wrote that he had wished to avenge himself for the vulgarities other socialists had inflicted on Mary Burns, his own mistress, and that concern for Moses Hess had been only secondarily on his mind. All this perhaps was human, but scarcely communitarian. What community could have survived the sexual antagonisms occasioned by a few activists such as Engels? Perhaps the strict sexual codes of the communist colonies were a precondition for their success.

IV

Never compelled to lead a communitarian existence, never a participant in communist experiences, it was Engels indeed who was the scientific Utopian in rendering judgments that were founded on wishes rather than fact. He never coped with the question of the quality of communist life as did Hawthorne. Engels oddly enough was familiar in later years with Hawthorne's *Scarlet Letter* because it was dramatized by Edward Aveling.[49] But probably he never read Hawthorne's short stories of Shaker life, "The Shaker Bridal" and "The Canterbury Pilgrims," which were founded on direct observation and searching analysis. In the second story, a young Shaker boy and girl, fleeing

[48] *MEGA* (Berlin, 1929), Dritte Abteilung, Band 1, pp. 91–92, 29, 24. The translated passage is taken from Elliott Erikson, *Karl Marx and the Communist Manifesto,* a doctoral thesis at Stanford University, February 1954, Doctoral Dissertation Series, Publication No. 8215, University Microfilms, Ann Arbor, pp. 224–25.

[49] Frederick Engels, Paul and Laura Lafargue, *Correspondence,* trans. Yvonne Kapp (Moscow, 1960), Vol. 2, p. 121. Cf. Lewis S. Feuer, "Marxian Tragedians," *supra.*

the community, encounter a party of travelers who are coming to join the "cold and passionless society." They include a variety of persons estranged from American society, a poet who has not won the ear of his countrymen, a "ruined merchant" who wishes to become a communist manager, and a laborer, with his wife and children, who has grown poorer and poorer till he has only two alternatives, to go west to Oregon, or join the Shaker village.[50] The wife has seen love wear away under misery, and when the hungry children cry out, they cannot help but go on to the communitarian enclave. The young lovers, however, still seek the world of individuals. And "The Shaker Bridal" likewise deals with the communitarian alienation and the fate of individual love under communism. Two childhood lovers who once were driven by poverty into a Shaker village are now in their thirties about to be chosen as its Father and Mother. The man had come to the Shakers as "to a tomb, willing to lie down in its gloom and coldness, for the sake of its peace and quiet." They have overcome "human frailties and affections" in this society where men boast they have never clasped a woman's hand in their own, and where fathers never take their children on their knees. Having destroyed themselves, they would see the world destroyed, and look forward to the day "when children shall no more be born and die," and when the sun will "go down, never more to rise on a world of sin and sorrow." At the ceremony, the woman in her being finally rebels against the Communal Leviathan; she shudders "as if there were something awful and horrible in her situation and destiny" and falls dead at her childhood lover's feet. Thus Hawthorne searched into the inner fate of the human beings in the communist colonies Engels extolled.

[50] The so-called "safety-valve" concept of the frontier seems to have been taken for granted at this time in America. Sir Charles Lyell wrote, in 1845, that American democrats doubted the workability of a universal male franchise for England, "where there is no outlet in the Far West, no safety-valve for the escape of the redundant inhabitants. . . ." Sir Charles Lyell, *Travels in North America* (London, 1856), I, 227.

Would the superstructure that the communist foundation required have perforce to be repressive, anti-humanist? Engels and Marx instinctively turned from such questions; Marx later argued that the dialectical social science could not enable one to predict future social forms but only to make explicit present tendencies. "No question," he wrote, "can be solved unless the elements of its solution are involved in its terms,"[51] and presumably the terms were not as yet given. Withal, they were confident in affirming that communist society would witness the free development of all, the transition from the realm of necessity to the kingdom of freedom. How could they use the dialectical method in this predictive fashion when their method itself presumably precluded such predictions? The communist colonies were virtually the only empirical evidence Engels and Marx had for the quality of communist life, and they could sense how quickly they tended to become personal dictatorships. George Ripley kept Brook Farm alive by his magnetic leadership, but there were others beside Hawthorne who became restive with his judicious guidance. And Hawthorne in his remarkable *The Blithedale Romance* drew a fictional portrait of George Ripley, Brook Farm's leader, in the guise of the all-dominating and all-directing Hollingsworth, whom the "mighty purpose" of "philanthropy" (the spirit of the do-gooder) transforms into a "cold, spectral monster" who sees no human beings but only the raw material for proselytes. Owen, Rapp, and Bäumler were benevolent dictators.

Communitarian opinion, moreover, tended to be cruelly despotic; self-righteous mediocrities shaped the dominant pattern of communist life. "In the American social communities," wrote Ralph Waldo Emerson, "the gossip found such vent and sway as to become despotic. The institutions were whispering galleries, in which the adored Saxon privacy was lost. Married women I believe uniformly decided against the community. . . ." Was communist so-

[51] Marx and Engels, *Correspondence 1846–1895*, p. 386.

ciety a kingdom of freedom? This was a question Engels and Marx were glad to prorogue as they turned from community-construction to class struggle. With one's energies absorbed in the tactics of struggle and the proletarian conquest of power, one could claim leave to repress the overriding problem of direction—whither society? With their closure on the study of communist colonies, Engels and Marx were also ridding themselves of responsibility for the empirical study of socialism. They were drawing instead a promissory note on history, without the warrant of their scientific solvency.

Curiously, socialist colonizers such as the Brook Farmers felt like Marx and Engels that they were, above all, the exponents of "social science." Indeed, the use of "social science" was first introduced by the publication of *Phalanx or Journal of Social Science, Devoted to the Cause of Association and Social Reform,* twenty-three numbers of which appeared in New York from October 5, 1843, to May 28, 1845. The Brook Farm communists wrote in their constitution in 1844 that they proposed to secure "to the Association the benefits of the highest discoveries in social science." "It is an essential characteristic of the new Social Science," said Charles A. Dana to the New England Fourier Society in 1844, "that it is pacific and not destructive. It does not so much seek to overturn the old order of things, as to supplant it. . . ."[52] This was no call to class struggle but rather a reasoned advocacy of socialist pilot experiments which would then, in competitive coexistence with the capitalistic environment, prove their superiority. There was a kind of Darwinian flavor to the Brook Farmers' conception of social evolution. It would not come about through dialectical catastrophe, leap, or revolution. Rather, each socialist colony

[52] *Autobiography of Brook Farm,* pp. 224, 100, 109. By contrast, the first use of "sociology" in the United States seems to have been George Fitzhugh's *Sociology for the South* (1854), a book written in "scientific" terms in advocacy of the slave system. Cf. *Ante-Bellum Writings of George Fitzhugh and Hinton Rowan Helper on Slavery,* ed. Harvey Wish (New York, 1960), p. 45.

was like a variation in the social species; and the socialistic variations would tend to perpetuate themselves and survive over their capitalistic rivals through the struggle for existence. The new social science seemed to demonstrate a law of Sociological Selection. This was, indeed, an inevitability of gradualism through the cumulation of socialist variations.

The American transcendentalist communists, like Marx and Engels, extolled the guiding wisdom of Fourier and Feuerbach. Like Engels, George Ripley, with the credentials of the new social science, took note of the Working Men's Movement as "proof among ten thousand others of the correctness of the views of social progress set forth by the immortal Fourier." The workingmen were protesting the "sovereignty of combined capital; and with a strong instinct, if not a clear consciousness of the strength of union, are forming systematic organizations. . . . They are an important step in the progress of Humanity towards its destined goal." So wrote Ripley in *The Harbinger* for June 20, 1846, even as Engels, holding to the same philosophy, was expressing similar communitarian longings. Ripley combined his transcendentalist idealism with Fourier's psychological theories in a way similar to Engels' synthesis of Feuerbach with Fourier. And like Engels, Ripley at this time still looked to the middle class as well as the workingmen to lead the way to communism. Fourier was unfortunate, wrote Ripley, in having in France "no intelligent middling classes" to whom to appeal. The American Associationists, on the other hand, could, he said, "depend on the intelligence, the sense of justice, the faith in progress, the practical skill and energy, and the material resources, which will be consecrated to this cause by the great middling classes of American society. . . ."[53] Transcendentalism was the philosophy of American socialism at a time when, as Frothingham put it, "socialism was spreading," and "seemed, to enthusiastic believers, to be fast assuming in the United States a national char-

[53] *Autobiography of Brook Farm,* pp. 164, 192.

acter."[54] Charles A. Dana, who wrote Brook Farm's Articles of Association, many years later clarified the transcendentalist inspiration: "In the party of Transcendental philosophers," said Dana, "the idea early arose . . . that democracy . . . was not enough . . . it should be raised up into life and be made social. The principle of equality should be extended. . . . That could only be accomplished by the reform of society. . . . And that was what inspired the socialistic movement which began about 1835 or 1838."[55] Engels in his communitarian phase could well call the transcendentalists his comrades. They would have shared his enthusiasm for Feuerbach. Theodore Parker, for instance, "was intimate with the thoughts of Feuerbach," and says the historian of transcendentalism, O. B. Frothingham, "Feuerbach would have taken him by the hand as a brother."[56]

Clearly the communitarian, associationist movement seemed very much in the 1840s to the young social scientists of the world, Mill, Ripley, Marx, and Engels, the visible embryonic formation of the next stage. It was the root-predicament of Marx's dialectic method that it involved the extrapolation of some observable present trend. For in any given present, there are alternative, competing trends; some trends furthermore turn out to be self-limiting. If an observer in 1845 could perceive the genesis of communist colonies, he could also discern the burgeonings of a managerial class, the strivings of the new intellectuals, the beginnings of trade-unionism, and the spread of public education. Which of these trends would prove dominant? The one toward a managerial society? Or that toward a democratic, reformed capitalism? Or a scientific technoc-

---

[54] Octavius Brooks Frothingham, *Transcendentalism in New England* (New York, 1876), p. 170.

[55] Charles A. Dana, "Brook Farm," in James Harrison Wilson, *The Life of Charles A. Dana* (New York, 1907), p. 521.

[56] Octavius Brooks Frothingham, *Theodore Parker: A Biography* (Boston, 1874), pp. 566–67; *Recollections and Impressions 1822–1890* (New York, 1891), p. 61. Ripley, on the other hand, found Feuerbach "crabbed and dogmatic in his atheism." Octavius Brooks Frothingham, *George Ripley* (Boston, 1883), p. 229.

racy? Or a society of decentralized communities? Marx's method involved a selective, arbitrary emphasis on one theme, an intuitive grasping of the drift of history; his own ethical longings would lead him to choose one trend and repress the others. Moreover, there is what we might call a polar-equilibrium principle in history; a given trend through its operations calls into existence a countertrend; instead of a dialectical transformation into a new society, one may see a new equilibrium that reinstates the old society reformed. Engels thought in 1845 that the communist communities were the nuclei of the new society; his social science was from the outset blended with social nescience, in that strange heady mixture of empirical richness, ethical power, summons to action, prophecy, and misprediction, in which all the ingredients fluctuated uncontrollably and indeterminately.

v

The dream of decentralized communist societies on the model of the American Utopias has always remained alive as a recessive theme in the socialist unconscious. Allow Marx, Engels, Lenin, or Trotsky to speculate as to their true goal, and despite their authoritarian drives, they will fall back into a vision of society as a collection of Brook Farms. Marx, writing his defenses of the Paris Commune, suddenly defined its inner aim as a society of "cooperative production," in which "united cooperative societies are to regulate national production upon a common plan." Decentralized communes, "the political form of even the smallest country hamlet," were to administer their common affairs; only a few functions would remain to the central government.[57] Engels, at the end of his life, was angered by what he called the "State socialism" of Jean Jaurès; it lacked, indeed, the Utopian communitarian

[57] Karl Marx and Friedrich Engels, *Basic Writings on Politics and Philosophy,* ed. Lewis S. Feuer (New York, 1959), pp. 367, 370.

element.[58] When he criticized the German party's state socialist language and proposals in 1875, he proposed, almost sentimentally, "to replace *state* everywhere by 'community,' a good old German word which can very well represent the French word 'commune.'" And in 1891 he was still explaining to German state socialists that he meant each commune to enjoy "complete self-government on the American pattern."[59]

Most remarkable were the dreams of Utopian communities with which Lenin and Trotsky, in the midst of revolution, civil war, their own terrorism against anarchists and Kronstadt decentralizers, comforted themselves. Trotsky recalled in 1937:

The author of these lines discussed with Lenin more than once the possibility of allotting to the anarchists certain territories where, with the consent of the local population, they would carry out their stateless experiment. But civil war, blockade, and hunger left no room for such plans. The Kronstadt insurrection? But the revolutionary government naturally could not "present" to the insurrectionary sailors the fortress which protected the capital only because the reactionary peasant-soldier rebellion was joined by a few doubtful anarchists.[60]

Beneath the Promethean urge to lay violent hands on the Old Social Order and to destroy it, there always survived the conception of the Idyllic Community in which conflict would vanish and a strange peace would fill the totality of things.

[58] Engels, Paul and Laura Lafargue, *Correspondence*, Vol. 3, p. 325.

[59] Karl Marx and Frederick Engels, *Critique of the Gotha Programme, A Contribution to the Critique of the Social-Democratic Draft Programme of 1891* (Moscow, 1959), pp. 42, 60.

[60] Leon Trotsky, *Stalinism and Bolshevism* (New York, 1937), pp. 22–23. Also cf. Victor Serge, *Memoirs of a Revolutionary 1901–1941*, trans. Peter Sedgwick (London, 1963), p. 119. In the early stages of the revolution, anarchists collaborated with the Bolsheviks. The Bolshevik power was soon, however, suppressing them. Emma Goldman, *My Further Disillusionment in Russia* (New York, 1924), pp. 83 ff.; *My Disillusionment in Russia* (New York, 1923), pp. 47 ff.

Such, then, was the episode of Engels and Marx's entry into communism by way of Utopia.[61] Engels, we might note, always kept Marx informed of his propaganda for the formation of communities. Although only Engels' letters to Marx for this period are extant, they indicate only a concord between the two friends. Within two years, however, the adventure into community was put aside. When Marx and Engels wrote *The German Ideology* in the first half of 1846, they dated the founding of the "social democratic school" in North America as of the year 1829.[62] This was the year in which the Workingmen's Party of New York was organized. Communism, in short, was being identified with political class struggle, and differentiated from the Shaker or Rappite communal withdrawal.

Indeed, the most thorough rejection of the communities was finally published in September 1847 in the *Kommunistiche Zeitschrift* (Communist Journal), the organ of the London members of the Communist League, under the aegis of Marx and Engels. The critique of communities, based on practical, philosophical, and political grounds, was made by way of an article against "Citizen Cabet's Emigration Scheme," the proposed Icaria in America.

[61] Arthur Bestor, in his noteworthy *Backwoods Utopias*, has argued that in America alone was there a continuous evolution from an earlier religious socialism to the secular socialism of the nineteenth century: "In Europe, by contrast, there was a hiatus." Professor Bestor also remarks that Karl Marx read nothing on the history of religious movements. Actually, however, Engels' study of the American religious communist colonies and Marx's tribute to Wilhelm Weitling, the religious socialist, as a pathfinder, show a similar continuous evolution in European socialism from a religious to a secular form. Moreover, not only did Engels write *The Peasant War in Germany*, a study of mystical, religious communism, but Marx also in 1850 tried to come to terms with Guizot's interpretation of the Cromwellian revolution. Cf. Arthur Eugene Bestor, Jr., *Backwoods Utopias: The Sectarian and Owenite Phases of Communitarian Socialism in America: 1663–1829* (Philadelphia, 1950), pp. 38–39.

[62] Marx and Engels, *The German Ideology*, p. 123.

Such a community, said the Marxists, is "impossible of accomplishment at the present time" because the emigrants, "though they be zealous communists," would still be tainted "with all the faults and prejudices of contemporary society," which they would not be able suddenly to discard. Quarrels would arise among the members which European spies would exacerbate "until the whole little communistic society becomes completely disintegrated." The emigrants, moreover, would most likely be industrial workers who would not adapt themselves easily to the soil. Privations, sicknesses, and the deprivation of "amenities which even the poorest European worker sometimes has at his command" would sap their enthusiasm.

To these practical objections to the communities, the first Marxists added a philosophical one deeply founded on Marx's conception of social change. A communist society, said the Marxist journal, cannot be envisaged "without its having first passed through a period of transition, and indeed a democratic period of transition, during which personal property would gradually become merged into social property; for communists recognize the principle of personal freedom (as, probably, do the Icarians likewise). A leap, such as Cabet contemplates, in the sequence of events is as impossible from a communist outlook as, from a farmer's outlook, would be a harvest when there has been no seed-time." In short, the communist colonies, from the Marxist standpoint, were trying to leap a stage in the gradual dialectical-evolutionary process.

The failure of such communities, warned the Marxists, would set back the cause of the proletariat "to yet further decades of wretchedness and poverty." If a colony did manage to establish communism "among a few hundred or a few thousand persons," it would only be by its becoming "exclusivist or sectarian in character. An example is furnished us," they continued, "by Rapp's experiment in America." And as sectarians, the communist colonizers would suffer persecution "at the hands of their American neighbors." Take heed, wrote the Marxists, of the persecutions which the Mormons have had to undergo: "We would advise every one who is contemplating emigration with Cabet to America to read a report of the persecutions which the Mormons, a religious sect based upon communist principles, have had to endure and are still enduring." Gone was Engels' pristine enthusiasm of two years earlier for the Rappites and the other religious communist pioneers. Now the Marxist comrades spoke for the primacy of Europe over America as the continent for social revolution: "Brothers, let us man the breach here, in old Europe; let us remain here to work and fight; for in Europe alone are all the elements ready for the establishment of a society based on the community of goods. Such a society will be inaugurated here if it is ever going to be inaugurated at all."[63]

Five months later in the *Communist Manifesto,* composed for this same Communist League, Marx and Engels ridiculed the efforts "to march straightway into the social New Jerusalem," and consigned to the ineffectual in history those who "still dream of experimental realization of their social utopias, of founding isolated *'phalanstères,'* of establishing 'home colonies,' of setting up a 'Little Icaria' —duodecimo editions of the New Jerusalem. . . ." In truth, they were mocking at something within themselves. For Utopian aspiration is less a stage in the social development of the proletariat as Marx would have it than a recurrent psychological phenomenon in all mankind, a universal theme of history, which perdures, as Lewis Mumford has said, as long as actual life falls short of its ideal possibilities, as long as people experience the trauma of discovery that society is not *communitas* but *divisum.*[64]

---

[63] *The Communist Manifesto of Karl Marx and Friedrich Engels,* ed. D. Ryazanoff, trans. Eden and Cedar Paul (London, 1930), pp. 20, 296–97.

[64] Lewis Mumford, *The Story of Utopias* (new ed.; New York, 1962), p. 7.

VI

In November 1847, Karl Marx wrote: "Socialism and communism did not originate in Germany, but in England, France and North America."[65]

When Marx wrote of the North American origin of socialism and communism, he had in mind curiously not the communist colonies that had so engaged Engels' involvement but rather the little-known Workingmen's party of New York, born on April 23, 1829, in the aftermath of a winter's depression; it made a vigorous showing at the polls that year when it received six thousand votes in New York City—28 per cent of the total electorate—but gradually declined during the next two years as an independent organization.[66] When Karl Grün, a German "true socialist," said that the Americans were a prosaic lot who would have to learn their socialism from the Germans, Marx rebuked him sarcastically in *The German Ideology:* "they [the North Americans] have had, since 1829, their own social democratic school, . . ."[67]

Marx learned of this movement from a book by Thomas Hamilton, a British military officer and novelist, entitled *Men and Manners in America*, which was published in London in 1833. Its two volumes enjoyed a wide popularity; the book was reprinted the following year in

[65] Karl Marx, "Die moralisierende Kritik und die kritisierende Moral. Beitrag zur Deutschen Kulturgeschichte. Gegen Carl Heinzen von Karl Marx," *MEGA* (Berlin, 1932), Erste Abteilung, Band 6, p. 308. Translated in Karl Marx, *Selected Essays*, trans. H. J. Stenning (New York: International Publishers, 1926), p. 140.

[66] Walter Hugins, *Jacksonian Democracy and the Working Class: A Study of the New York Workingmen's Movement, 1829–1837* (Stanford, Calif.: Stanford University Press, 1960), p. 15. Nathan Fine, *Labor and Farmer Parties in the United States 1828–1928* (New York: Rand School of Social Science, 1928), p. 16.

[67] Karl Marx and Friedrich Engels, *The German Ideology*, Parts I and III, ed. R. Pascal (New York: International Publishers, 1939), p. 123.

Boston, and within ten years, was translated into French, twice translated into German, and republished in a new English edition. During the mid-forties Marx was reading widely in the sociology and politics of the United States. He studied Tocqueville, Beaumont, and Hamilton, and the constitutions of such American states as Pennsylvania and New Hampshire. When he wrote his warped essay *On the Jewish Question* in 1844, he drew on these writers for the concrete facts concerning the status of religious belief and practice in the United States. America was of crucial importance in the discussion of the religious question because it indicated, as a model, how religion would fare in a fully developed bourgeois society in which political emancipation had been achieved. Despite the absence of a state religion, despite the constitutional bars against religious requirements, "North America is pre-eminently the country of religiosity, as Beaumont, Tocqueville and the Englishman Hamilton assure us with one voice." From Beaumont's feeling-laden novel of the tragedy of slavery, *Marie*, Marx drew evidence that American civilization had become Judaized because it was commercialized. "The practical domination of Judaism over the Christian world has reached a point in North America that the preaching of the Gospel itself, the Church ministry has become an article of commerce. . . ." He cited passages from Beaumont: "In the eyes of a large number, the ministry is a commercial career." Yet, "nobody in the United States believes that a man without religion might be an honest man." He drew most heavily, however, from Thomas Hamilton's *Men and Manners in America:*

"The pious and politically free inhabitant of New England," relates Colonel Hamilton, "is a kind of Laokoon, who does not make even the slightest effort to free himself from the serpents which are throttling him. Mammon is his god, he prays to him, not merely with his lips, but with all the force of his body and mind.

"In his eyes, the world is nothing more than a Stock Exchange, and he is convinced that here below he has no other destiny than to become richer than his neighbors."

Hamilton, moreover, said Marx, had perceived accurately that political emancipation in the United States, its abolition of property requirements for the vote and elective office, would inevitably lead to the abolition of private property. "Hamilton interprets this fact quite correctly from the political standpoint: 'The great multitude has won the victory over the property owners and the monied men.' Is not private property ideally abolished when the have-nots become the legislators of the haves?"[68]

The book of Thomas Hamilton, however, not those of Tocqueville and Beaumont, was the source of Marx's knowledge concerning the political theory and practice of the Workingmen's party of New York. Although the two young Frenchmen arrived in New York in May 1831, they never met any of the leaders of the Workingmen's party or came into contact with its political activities. Tocqueville's discussions and interviews were largely with disillusioned Federalists; as a sociological interviewer, his sample was distinctly unrepresentative. Tocqueville all his life remained a poor observer of working-class life. On the eve of the June days of the Revolution of 1848, with the working class preparing for insurrection, he listened to George Sand describing "the condition of the Paris workmen, their organization, their numbers, their arms, their preparations, their thoughts, their passions, their terrible resolves," and he "thought the picture overloaded." He conceded that subsequent events proved him wrong. Yet that interview with George Sand was "the first time" Tocqueville had had a discussion "with a person able and willing to tell me what

[68] Karl Marx, "On the Jewish Question," in *Selected Essays*, pp. 50, 51, 53, 72, 90, 91. Karl Marx, "Zur Judenfrage," in Karl Marx and Friedrich Engels, *Werke*, Band I, (Berlin, 1961), pp. 351–52, 354, 363, 373. For the last quotation from Hamilton, Marx cited Hamilton's book, *Die Menschen und die Sitten in den Vereinigten Staaten von Nordamerika*, Band I (Mannheim, 1834), pp. 146, 356. This book is not available to me. I have the impression that Marx ran two passages together.

was happening in the camp of our adversaries."[69] Tocqueville in America recognized, of course, the struggle between the working class and its masters, "the constant struggle for wages that is going on between these two classes." Unlike the Marxists, however, with their pessimist conviction in the increasing misery of the workers, Tocqueville held to the optimist view "that a slow and gradual rise of wages is one of the general laws of democratic communities." Where "wretchedness" prevailed among a section of the working class, it was, he believed, "an exception to the general rule," "a monstrous exception in the general aspect of society."[70] Tocqueville's proposed law of American development was basically at variance with that which, as we shall see, Hamilton derived from the Workingmen's party, and which found its way into Marx's standpoint.

Nor did the warmhearted Beaumont see the working-class misery and social ferment Hamilton reported. American society, wrote Beaumont, was thoroughly egalitarian; "I found not only political equality . . . but I could see social equality everywhere, in money matters, in the professions, in all their customs." Apart from the Negro slaves, all America was middle-class in economic conditions and attitudes; "all Americans are merchants," "businessmen." A laborer in America, said Beaumont, regards himself as helping his master, not as working for him, and he wishes no more than his lawful wages. Beaumont indeed reproached the "English author who has written with some skill on the customs of the United States, Hamilton," for having said that there was as much social inequality in the United States as in England.[71] But Hamilton, though he

[69] *The Recollections of Alexis de Tocqueville*, trans. Alexander Teixeira de Mattos, ed. J. P. Mayer (New York: Columbia University Press, 1949), p. 149.

[70] Alexis de Tocqueville, *Democracy in America*, trans. Henry Reeve, ed. Phillips Bradley (New York: Knopf, 1953), II, 160, 190–91.

[71] Gustave de Beaumont, *Marie, or, Slavery in the United States: A Novel of Jacksonian America*, trans. Barbara Chapman (Stanford, Calif.: Stanford University Press, 1958), pp. 221, 227, 230.

probably erred in another extreme, reported on a whole set of facts and ideas that had eluded the eyes of Beaumont and Tocqueville.

Thomas Hamilton (1789–1842), the son of a Glasgow professor of anatomy, had, after three winters at Glasgow University and a trial of commerce, served in the Peninsular Campaign, in which he was severely wounded. Retired from the army, he turned to literature and published in 1827 a successful novel, *Cyril Thornton,* in which his talent for sociological description showed itself in his picture of Scottish university life. He was a good friend of Walter Scott and William Wordsworth. Bereaved by the death of his wife in Italy at the end of 1829, Hamilton undertook a journey to America in October 1830.[72] *Men and Manners in America* was the product of his sociological exploration.

A week after he arrived, Thomas Hamilton came to know firsthand the Workingmen's party of New York. The twenty-fifth of November, in those days, was celebrated as "a grand-gala day" in New York to commemorate the anniversary of the evacuation of the city by the British. That year, however, it was determined "to get up a pageant of unusual splendour, in honour of the late Revolution in France," the Revolution of July 1830 which overthrew the Bourbon monarchy. "This resolution, I was informed," wrote Hamilton, "originated exclusively in the operative class, or *workies,* as they call themselves, in contradistinction to those who live in better houses, eat better dinners, read novels and poetry, and drink old Madeira instead of Yankee rum. The latter and more enviable class, however, having been taught caution by the results of the former French Revolution," had prudently determined to join in

[72] John Veitch, *Memoir of Sir William Hamilton, Bart.* (Edinburgh, 1869), pp. 129–30; "Death of Thomas Hamilton, Esq.," *Blackwood's Magazine,* 53 (1843), 280; T. B., "Thomas Hamilton," *The Dictionary of National Biography,* ed. Sir Leslie Stephen and Sir Sidney Lee (London: Oxford University Press, reprinted 1921–22), VIII, 1097; "Thomas Hamilton," *Appleton's Cyclopaedia of American Biography,* ed. James Grant Wilson and John Fiske (New York, 1887), III, 65.

the pageant.[73] Hamilton described the festive procession of trades:

Butchers on horseback, or drawn in a sort of rustic arbour or shambles, tastefully festooned with sausages. Tailors, with cockades and breast-knots of ribbon, pacing to music, with banners representative of various garments, waving proudly in the wind. Blacksmiths, with forge and bellows. Caravans of cobblers most seducingly appareled, and working at their trade on a locomotive platform, which displayed their persons to the best advantage. And carpenters too. . . .[74]

Beneath the holiday mood, Hamilton found, however, as time progressed, that there were social and economic forces at work of the first magnitude.

In a chapter on New York, Thomas Hamilton set down his reflections on the impact of increasing industrialization on political parties:

In that city a separation is rapidly taking place between the different orders of society. The operative class have already formed themselves into a society, under the name of "The Workies," in direct opposition to those who, more favoured by nature or fortune, enjoy the luxuries of life without the necessity of manual labour. These people make no secret of their demands which, to do them justice, are few and emphatic. They are published in the newspapers, and may be read on half the walls of New York.

Hamilton distinguished clearly between the two factions of the Workingmen's party, the Moderates and the Extreme Left. The Moderates were concerned primarily with achieving equality of educational opportunity, "equal and universal education." The Extreme Left went much further in its demands:

There are others who go still further, and boldly advocate the introduction of an AGRARIAN LAW, and a periodical division

[73] Thomas Hamilton, *Men and Manners in America* (Edinburgh and London, 1833), I, 59–60.
[74] *Ibid.*, p. 62.

of property. These unquestionably constitute the *extrême gauche* of the Worky Parliament, but still they only follow out the principles of their less violent neighbours, and eloquently dilate on the justice and propriety of every individual being equally supplied with food and clothing; on the monstrous iniquity of one man riding in his carriage while another walks on foot. . . .[75]

Was this the first application to American politics of the term *extrême gauche?* These men of the left had a simple ideology: "only equalize property," and society would not be divided into classes, one that drank champagne and the other water, but, said Hamilton sardonically, "both would have brandy, a consummation worthy of centuries of struggle to attain."

"All this is nonsense undoubtedly," wrote the Tory Hamilton, yet this party was "strong in New York," and its influence in the municipal election had been "strongly felt." Above all, however, Hamilton saw in this Workingmen's party the portent of the future, for it would be the political voice of an ever increasing, ever more miserable working class:

There can be no doubt that as population becomes more dense, and the supply of labour shall equal, or exceed the demand for it, the strength of this party must be enormously augmented. Their ranks will always be recruited by the needy, the idle and the profligate, and like a rolling snowball it will gather strength and volume as it proceeds, until at last it comes down with thundering with the force and desolation of an avalanche.

The event may be distant, but it is not the less certain on that account.

The settlement of the Western lands still unoccupied, an "immense extent of fertile territory," would, continued Hamilton, "delay the day of ruin." When the frontier would be gone, however, then would commence "the trial of the American constitution; and until the trial has been passed, it is nonsense to appeal to its stability."

[75] *Ibid.,* pp. 299–301.

This period of trial, Hamilton reckoned, would not be very distant. Within half a century, the American people would number about fifty millions, and "the pressure of population, on the means of subsistence" would become very great, especially in the Atlantic states. Hamilton's forecast had the idiom of the later Marxian analysis: "Poverty and misery will be abroad; the great majority of the people will be without property of any kind, except the thews and sinews with which God has endowed them; they will choose legislators under the immediate pressure of privation." Security of property would vanish in this electoral uprising of a propertyless working class.

The growth of huge industrial cities, moreover, with a population at the mercy of the industrial cycle of prosperity and depression, made "inevitable," said Hamilton, the passage of political power to the *extrême gauche* of the Workingmen's party:

Huge manufacturing cities will spring up in various quarters of the Union, the population will congregate in masses. . . . Millions of men will depend for subsistence on the demand for a particular manufacture, and yet this demand will of necessity be liable to perpetual fluctuation. When the pendulum vibrates in one direction, there will be an influx of wealth and prosperity; when it vibrates in the other, misery, discontent, and turbulence will spread through the land. . . . Let it be remembered that in this suffering class will be practically deposited the whole political power of the state; that there can be no military force to maintain civil order, and protect property; and to what quarter, I should be glad to know, is the rich man to look for security, either of person or fortune?

The workings of the democratic republic in the United States would, according to Hamilton, enable the transfer of political power to the working class to be made without violence. "There will be no occasion however for convulsion or violence. The *Worky* convention will only have to choose representatives of their own principles, in order to accomplish a general system of spoliation, in the most legal and constitutional manner." Even if the federal government were not so inclined, individual state governments could undertake "to dispose of the property within their own limits as they think proper, and whenever a *numerical* majority of the people shall be in favour of an Agrarian law, there exists no counteracting influence to prevent, or even to retard its adoption." Hamilton had discussed the prospect of these future developments "with many of the most eminent Americans of the Union"; without exception, all had agreed that such a future period of trial was "according to all human calculation inevitable." Democracy seemed to lead "necessarily . . . to anarchy and spoliation. . . . In England the journey would be performed with railway velocity." In the United States, it would take a generation or two longer, "but the termination is the same." What preserved America, for the present, from "revolutionary contention" was that "the great majority of the people are possessed of property"; but "another state of things must necessarily arise." "The weapons of this fearful contest are already forged; the hands will soon be born that are to wield them." Hamilton's own allegiances were clear. The working class was moved by "hunger, rapacity, and physical power," but "reason, justice, and helplessness" were the attributes of the propertied.[76]

To Marx, the book *Men and Manners in America* told the first story of an organized political party of labor in the world's history. Actually, as Helen L. Sumner pointed out, it was the Workingmen's party organized in Philadelphia a few months before, in July 1828, that was "the first labor party in the world."[77] The New York party can claim, however, to have been the first to elect an exclusively independent labor candidate to the legislature—

[76] *Ibid.,* pp. 302–10. Hamilton's discussion of American politics, notes Jane Mesick, was "by way of warning to his own country." Jane Louise Mesick, *The English Traveller in America 1785–1835* (New York: Columbia University Press, 1922), p. 339. Also cf. Dixon Ryan Fox, *The Decline of Aristocracy in the Politics of New York* (New York: Columbia University Press, 1919), p. 357.

[77] John R. Commons *et al., History of Labour in the United States* (New York: Macmillan, 1953), I, 169, 195.

Ebenezer Ford, a carpenter. The American events, above all, were an indication of what the course of history would be as other countries became republican and bourgeois. Marx insisted that the American bourgeois republic itself exemplified most sharply the social contradictions of capitalism and that socialism and communism consequently had their origin there. The more developed a bourgeois society was,

all the more acutely does the social question obtrude itself, in France more acutely than in Germany, in England more acutely than in France . . . in the Republic more acutely than in the constitutional monarchy. Thus, for example, the crises in the credit system and in speculation, etc., are nowhere more acute than in North America. Nowhere, too, does social inequality obtrude itself more harshly than in the Eastern States of North America, because it is nowhere less glossed over by political inequality.

Special conditions in America had mitigated the development of pauperism. But now, "pauperism is making the most delightful progress."[78] America was not exempt from the law of history; it was the law's best illustration. Their philosophy of history led Marx and Engels to exaggerated expectations concerning the imminence of revolution in the New World. Engels in 1848 surveyed the revolutionary movements and announced that the proletariat in the United States was "in open rebellion against the ruling bourgeoisie."[79] There were German democrats such as Carl Heinzen who extolled the American political and social system; Heinzen indeed polemicized with vigor against Marx as an "ape" who hopped from Hegelian thesis to antithesis in the "barbarous nonsense" of economic determinism, and who proposed to destroy human freedom in his "communist factory and barracks state."[80] Marx

[78] Marx, Selected Essays, pp. 143–44.

[79] D. Ryazanoff, ed., The Communist Manifesto of Karl Marx and Friedrich Engels (New York, 1930).

[80] Carl Wittke, Against the Current: The Life of Karl Heinzen (1809–80) (Chicago: University of Chicago Press, 1945), pp. 237–

and Engels were desperately concerned to refute the claim that the American democracy was exempt from their dialectical laws of history.

The Workingmen's party had no clear conception of the socialized ownership of the means of production. Nevertheless, in two important respects, it would have seemed to Marx to constitute a communist party. In the first place, it was a party of the working class, the "operative class," which proposed as soon as it could to win the political power of the state, and then to reorganize the economy as seemed best for the interests of the working class. It was from the political standpoint wholly different from the Fourierist Associationist movement. The Associationists proliferated in America at this time but they remained essentially a nonpolitical movement. They did not propose to carry their program to the polls but solely to establish their phalanxes with their own capital, and without any regard to the conflict of political parties. They did not aspire to political power. Moreover, as Henry E. Hoagland said, they brought "a middle-class philosophy of aiding the depressed masses." A most distinguished list of American intellectuals supported Associationism but entirely without any notion of committing themselves to class struggle.[81] Secondly, a rudimentary communistic philosophy had appeared among the Workies—agrarianism. Their program for the periodic division of property was not clearly outlined by Hamilton, but it was clear, at any rate, that they proposed to achieve economic equality by "spoliation" and whatever other means were required. Given the increase of industrialization, Marx could expect that Workyism, with its ideology of class struggle, would pass beyond its primitive expression of agrarianism to fully developed communism. The *extrême gauche* of the Workies did not simply propose as did the later National Reformers a more equitable way of apportioning the unsettled frontier lands

---

43. Also cf. Carl Wittke, *The Utopian Communist: A Biography of Wilhelm Weitling, Nineteenth Century Reformer* (Baton Rouge, 1950), pp. 114–16.

[81] Commons, *History of Labour in the United States*, I, 502.

to actual settlers; rather, they proposed confiscation, "spoliation," expropriation of the existing landholders; they were a revolutionary party.

VII

From its North American inception, workingmen and intellectuals diverged in their conceptions of socialism. In his momentous *What Is to Be Done?* Lenin declared that socialist consciousness could not arise among the workers through their own experience and thought, but that it "could only be brought to them from without. The history of all countries shows that the working class, exclusively by its own effort, is able to develop only trade-union consciousness. . . . The theory of Socialism, however, grew out of the philosophic, historical and economic theories that were elaborated by the educated representatives of the propertied classes, the intellectuals."[82] Lenin's viewpoint in one form or another is held by most students of the history of socialism and the labor movement, yet it is surprising that it has not been submitted to a rigorous empirical test. Does the North American origin of socialism gibe with Lenin's doctrine that socialist consciousness cannot be the spontaneous creation of the working class?

The agrarians, the forebears of socialist consciousness in the Workingmen's party, were not intellectuals. Most of the leaders of the Workingmen's party, writes Edward Pessen, "seemed to favor a kind of socialism."[83] The leaders of the Moderate faction, however, were intellectuals—Robert Dale Owen, Frances Wright, and George Henry Evans—they vigorously advocated a scheme for universal education that resembled Plato's project for the education of the Guardians. Their "educational communism" envisaged an upbringing for all children till the age of

[82] V. I. Lenin, *What Is to Be Done?* (New York: International Publishers, 1931), pp. 32–33.

[83] Edward Pessen, "The Workingmen's Movement of the Jacksonian Era," *Mississippi Valley Historical Review*, 43 (1956), 438.

twenty-one in state boarding schools where they would be fed, clothed, and lodged, and wear a uniform dress.[84] America's first socialist intellectuals thus already showed an authoritarian bias. Their program was subsequently disavowed by the executive committee of the party, which was sensitive to the criticism that the party was led by enemies of the American home; the committee, on the contrary, endorsed simply "a republican system of education." The agrarian group was led by Thomas Skidmore, a machinist, who in the fall of 1829 was the "undisputed leader" of the Workingmen's party as a whole.[85] The party at the outset emphasized its working-class character. When, at its second organization meeting on April 28, 1829, a Committee of Fifty was set up to prepare a report and manage its affairs, "great care was taken to have no 'Boss' on the committee . . . [so] a large majority . . . were journeymen," wrote George Henry Evans. The report adopted on October 19 invited all fellow citizens "who live on their own labor, AND NONE OTHER" to join in the nomination of workingmen for election to the legislature. Skidmore's domineering ways and extreme ideas, however, proved his undoing, and he was read out of the party a few months later. He charged at that time that nineteen of the seventy delegates were "rich men, living on the labor of others," and then organized the first splinter group in the history of the American socialist movement, the "Original Workingmen's Party," he called it, "for those and those only who live by the labor of their hands."[86]

[84] Frank T. Carlton, "The Workingmen's Party of New York City, 1829–1831," *Political Science Quarterly*, 22 (1907), 405. Richard William Leopold, *Robert Dale Owen* (Cambridge, Mass.: Harvard University Press, 1940), pp. 85 ff. Robert Dale Owen, *Threading My Way* (New York, 1847), pp. 296–99. For the career of George Henry Evans, cf. Helene Sara Zahler, *Eastern Workingmen and National Land Policy, 1829–1862* (New York, 1941), pp. 23, 33–41.

[85] Edward Pessen, "Thomas Skidmore, Agrarian Reformer in the Early American Labor Movement," *New York History*, 35 (1954), 280.

[86] Carlton, *op. cit.*, p. 406. Hugins, *op. cit.*, p. 14.

Thomas Skidmore, machinist, was the primal forebear, as far as there was one, of the socialist movement and the socialist consciousness. Skidmore was the prototype of what we might call the "worker-intellectual" in the American labor movement. Students of the annals of trade-unionism and labor parties invariably come across worker-intellectuals who germinate ideas, at the critical moments when organizations are in the first stage of self-formation, from their own experience, reading, reflection, and consciousness. The "worker-intellectual" is a workingman with the soul of an intellectual, a workingman become articulate, a worker with his hands who has refused to allow his consciousness to atrophy or become the agent of self-reproach but who would call the master's social system before an impartial tribunal. The "worker-intellectual" will speak of justice, the human aspiration, and status; he has the prophet's fervor as he condemns the exploiter. The economic struggle for him is not simply one over the division of the gross national product; it is a struggle between the men of evil and the men of good. Karl Marx knew several such worker-intellectuals, of whom the most imposing was Wilhelm Weitling; at first enthusiastic about him, Marx later ousted him with his dialectical weapons from the communist movement; the hegemony of the political intellectual over the workers was established. The "worker-intellectual" will be found even among the lowliest in labor's ranks. Carleton Parker, wandering among the I.W.W. halls, was amazed by their abstract discussions, and found in their libraries not only books of Marx and Kautsky but "dog-eared," dull and theoretical pamphlets of their own leaders.[87] Thomas Skidmore was a man of this mold.

In his book *The Rights of Man to Property,* Skidmore addressed himself to the working class, to those who lived by their own labor. They were, as Marx later said, to

---

[87] Carleton H. Parker, *The Casual Laborer and Other Essays* (New York: Harcourt, Brace & Howe, 1920), p. 103.

achieve their own emancipation. In large capital letters, Skidmore wrote: "It will be for those who are suffering the evils . . . to lead the way. . . . It is to be the result of the combined exertions of great numbers of men." "The poor and middling classes" must finally understand that "he who commands the property of a State, or even an inordinate portion of it, has the liberty and the happiness of its citizens in its own keeping." "He who . . . can give me employment, or bid me wander about in idleness, is my master; and it is the utmost folly for me to boast of being anything but a slave."[88] Such words condemned the system of wage labor. Without proposing a planned economy, Skidmore envisaged the abolition of all forms of what Marx called surplus value. In the last pages of his book, Skidmore wrote: "Take away from the possessors of the world their dividends, their rents, their profits; in one word, that which they receive from the *use* of it, and which belongs, freely belongs, to one as much as another. . . ." He called for a society in which there would be "no lenders, no borrowers; no landlords, no tenants; no masters, no journeymen; no Wealth, no Want." With such a renovated social order, "the present condition of the human race . . . would be annihilated for ever." He opposed Robert Owen's organization of the factory at New Lanark, Scotland, because despite Owen's purity of motive and executive talent, he and his associates still drew an annual interest on their capital.[89] It was in such passages that Skidmore's agrarianism verged on socialism.

The idiom and generalizations of historical materialism seemed to come spontaneously to the machinist Skidmore. It was an absurdity no longer to be tolerated "that a very great part, of the human race, are doomed, of right, to the slavery of toil, while others are born, only to enjoy." The leader of the Workingmen's party indicated his goal like a social geometer writing Q.E.D. at the end of the

[88] *Ibid.,* pp. 387–88.
[89] *Ibid.,* p. 385.

theorem he has proved: "I have shewn enough to justify my fellow citizens in pulling down the present edifice of society, and to induce them to build a new one in its stead. . . ."[90]

Probably Marx never heard of Thomas Skidmore, but through the intervention of the British Captain Hamilton, he read of the first labor party in the history of the world that had elected a legislative representative, and had an agrarian ideology pregnant with socialist potentialities. He read how the triumph of this movement was feared to be inevitable in an industrial civilization. Thus, the vision of a workingmen's state was first born among Skidmore and his fellow "worker-intellectuals." The socialist consciousness was not given to them from without by intellectuals from the propertied classes, as Lenin would have had it. Later Marx and Engels took up socialist ideas that had arisen spontaneously among the workingmen, and, processing them through Hegelian and Ricardian machinery, gave them a so-called "scientific" form. The socialist consciousness itself, however, first appeared among the agrarians, many of them anonymous, of the Workingmen's party of New York. It was in America too that the workingmen's protest first took shape in a political party with electoral support. In this sense, the North American origin of socialism and communism provided a model of what could be expected to occur when democracy would have been established in the European countries.

The sanguine expectations of Marx and Engels for social revolution in America vanished after the European defeat of 1848. They became aware that America took the finest of their fellow German revolutionists, and transformed them into upstanding pillars of the republic. "After the failure of the Revolution of 1848," said Marx in his inaugural address to the Working Men's International Associa-

---

[90] *Ibid.*, pp. 67, 126, 125, 4–6. Daniel De Leon, the leader of the Socialist Labor party, quoted frequently from Skidmore's book. Cf. Arnold Petersen, *Daniel De Leon* (New York, 1931), p. 5.

tion, "the most advanced sons of labor fled in despair to the Transatlantic Republic."[91] Their close friend, Joseph Weydemeyer, tired of an unemployed exile in Switzerland, and wishing to make a living for his wife and children, decided in 1851 to emigrate to America. Engels wrote deploring the necessity for that decision:

> . . . the available Germans who are worth anything become easily Americanized and give up any thought of returning. Then too we must consider the special conditions in America: the ease with which the overflow population settles on the land, the necessarily increasing tempo of the country's prosperity which makes people consider bourgeois conditions as a *beau idéal*. Those Germans who think of returning home are for the most part only demoralized individuals. . . .

Marx, too, expressed his fear that Weydemeyer would lose himself "somewhere in the Far West."[92] Weydemeyer in later years served with distinction as a colonel in the Union Army during the Civil War. Marx himself by a narrow margin decided not to emigrate to the United States to found a newspaper. If he had, who knows? Perhaps he would have found himself as General Marx in Lincoln's army, or served as Carl Schurz did later, in the President's cabinet. And Marxian socialism would have been a branch of American democratic theory.

Meanwhile, however, it was part of the drama of alternation of ideas, that socialism, springing up almost namelessly in America, a vision born of the working-class consciousness in 1829 in New York, was then adopted and recast by the German intellectuals, Marx and Engels, and should

---

[91] Karl Marx, "Inaugural Address of the Working Men's International Association, September 28, 1864, in Karl Marx and Frederick Engels, *Selected Works* (Moscow, 1955), I, 381.

[92] Karl Obermann, *Joseph Weydemeyer: Pioneer of American Socialism* (New York: International Publishers, 1947), pp. 28–29. Franz Mehring, *Karl Marx: The Story of His Life* (New York: Humanities Press, 1961), p. 240.

have been claimed three-quarters of a century later by Lenin on behalf of intellectuals and their hegemony.[93]

[93] Several months after this essay was circulated in mimeographed form, an important article was published by Maximilien Rubel which remarkably confirmed my reconstruction of Marx's studies of Thomas Hamilton's book on America. Rubel, working with the unpublished notebooks of Marx at the International Institute for Social History in Amsterdam, found in them about fifty passages from the German translation of Hamilton's book published in 1834. These passages Marx had written down in 1843. Rubel quotes at length from five of them. They coincide exactly with those which I had inferred from internal evidence Marx must have used as the basis for his statement that socialism originated in North America. Rubel states aptly: "In Thomas Hamilton he found what Tocqueville failed to notice: the revolutionary implications of American democracy." Cf. Maximilien Rubel, "Notes on Marx's Conception of Democracy," *New Politics*, 1 (1962), 83–85.

Neo-Primitivism:
The New Marxism of the
Alienated Intellectuals

An ideology can have a career very different from what
its founder intended. If Marx were alive today, he would
be astounded by the latest stage of Marxism. When he and
Engels wrote the *Communist Manifesto* in 1848, and when
he published *Capital* in 1867, he expected that he was
providing the workers' movement with a science; a hundred years later his doctrine is largely ignored by industrial workers. Instead, Marxism has become the ideology
of Alienated Intellectuals. When Marx was politically active a hundred years ago, he looked to the initiative of the
International Workingmen's Association as the historical
agent of the world's socialism. He saw the peasantry as a
retarding force, sunk in the "idiocy of rural life." A century later Lin Piao, Minister of Defense in Mao's Communist China, proclaims the war of the countryside against
the cities, and summons the peasants of Asia, Africa, and
Latin America to lead the world through "people's wars"
to communism; the American and European workers are
regarded as having succumbed to capitalist affluence.[1] A
century ago Marx hailed the workers' trade-unions and
political parties as their instruments for educating themselves to a cultural and political level that would bring
them to rule. He utterly rejected any actions of terrorist
violence or attempted seizures of power by bands of intellectuals. A hundred years later, Fidel Castro, Che Guevara, and Régis Debray assert that the guerrilla action of
armed intellectuals is the necessary step for opening their
road to power. Indeed, the students, the youthful intel-

[1] *New York Times*, September 4, 1965. Also cf. "Radio Discussions in Moscow," *Survey*, No. 63 (April, 1967), p. 28.

lectuals exempt from the workings of economic causation, are hailed today as the activators of an otherwise immobile historical dialectic.

The phenomenon of the revolutionary student intellectual was a new one in Marx's lifetime: he was troubled by it but never fully understood it. The student unrest seemed to him epiphenomenal to some deeper movement, and could therefore be disregarded. "The stupid nonsense the Russian students are perpetrating," wrote Marx in 1877, was "merely a symptom, worthless in itself. But it is a symptom. All sections of Russian society are in full decomposition economically, morally, and intellectually."[2] Sometimes the intellectuals seemed to Marx self-destructive in their idealism; at other times they seemed ambitious for places of power, and desirous of using the workers' movement to achieve their ambitions. What Marx could never have possibly discerned was that the intellectuals would remake Marxism into an ideology that is frankly neo-barbarian, that is, anti-intellectual, anti-urban, anti-working class, anti-Western. For many years Marx fought an uncompromising battle against his anarchist adversary, Mikhail Bakunin; he drove the Russian and his followers from the International and believed he had put their ideas to rout. Bakunin, indeed, broken by Marx's vilifications, retired to die. From the vantage of a hundred years, however, it seems that Bakunin is taking his revenge upon Marx. The revolutionaries today, the intellectuals and student activists, are Marxist in form but Bakuninist in content.

What are the tenets of this new Bakuninist-Marxism? We can list them bearing in mind that they are found in varying proportions in different movements and sub-movements:

(1) The Neo-Marxist intellectual rejects the notion that the labor movement is a progressive force in contemporary history. Like C. Wright Mills, he regards such a "labor

---

[2] Karl Marx and Frederick Engels, *Letters to Americans 1848–1895*, to L. E. Mins (New York, 1953), p. 115.

metaphysic" as a "legacy from Victorian Marxism that is now quite unrealistic."[3]

(2) The Neo-Marxist believes that the Alienated Intellectuals will be the principal agents in fashioning the new society. In this respect, they revert to the view of Louis Auguste Blanqui, the indefatigable organizer in Paris for forty years of secret clubs of déclassés, recruited mostly from Left Bank students and nonstudents, who planned and plotted for the seizure of power by their elite, and their proclamation of a dictatorship in the name of the proletariat.

(3) The Neo-Marxist, rejecting the impersonal determinism of economic processes and slow cumulative social movements, believes in the personal voluntarism of individual guerrilla action as the igniting agency of the System; not the immanent development of the System, but the Confrontation of the System by the Individual.

(4) The Neo-Marxist regards the peasantry of backward countries as offering a far more revolutionary potential than the proletariat of advanced societies.

(5) The Neo-Marxist tends to regard the colored races of Asia, Africa, and Latin America as the "proletariat" (in a higher sense) engaged in a war of liberation from the "bourgeois" white race of North America and Europe.

(6) The Neo-Marxist is anti-urban, and sees the countryside in the present epoch waging an implacable war against the degenerate, exploiting cities; he revives in this sense the classical Populist doctrine of an antagonism of the soil-dwellers against decadent urban civilization.

(7) The Neo-Marxist, because he is an Alienated Intellectual, holds to an ideology of anti-intellectualism; he wishes not so much to raise the cultural level of the masses as rather to lower himself to the level of their lowest stratum; whether in language, gait, dress, morals, and manners, he tries to identify himself with the behavior of the lowliest as he sees them, and to rid himself of the trappings

[3] C. Wright Mills, "On the New Left," *Studies on the Left,* Vol. II, No. 1 (1961), pp. 70–71.

of bourgeois culture; he is what we might call a neo-primitivist.

(8) The Neo-Marxist believes that the younger genera-tion, those under thirty, or even twenty-five, are uniquely endowed with revolutionary instincts; he combines the no-tion of generational struggle with that of class struggle, and above all, with elitism and primitivist instinctivism, revert-ing in underlying tone to the view of the Russian student revolutionist, P. N. Tkachev, that all people over twenty-five years of age should forthwith be executed.[4]

(9) The Neo-Marxist will consequently not wait on the processes of the economic decline of capitalism; indeed, what he fears most is the stability and affluence of the capi-talist economy, and its capacity for de-revolutionizing the masses with material goods; he has become doubtful that some economic law preordains the decay of capitalist civi-lization; all the more therefore does he advocate the tactic of continuous insurrection and terrorism to disrupt and dislocate the System, to "bring it to a grinding halt."

Ten and fifteen years ago, when African nations were achieving their independence, there also emerged a strange mixture of tribalism and Marxism. Jomo Kenyatta, a Marx-ist alienated from the primitive customs of his own people, tried desperately to find a cultural mooring among them. Kwame Nkrumah made mandatory a tribal blood ritual in The Circle, a revolutionary African student group he helped to found; he synthesized Trotskyism with tribalism. Thus the future Prime Ministers of Kenya and Ghana, both Alienated Intellectuals, struggled for a reidentification with tribal culture. They fused primitivism with Marxism largely because their peoples whom they were undertaking to lead politically lived at a primitive level of social and material existence. The Neo-Marxist today, however, is often an intellectual who is consciously regressing to primi-tivism. His neo-primitivism does not arise from tribal con-ditions of life; rather it is a conscious protest against the

[4] Albert L. Weeks, *The First Bolshevik: A Political Biography of Peter Tkachev* (New York, 1968), p. 64.

values of Western civilization, an assertion, often by Westerners themselves, of a neo-barbarian standpoint. The neo-primitivist intellectual, glorifying violence, wishes scientific reason to abdicate in favor of the revolutionary instincts. If classical thinkers such as Marx and Freud wished to supplant the unconscious with the conscious, the id with ego, the neo-primitivist wishes to replace the reason with the id, the consciousness with the rule of unconscious drives.

Régis Debray is the most recent exponent of neo-primitivist Marxism. Himself the child of wealthy parents, a graduate of the Ecole Normale, twenty-seven years old, a creature of ideas, his mind filled with Marxist and Sartrean idea-images, with no stabilizing ballast of experience, perceiving social realities through a political a priori more transcendental than the Kantian, a man who, never having had to earn his own living, has never had real obstacles on which to expend his plentiful aggressive energies, here indeed is an exemplar of the Alienated Intellectual, with the credentials for formulating the precepts of the new ideological stage, that of Bakuninist-Marxism. Having fallen under the spell of Che Guevara and Fidel Castro, Debray expounds in his *Revolution in the Revolution?* the new primacy of the student turned guerrilla fighter. "The irony of history has willed, by virtue of the social situation of many Latin American countries, the assignment of precisely this vanguard role to students and revolutionary intellectuals, who have had to unleash, or rather initiate, the highest forms of class struggle." Their basic principle, "insurrectional activity is today the number one political activity," is also their principle of self-therapy; guerrilla activity enables them to overcome the anxieties of bourgeois infantilism, their special illness: "Nothing like getting out to realize to what extent these lukewarm incubators make one infantile and bourgeois." And what are these maternal incubators, these Oedipal ties, which the *guerrillero* is trying to sever? House, running water, a roof, electricity, stores. In the so-called virgin forest, he can undertake "to erase the marks left on his body by the incubator—his weakness." In the mountain he recovers his manhood, and he finds the mountain his appropriate symbol. He endorses Fidel Castro's exhortation of 1957: "The most fitting slogan of the day ought to be, All guns, all bullets, and all resources to the Sierra." The *guerrillero's* experience brings a new sense of comradeship to replace the bourgeois psychology: "The first law of guerrilla life is that no one survives it alone. . . . Petty bourgeois psychology melts like snow under the summer sun, undermining the ideology of the same stratum. Where else could such an encounter, such an alliance, take place?" As they share their burdens, lightening each others' knapsacks, the *guerrillero,* according to Debray, feels himself shedding class egoism, and living communism in a historic leap from the bourgeois constraints. Thus too Mao Tse-tung and his disciples cherish the days of the Long March and the memory of their communist enclave in Yenan.

The civilization of the cities, egoistic, competitive, industrial, intellectual, is an emasculating force, says the Alienated Intellectual. He must decivilize, deculturate himself. At the same time, the Neo-Marxist, as a generational rebel, aims to undermine the hegemony of the older generation in Marxism. He demands a new generational style, a new tactic, that will stamp the obsolescence of the old. Thus Régis Debray says that in Latin America "there is a close tie between biology and ideology," and that elderly men cannot fit into the ranks of the mountain guerrillas; the guerrilla fighter thus supplants the party militant; Father Marx and Old Man Lenin are superseded by Fidel and Che; a "rejuvenation" (in Debray's word) of the party takes place; the revolutionary movement accomplishes a tactical parricide.

The guerrilla fighters meanwhile, according to Debray, remold the passive psychology of the peasantry. Day by day the guerrillas "destroy the idea of the unassailability" of the existing order, "that age-old accumulation of fear and humility vis-à-vis the patron, the policeman, the *guardia rural. . . .*" The enemy's strength is shown to be bluster; the guerrilla's ambush and terrorism prove "that a soldier and a policeman are no more bullet-proof than anyone else."[5]

Sixty-five years ago, Lenin in 1903 created the new conception of a Bolshevik party—the party of professional revolutionists engaged in propaganda and agitation, editing newspapers, writing clandestine leaflets, meeting in secret cells to read Marxist classics, waging electoral campaigns for the Duma's seats, teaching the workers that they must one day violently overthrow the bourgeois regime. Now there is a Neo-Bakuninist-Marxist conception of the party: "The guerrilla force is the party in embryo." Gone is the concern for political coalitions and alliances; the new vanguard builds itself without benefit of a party apparatus. The virtues of the new revolutionist are also of a different order from the old. "You are capable of creating cadres who can endure torture and imprisonment in silence," said Che Guevara to Party comrades, "but not of training cadres who can capture a machine-gun nest."[6] The guerrilla movement, says Debray, has ended "the divorce of several decades' duration between Marxist theory and revolutionary practice."

Raymond Aron once said Marxism was the opiate of the intellectuals; we may add: Neo-Bakuninist Marxism is the hallucinogenic of the Alienated Intellectuals. The quest for manhood and identity through guerrilla warfare is a recurrent theme among them. Between the two world wars, for instance, T. E. Lawrence became something of an idol among young English intellectuals. Here was a man of books who had betaken himself among Arab nomads of the desert, and proved his manhood in guerrilla warfare, raiding the enemy's communication lines, living life primitively, with tent and camel, acknowledging the homosexual community of his comrades-in-arms, and then writing the definitive essay on guerrilla warfare for the *Encyclopedia Britannica*. What Lawrence of Arabia was with his primi-

[5] Régis Debray, "Revolution in the Revolution?" *Monthly Review*, Vol. 19, No. 3 (July–August 1967), pp. 21, 51, 52, 71, 76, 102, 111, 112.

[6] *Ibid.*, pp. 103, 106, 107.

tivist and guerrilla mystique for the English middle-class alienated youth in the twenties and thirties, Che Guevara of Cuba and Bolivia is for the estranged youth of the mid-sixties. Lawrence could never adjust himself to ordinary, prosaic society and had to live by a cult of death. Che Guevara could not attune himself to the socialist bureaucratic society of Cuba, but had to seek out the Bolivian mountains in a death quest.

If Marx's specter stood over the world during the years of the depression, it is clear that it is Bakunin's specter that animates the revolutionary movements today. Marx ridiculed Bakunin as "one of the most ignorant men in the field of social theory,"[7] yet it transpires that his anarchist adversary was far more prescient, far more intuitive in grasping the dynamic of the revolutionary drive. To be sure, Bakunin lacked Marx's erudition and dialectical skill. During his twelve years of imprisonment and Siberian exile, Bakunin could not pursue daily studies and note-taking as Marx did in the reading room of the British Museum. But Bakunin, having escaped and returned to his revolutionist's calling, mixed naturally with workingmen's and students' circles. He grasped far more deeply than the bookworm Marx ever did the nature of the revolutionary "instincts." It was during the latter sixties that Bakunin, challenging Marx's hegemony in the International Workingmen's Association, wrote a series of pamphlets that history has demonstrated to have been the most prophetic criticisms of Marxism.

The social revolution of our time, said Bakunin, is primarily an uprising of the "uncivilized," the so-called "inferior races." What drives them is the "instinctive passion of the masses for equality." Marx, according to Bakunin, had failed to understand the psychology of revolution. Marx, holding to a mechanical law of stages of social evolution, looked to the workers of the "most advanced

[7] Karl Marx, *Letters to Dr. Kugelmann* (New York, 1934), p. 103. Marx wrote that Bakunin's tone was that of those "accustomed to attack western civilisation to palliate their own barbarism." *Ibid.,* p. 102.

countries" in "which modern capitalist production has reached its highest degree of development" to initiate and guide the revolution. Marx held up England as a model of the world's future evolution, saying, "De te fabula narratur." The creed of political primitivism and anti-civilization, however, permeates the new revolutionary movements. Not the stage of industrial evolution, says Bakunin, is the primary determinant, but rather "the intensity of the instinct of revolt, . . . This instinct is a fact which is completely primordial and animal, . . ." This instinct of revolt is enfeebled among civilized peoples, "whether it is that it has been exhausted during their previous development, or whether, finally they were originally less endowed with it than were others." The true proletariat of modern times, said Bakunin, is not the industrial workers of "advanced" countries, but rather "that great mass, those millions of non-civilized, disinherited, wretched and illiterates"; this "rabble," "very nearly unpolluted by all bourgeois civilization," will inaugurate the Social Revolution.[8] The so-called "inferior races," who have either rejected or remained unaffected by bourgeois civilization, will be, declared Bakunin, the makers of the Revolution.

Curiously, this ideology of anti-civilization had a strong attractive power for Bakunin and his intellectual disciples. Revolutionary students were ready to revolt against their fathers' civilization. The potent social mixture of modern times between the neo-primitivist intellectual and the culturally primitive peasant was fashioned in Bakunin's social alchemy: "I believe exclusively in the peasant community and in the educated community of irreconcilable youths. . . . A phalanx forty thousand strong, these youths, whether they know it or not, belong to the revolution." Engels, Marx's collaborator, could muster in 1870 no enthusiasm for the prospect of an alliance between the student nihilists and a backward people. They seemed to him

[8] *Michel Bakounine et les Conflits dans l'Internationale, 1872,* ed. Arthur Lehning (Leiden, 1965), pp. 153–54, 163–65. Michael Bakunin, *Marxism, Freedom, and the State,* trans. K. J. Kenafick (London, 1950), pp. 48–51.

a menacing amalgam threatening to disintegrate Western progress: "How awful for the world . . . that there are 40,000 revolutionary students in Russia. If there is anything which might ruin the western European movement, then it would have been this import of 40,000 more or less educated, ambitious, hungry Russian nihilists; all of them officer candidates without an army."[9] The primitivist impulse waxed strong among Bakunin's disciples who studied the *Catechism of the Revolutionist,* a forerunner of Che Guevara's and Régis Debray's manuals on the vocation of the guerrilla warrior: "The revolutionist is a doomed man. . . . Everything in him is absorbed by one exclusive interest, one thought, one passion—the revolution. . . . He knows only one science, the science of destruction. . . . The object is but one—the quickest possible destruction of that ignoble system. . . . Day and night he must have one thought, one aim—inexorable destruction."[10]

Lenin, we now see, was the intermediary in imparting this neo-barbarian ingredient to Marxism. Seventy per cent of the world's population, said Lenin in 1920, lived in backward Asian countries, and the Soviet form of society could be directly adapted to these precapitalist systems. Three years later, he said that the outcome of the world struggle would be determined by the fact that the backward countries had "the overwhelming majority of the population of the globe."[11] Maturation and growth in the advanced countries were no trustworthy road to communism; the resentment of the backward was the reliable mainspring of the world's revolution. To this Bakuninist idea, Lin Piao,

[9] G. M. Stekloff, *History of the First International,* trans. Eden and Cedar Paul (London, 1928), p. 166. Max Nomad, *Apostles of Revolution,* rev. ed. (New York, 1961), p. 133. Shlomo Avineri, "Feuer on Marx and the Intellectuals," *Survey,* No. 62 (January 1967), p. 154.

[10] Max Nomad, *op. cit.,* pp. 230–31.

[11] V. I. Lenin, "Report of the Commission on National and Colonial Questions to the Second Congress of the Communist International" (1920), in *The National Liberation Movement in the East,* trans. M. Levin (Moscow, 1957), pp. 265, 267; "Better Fewer, But Better" (1923), *op. cit.,* p. 315.

Mao's Minister of Defense, gave frank expression in 1965. Mao's strategy, he said, was "the establishment of rural revolutionary base areas and the encirclement of cities." The peasants constitute, he said, "the main force" of the revolution against the imperialists: "The contradiction between the revolutionary peoples of Asia, Africa and Latin America and the imperialists headed by the United States is the principal contradiction in the contemporary world." "Taking the entire globe, if North America and Western Europe can be called the cities of the world, then Asia, Africa and Latin America constitute the rural areas of the world. . . . In a sense, the contemporary world revolution also presents a picture of the encirclement of cities by the rural areas."

Thus Bakunin's neo-primitivist ideology prevails among the new generation of Marxists. Bakunin's anarchism, of course, plays little part, but his definitions of the roles of intellectuals, peasants, violence, and the revolutionary instinct have carried the day. Why, however, are Western intellectuals among those drawn to primitivism, to the extolling of violence, to "creative vandalism"?[12] The Bakuninist neo-primitivism is the most recent symptom of a collapse of character in many intellectuals. There were Roman intellectuals who when their empire was invaded welcomed the triumph of the Huns and Vandals as importing a higher primitivism to replace their guilt-ridden civilization.[13] What has been taking place in much of our society is not the "secession of the proletariat," which Toynbee feared, but the "secession of the intellectuals." Part of the malaise springs from the multiplication of a vast corps of literary and aesthetic intellectuals without high competence or talents, often semi-educated, but who none-

[12] See the issue on "Creative Vandalism," *Anarchy,* No. 61 (March 1966).

[13] *Seven Books of History against the Pagans: The Apology of Paulus Orosius,* trans. L. W. Raymond (New York, 1963), p. 392. Salvian, *On the Government of God,* trans. E. M. Sanford (New York, 1930), pp. 109, 217. J. B. Bury, *History of the Later Roman Empire* (London, 1923), I, 283–85.

theless feel themselves as most properly qualified (in Shelley's phrase) to be the legislators of mankind. Society, they feel, is not proffering them the places they merit. The Alienated Intellectuals, beginning with Blanqui and Bakunin, have tended to be anti-Semitic largely, one suspects, because the persecuted Jews refused to secede from the System but generally cultivated their professional and technical powers and skills till the System recognized them. For every Trotsky there were a hundred doctors, dentists, druggists, teachers, engineers. Chaim Weizmann, insistent on doing his seven hours a day of chemistry, and refusing to be an ideological man, was much more representative of the Jews than their handful of professional revolutionists.[14] The Alienated Intellectuals have also their men of unusual abilities: they are the restless chieftains of the new intellectual tribes, the new sects and movements, who see themselves as the philosopher-kings of the new society. The new elite strives for power, longing to replace the succession of businessmen, lawyers, engineers, and soldiers who have hitherto provided the governing elites. But there is a deeper malady too whose operations can only be obscurely sensed. The intellectual too often suffers from a Hamlet complex: he often feels that intellect has disabled him, unmanned him, feminized him, deprived him of the capacities for will and action; he wishes to recover his manliness, to have his every word transmuted to action. His neo-primitivism is a rebellion against what he feels his intellect has done to emasculate him. The cult of violence is a reversion to the primitive rites of passage from adolescence.

The neo-primitivist intellectual drawn to "guerrilla warfare" is moved by an atavistic longing for the unrestraints of savagery. To stalk the System, to strike at it suddenly from ambush, to feel the exhilaration of maiming and decapitating authority, all this exhilarates the unmanned Alienated Intellectual. "Guerrilla warfare" is precisely a

[14] Chaim Weizmann, *Trial and Error: The Autobiography of Chaim Weizmann* (New York, 1949), pp. 37–38, 64.

projective tactic of those haunted by fears concerning their masculinity. To its ideologists it has the attractions of a psychological restorative, a quick access to "reality," self-assertion, and community. The Alienated Intellectual, with his surplus free-floating energies, lives all the more in a world of myth and fantasy, far from the science that Marx extolled. It is perhaps characteristic of the neo-primitivism that myth has become the privileged ideological category for so many intellectuals. We have yet to cope honestly and directly with this problem. One thing, however, is clear: that the neo-primitivist who, like Bakunin, uses political action to project on a social scale his private maladies finally becomes the progenitor of a society in which his malady is magnified and transmitted a thousandfold. Bakuninist-Marxism will be a tragic chapter in the history of the intellectual class, the worst of their treasons because the one most self-destructive.

A Neo-Marxist Conception
of Social Science

During the 1950s C. Wright Mills was outstanding among American sociologists for his courage in confronting the most central issues of our time. His name has become a byword in the academic world as one unafraid to say the unpopular thing. In *The Sociological Imagination* (New York: Oxford University Press, 1959) Mills tried to do for this generation of social scientists what Veblen did for his. Where Veblen called for the overthrow of the pecuniary culture which distorted pure science, Mills saw the enemy as the "research bureaucracy" which has "expropriated" the means of social science research. His book, to put it bluntly, calls upon social scientists to overthrow the research bureaucracy and "in some collective way" to take "full control over these means of research" (p. 106). "The bureaucratization of social study," according to Mills, is the general trend today. The two dominant styles of research, "grand theory" and "abstracted empiricism," are handmaidens of the bureaucratic power elite; the one provides it with ideological defense, the other makes its authority more efficient and effective (p. 117).

Certainly, it is true that many social scientists share the values and political standpoint of the American managerial class. The most creative group of American sociologists has evolved from youthful radicalism to adherence to what a sardonic critic might call the "allrightnik" view of American society. They have expressed in scientific terms an experience not unlike that recorded in Harry Golden's *Only in America*. Mills's book would rebuke this school of thought. He believes that they have surrendered the promise of social science for bureaucratic rewards. Their existence, moreover, has determined their consciousness; bureaucratic existence, Mills holds, has made for bureaucratic modes of thought.

As the basis for his critique of bureaucratic modes of thought Mills sets forth what we might call a "Neo-Marxist" methodology of social science. "Abstracted empiricism," the collection of facts "by a bureaucratically guided set of usually semiskilled individuals," is held to be founded on the fallacious "building block" theory that a cumulation of specific studies can produce a social science. Its problems are not defined with reference to "the basic idea of historical social structure." Devoid of "substantive propositions or theories," its principal function, Mills says, is to provide jobs for semiskilled technicians who invoke the scientific method to hide their intellectual poverty. As for "grand theory," the pompous sister of "abstracted empiricism," it consists of "empty formalities," an "associating and dissociating of concepts," which never connect with problems in their historical context. Mills holds that the whole effort at grand theory is ill-founded; "there is no 'grand theory,' no one universal scheme in terms of which we can understand the unity of social structure" (p. 46). He translates several passages of grand theory from Parsons' ponderous prose into everyday English; the effect is wholesome.

How valid is Mills's arraignment of present-day social science? Mills charges, as the Marxists used to, that the "political meaning" of abstracted empiricism is to eliminate "the great social problems and human issues of our time from inquiry" (p. 73). I wish he had written down, from his own considerable experience, several sample case studies of the professional evolution of graduate students, and had indicated how, in his opinion, they have been led by institutional pressure to betray their vocation as social scientists. It would have meant more than his rather familiar methodological polemic. But, unfortunately, Mills offers no concrete evidence on this point. Many graduate students whom I know do not fit into Mills's picture. They are going off to Tanganyika to study African trade-unions, or to Malaya to examine the process of colonial self-liberation, or to India to study its Communist party. They study problems of interracial housing, work dissatisfaction, and the varieties of political experience. They do not often propose sweeping theories, and sometimes their contribution is rather in the collection of a novel body of facts. But here three things should be borne in mind. Originality in theory is a rare and unusual gift. A Newton, an Einstein, a Marx, or a Freud has an isolated greatness that stands out among a legion of their more earth-bound associates. If many young social scientists turn to modest empirical studies, it is not necessarily because political fears make them avoid theory. Rather, like their physicist friends, they look for problems which are within the limits of their abilities. It will not do to deride their labor, as Mills does, or to see a political cowardice in every human limitation. Secondly, there is far more to the "building block" theory of science than Mills is prepared to allow. Darwin made use of the observations of innumerable collectors and then plied them with questions. The "vulgar empiricist," whom Mills and the Marxists scorn, has contributed much to the daily life-blood of science. Thirdly, the theoretical problems themselves are more beset with difficulties than they were once thought to be. Simple certitudes have given way to intricate uncertainties. Mills's own book begins with the tone of imperative points but before it ends they have metamorphosed into question marks.

The taint of foundation finance is for Mills the original sin of contemporary American social science; he also has a refreshing hatred for research teams. Nevertheless, it is astonishing that his book does not even mention *An American Dilemma*, a work of "bureaucratic social science," the product of research teams working under Myrdal, financed by a foundation, and yet, nonetheless, a work which affected greatly the intellectual climate, provided documentation for the Supreme Court's decision against racial segregation in the public schools, and contributed to the most significant recent effort in American social reconstruction. An ingredient of bureaucratic guidance, indeed, is not incompatible with the advancement of science. The Royal

Society did a great work when it sent Eddington to Principe in 1919 to photograph the eclipse of the sun and test Einstein's theory; and in the eighteenth century the British government helped science as well as navigation by offering a prize for improvements in the chronometer. Our ultimate demand from any social organization for research is that the individual scientist retain his own basic choice of problems and methods; therefore, safeguards are required that the bureaucratic component may never become dominant.

To what degree, however, have the social sciences become bureaucratized? The contributor to sociological journals and meetings is still likely to be a yeoman researcher, cultivating his own material, and vassal to no foundational feudal fief. Among the projects assisted by grants of some kind there is little indication that the work itself was "bureaucratically guided." The technology of social science research does not have the degree of bureaucratic potential possessed by the technology of physical research. A few years ago P. W. Bridgman sadly noted that the new experimental techniques were making it extremely difficult for the individual physicist to work on his own. Happily, the technology of social science research has not made the dominance of a bureaucracy inevitable. Neither the small-scale investigator of "milieus" nor the large-scale theorist of whole societies need abandon their status as intellectual entrepreneurs; the capital requirements of their research still remain minimal. The individual researcher can still fare forth with his own means of doggedness as W. E. B. Du Bois did in 1896 to write *The Philadelphia Negro*. And the American radical tradition persists more vigorously among sociologists than among any other group of social scientists. Meanwhile, what is needed is a factual study of the degree to which academic managerialism has affected the direction and character of sociological research in the United States.

Mills rejects grand theory because, as a Neo-Marxist, he holds that every sociological theory must be restricted in its domain to some particular social structure. We should be guided, he says, by "what Marx called the 'principle of historical specificity' " (p. 149). (Actually Marx never used this expression; it was introduced by his expositors, notably Karl Korsch.) Thus, according to Mills, the idea of a human nature common to man as man violates the guiding principle of historical specificity. Even the relevance of history itself to the study of societies is held by Mills to be subject to this principle; the past is much more important in the workings of societies with a feudal heritage than it is in the United States.

There is, to my mind, a bit of obscurantism in "the principle of historical specification" which, at the present time, would obstruct the advance of social science. The principle rightly warns us to specify clearly the variables in our sociological laws; do not, for instance, enunciate as a law for all economic systems what may be true only of a competitive capitalist one. The principle has its obvious counterpart in physics. Kepler's laws, for instance, are laws for the motions of planets, not for masses in general. But Kepler's laws turned out to be special cases of the Newtonian laws which did apply to all masses. And, in a similar sense, the laws of different societies might likewise be special cases of the operation of universal psychological and sociological laws. To specify the historical structure would simply, then, be to state the initial social conditions that would bound the operation of the universal laws in the specific historical situation. We cannot, indeed, understand how one social system evolves into another without using some guiding laws of a common human nature; the revolt of men against their society's mores and values would be otherwise unintelligible. For all Marx's presumable adherence to the "principle of historical specification," he had no hesitance about making trans-historical generalizations. He set forth general laws concerning "all ruling classes," "all ideologies," "all modes of exploitation," and "all history." As for the hypothesis that the past itself is less important for American-type societies than others, that too could be formulated in some cross-societal law. We might say, for example: for all societies composed of immigrants the influence of the past will vary inversely with the novelty of the social circumstances.

The study of particular social structures should finally, if the history of science is a guide, lead to some general theory of human societies. In chemistry, after the laws of many particular elements were ascertained, the periodic law was discovered into which the properties of most elements fitted with regularity. This led to a universal theory of the constitution and transmutation of elements, their rise and decay. Why foreclose, as Mills does, the possibility of a similar evolution of sociological theory? Mills's animus against Parsons' theory has led him to overreach himself to a point where he would make impossible a theory of social change. Mills properly asks sociologists not to neglect "a fully comparative understanding" of the social structures in world history. Has the record of achievement, however, been so bleak? Hypotheses such as Wittfogel's concerning Asian societies have provoked a considerable discussion, and there are now journals devoted precisely to such comparative studies.

Examples of Marxo-Veblenite apriorism abound in Mills's book. He writes that social workers and teachers have an "occupational incapacity to rise above a series of cases" and cannot confront the problem of society as a whole. Actually, the generation of Jane Addams and Florence Kelley was stanchly socialist in its philosophy, while teachers were the most numerous occupational group among the communists. Mills laments that "there is no left-wing press" that the "average academician" would normally read. To which it is fair to reply that the left-wing press is still here, a proliferation of weeklies, monthlies, and quarterlies largely unread because, apart from the effects of prosperity and purges, so many of them have been discredited as political guides. Mills believes that, if there were genuine intellectual competition, "grand theory and abstracted empiricism would not have gained such ascendancy as they have." In Britain, however, where presumably a research bureaucracy has not corrupted social scientists, styles of research similar to the American prevail. The new trend of "Titmussism," which occupies itself with sociological problems of the welfare state, especially attracts young leftist intellectuals; they are "abstracted empiricists." Japanese sociologists, from conservative to communist, are likewise using American-fashioned methods. Polish Marxist sociologists are likewise enthusiastic about American modes of research. If we had a soviet of sociologists, or if instead we used the antitrust laws to break up foundation research, would the leading persons and trends in sociology be appreciably different from what they are?

The Neo-Marxism of Mills differs in one important respect from classical Marxism: it has lost the optimism characteristic of its forebear. The latter had a direction, a program as well as an indictment. Mills has the indictment without a direction. His "ideological meaning" therefore becomes vague just when one most expects him to have a clarity of leadership. He holds that the theories of socialism as well as of liberalism "have virtually collapsed as adequate explanations of the world" (p. 166). He is not cheerful about Soviet society, and he avows himself pessimistic about the chances of avoiding war and achieving freer societies (p. 193). He is as downcast by the intellectuals as he has been by every other class. Who would not be? Like a modern Jonah he cries: "Where is the intelligentsia that is carrying on the big discourse of the Western world?" Such names come to mind as Russell, Sartre, Camus, Linus Pauling, Silone, Pasternak; there have been intellectuals, principally European, who have been loyal to their calling. Nevertheless, the unofficial truce in the explosion of hydrogen bombs was, in large part, the achievement of a handful of American intellectuals who had not been absorbed into prosperous acquiescence. Mills himself has provided a model of forthright discussion the influence of which has been perhaps far greater than he thinks.

That there are dangers in bureaucracies no one will deny. What we need, however, is concern with their specific problems. We need to think about some code of ethics that will, for example, reduce the exploitation of research assistants by making plain their share in the authorship of new ideas and the discovery of facts. The customary perfunctory acknowledgments too often conceal the extraction of academic surplus value. We should seek ways of making research time and funds available to the isolated scholars in small institutions, and make of the latter centers to which young thinkers would willingly go.

As a sociological study of the sociological imagination, Mills's book seems to me to have missed the mark. It does not use the historical-comparative method it advocates; it cites little evidence for its generalizations; it is an editorial, written with honest gloom. As such, however, it has great importance. The rumors one hears of would-be research bureaucrats cannot be altogether fiction circulated by California beatniks. Where such trends of academic managerialism exist, their way will be made harder and their will to hegemony partially undone by Mills's powerful tract for sociologists.

Generational Conflict among
Soviet Marxists

I make no claim to being an "area specialist" on the Soviet Union, but for many years I have read the literature on Soviet society and ideology. For several years I attended courses in the Russian language, and acquired a stuttering knowledge. My hope in going to the Soviet Union was to engage in discussions with its philosophers, sociologists, and students, to speak with them while their doubts and searchings had not yet been blue-penciled out of existence by editorial committees, administrators, and bureaucrats. I was to find that it took a month or more to learn in the Soviet Union what needed only a week in Japan. One could meet readily in Japan, for instance, with a variety of factions in the Zengakuren, but in the Soviet Union my meetings with free student circles had to be arranged with caution. Where Marxist professors in Japan would speak freely of their different tendencies, among Soviet professors there was a conditioned preliminary response to profess a unanimous consensus in dialectical materialism, even when their differences were patently straining the consensus into dissension, and tearing the ideological garments at the seams.

During four and a half months, I talked with upwards of 150 Soviet philosophers and social scientists, sometimes for an hour, sometimes for five hours. At the Institute of Philosophy of the Soviet Academy of Sciences in Moscow, I gave five lectures to the research workers, ranging in number from twenty to fifty. I went to Tashkent to talk with the Institute of Philosophy and Law in Uzbekistan, and to Tbilisi, for long discussions with scholars at the Georgian Institute of Philosophy. At Leningrad, I inquired into the projects of the hard-working sociologists of the

Social Research Laboratory. Most of all, I learned from discussions with Soviet philosophers who raised objections and questions at my lectures.

My first lecture was on "The Development of Dewey's Pragmatism." The audience consisted largely of the Institute's Section on Bourgeois Philosophy and Sociology. I suggested this subject because I thought it would enable me to raise directly what I regarded as shortcomings and misstatements in the studies by Soviet ideologists of American philosophy. The discussion that followed showed how hard the Soviet ideological stance makes it for them to approach the history of ideas in an empirical spirit.

In the last few minutes of the lecture, I considered the allegation I found in Soviet books that Dewey was the philosopher of American imperialism. I said that from his first political writings, Dewey had been a critic of all imperialist ideology; that his essay on savage mind in 1902 had been directed against racist imperialism in the aftermath of the Spanish-American War; that he had lived in China for two years and had witnessed the May Fourth movement in 1919, and had written a series of remarkable articles defending its anti-imperialist program; that he had been a critic of American imperialism in Mexico; that he had been personally invited by Krupskaya, presumably on Lenin's behalf, to help in reorganizing Soviet education; that he had visited the Soviet Union in 1928, and written a series of warmly enthusiastic reports concerning the Soviet experiment; that, finally, the Soviet attacks on Dewey as an imperialist philosopher had begun only in the mid-thirties when Dewey criticized the Moscow trials and purges. "You yourselves," I said, "have since then come to recognize that with regard to these trials Dewey was right and Stalin was wrong."

The young philosophers in the audience listened intently and did not challenge these observations. But the chairman cautioned everybody to remember that I was giving my "personal opinions," and that they should bear in mind that Dewey had supported Trotsky, and that Trotsky had been trying to restore capitalism in the Soviet Union. It was amazing. These were not illiterates; these were the picked Soviet research workers on Western thought, and all had to acquiesce in this nonsense. Questions on my findings and method followed, and then the floor was taken by the Soviet authority on American pragmatism, Yuri Melvil. Dewey, he asserted, *was* the philosopher of American imperialism, and all the facts I had adduced were trivial; for "objectively" Dewey was a supporter of imperialism; he quoted from an American book which said that Dewey had become anti-communist long before it was fashionable to be so.

I prevailed on the chairman to allow me a few minutes to reply (it is the custom of the Communist party to allow its spokesman the last word). I pointed out what a "dogmatic Marxist" he was, for his dogmatism was such that no set of facts could possibly move him from his belief that Dewey "objectively" was a philosopher of imperialism; this was using "objectively" in an unverifiable sense to conform to dogmatic preconceptions. (There was a round of pleased laughter from the younger side of the room.) I then tried to show how the history of American philosophy did not confirm the Marxist formula that materialism was the progressive philosophy, and idealism the reactionary. Transcendentalism, for instance, was the philosophy of the most radical group of reformers in American history—the New Englanders, who, before the Civil War, dedicated themselves to socialist and abolitionist movements. I said I had once been a Marxist, but that my experience, and philosophical and sociological studies, had persuaded me there were basic limitations to Marxism.

It would be hard to exaggerate the degree to which the Stalinist era extirpated original philosophy and social science, and how its effects still persist. The sense of a continuing and supporting tradition of philosophical discussion is absent. I asked one young philosopher, the author of a work on English intuitionist ethics, if he could give me the title of a good history of Soviet philosophy; I remarked that in the United States we had several histories of American philosophy. He replied, after a moment's thought, that no such history of Soviet philosophy existed. The reason, he said, was simple: they had no need of one because, unlike America, they had no different schools of ideas; everybody worked within the framework of Marxist philosophy. This struck me as tantamount to admitting that the philosophical life of his country was so uninteresting that it didn't deserve to be written; why bother writing a history of commentaries and explications of the Truth which was already written clearly enough by Marx and Lenin? The young philosopher went on to add that a chapter on philosophy during the Lenin period had been prepared for the sixth volume of their collective history of philosophy, but it had been so much criticized that it had never been published. Clearly, silence about the destroyed generation of Soviet thinkers is still regarded as judicious.

An incident during the discussion of my second lecture on "The Sociology of Science" illustrated vividly the official obliteration of the Soviet philosophical past. I was presenting material which was published the following month in a book, *The Scientific Intellectual*. In reply to a question, I said that I disagreed with a seminal Marxist essay in this field. Someone asked to what essay I was referring. I answered it was an article by the Soviet scholar, B. Hessen, "The Social and Economic Roots of Newton's *Principia*," published in 1931 in a book called. . . . The chairman looked at my interpreter, an unspoken message seemed to flash between them, and the interpreter interrupted me: "We do not know anything of the author. I do not know his name." The chairman nodded assent. I looked at the audience. Not a word, not a question about the Soviet scholar to whom I had referred. In any normal gathering, the scholars would have been eager to get the exact reference to an important, neglected essay of one of their own countrymen. But with one glance they had been warned: Do not ask about this man. No doubt the book *Science at the Crossroads* was known to both the chairman and interpreter; its opening essay was by the still unrehabilitated Nikolai Bukharin, and Hessen himself evidently vanished during the Stalinist era. Their names are still enveloped in the collective repression of Soviet memory; references to their writings are to be avoided by the prudent Soviet scholar.

My third lecture was on "Contemporary American Thought." I chose this subject because I wanted to emphasize the tremendous variation in American philosophies, the "law of the spectrum," I called it, according to which the distribution of philosophies was primarily the outcome of differences in individual temperament, and the "law of the wings," in accordance with which every philosophical movement, whether pragmatism, idealism, or materialism, tended to evolve into right, left and center wings. I spoke of the generational differences among American philosophers—how the older philosophers were idealist, realist, or pragmatist, the middle-aged ones naturalist or positivist, and the younger ones, existentialist or ordinary linguisticians, and suggested that under normal conditions such a spectrum of philosophies would manifest itself in the Soviet Union, that this was typical of societies where the spectrum was not deflected by external pressure.

I was promptly challenged at that meeting and at subsequent discussions to apply these "laws" to Soviet philosophy. When I first did so, and pointed to the emerging diversity which I had encountered among Soviet philosophers, I was told that a few weeks of discussions were no sufficient basis for such a judgment; all Soviet philosophers were dialectical materialists. As the months went by, and the discussions accumulated, it became still more evident to me that a variety of conflicting philosophies is emerging in the Soviet Union, and that they are housed together under the rubric "dialectical materialism" in an unstable equilibrium. Dictatorial power, not intellectual agreement, imposes the harness of a planned ideology on recalcitrant temperaments. Nevertheless, even within the framework of the mandatory creed, one discerns the workings of the law of the spectrum. In the Soviet Union, the counterpart exists for every philosophical movement in Western Europe and

America. If planned ideology was eliminated, one might expect a flowering of these diverse philosophical trends.

Among the young philosophers, I found chiefly three trends: scientific realism, existentialism, and pragmatism. The scientific philosophers are (what I called) "scientific realists," that is, their "materialism" is simply a belief in the reality of the physical world. They are engaged in catching up with problems and readings which were central in American philosophy thirty-five years ago. I found circles, for instance, studying such works of Bertrand Russell as *Introduction to Mathematical Philosophy* and the more recent *Human Knowledge*. They are intrigued by the concepts of "structure" and "isomorphism," and talk very much in Russell's terms about how only the structure of the physical world can be known. They tend to reject Engels' theory of sensation as a "reflection" of the world, and find this to be "mirror-magic." They take the basic meaning of "reflection" to be "isomorphism." After the All-Union Conference on Cybernetics in March, they said that Academician Mitin, the Stalinist guardian of philosophic orthodoxy, had been forced to concede that there might be truth in the sign-theory of knowledge against which Lenin had polemicized. One of them remarked: "Ten years ago to have said 'symbols' would have brought down the cry 'idealism.' With no war, the progressive forces will rise." The scientific realist group is on friendly political terms with the Soviet existentialists, that is, they regard them as "moral people." They do not, however, think highly of the philosophical merits of the existentialists, who in their opinion have not yet broken with the Hegelian concept that contradictions can exist in reality.

What characterizes the Soviet existentialists? In the first place, they prefer to study the humanistic Marx of the *Economic and Philosophic Manuscripts,* the Marx of the concept of alienation. As one professor observed, "They are interested in Marx when he was not yet a Marxist." When I noted that this was the precise point—that they preferred the Marx who was not a Marxist—he retorted,

"They will evolve toward Marxism." The Soviet existentialists are concerned with problems of freedom and ethics that were banished from the consciousness in the Stalinist era; they are concerned with the quality of individual life rather than with the tactics of ideological class struggle. They enjoy reading such authors as Berdyaev and Solovyov, and take an interest in Freud. They find German existentialist philosophy more interesting than American thought, and feel themselves closer in spirit to the Germans than to the Americans. The Germans are said to be deeper, to raise at least the problems of existence even though they cannot solve them; the Americans are regarded as proponents of common sense, as relatively superficial.

Both the scientific realists and the existentialists are together in one camp as "anti-dogmatists." "The dogmatists," said a young philosopher, "are the previous people, the immoral ones, who fear that logical methods will unmask their foolish doctrines." "In what way," I asked, "are they immoral?" "They are immoral," he replied, "in their daily practice; they try to suppress their enemies administratively. When a person can prove something, he doesn't need illegal methods." The scientific realists and the existentialists regard each other as "socially progressive" because both oppose the dogmatic Stalinists. This fact of their political unity is perhaps an item of evidence against the historical-materialist theory of ideas, since, on the face of it, their philosophical differences correspond to no differences in politics, and this indeed may be the beginning of philosophy and the end of ideology in the Soviet Union.

The authorities, for ideological reasons, keep calling for dialectical logic, while the mathematical logicians argue that the development of Soviet technology in automation and computational machines requires their discipline. Technology wars with ideology. The young students of logic, however, recite *Principia Mathematica* with the same religious awe with which American graduate students used to approach logical arcana thirty years ago. The "dogmatists" fear mathematical logic primarily for one reason; they perceive that it lends itself to an admiration for clear thinking, and they do not relish the thought of logical instruments probing into their slogan-words and ideological sentences. The Department of Mathematics added to the general turbulence in 1962 by passing a resolution proposed by its logicians that the Chair of Logic in the Philosophical Faculty should be abolished. When a young logician-philosopher, Zinoviev, defended his thesis, there was, I was told, a "stormy" session between the dialectical and mathematical logicians. Zinoviev and his fellow logicians are trying to steer a course of ideological neutrality; they argue that they are workers on special problems, that, for instance, "when you try to show that in the system of Ackermann, some formula is not provable, it is impossible to say whether one is a dialectical materialist or not."

Another logician emphasizes that when he reviewed the work of Lukasiewicz, a Catholic, he criticized the latter's views on determinism, but differentiated between his logical achievements and general philosophical ideas. Thus the logicians aim to survive the ideological strife by trying to show the irrelevance of logic to both philosophy and ideology. The basic crossroads in Soviet thought, however, is between official *ideologism* and free *philosophy,* and the unspoken task of free philosophy in the Soviet Union is the critique of ideology.

Among the Soviet existentialists, one finds the unusual phenomenon of a return to the Bible for metaphor and stimulus in the exploration of the problems of man. Concerned as they are for the status of the individual and the achievement of his freedom, they are looking for a vocabulary that is not that of "class," "masses," and "party," but of humanity and the individual. Take, for instance, the young philosopher, Yuri Davydoff, author of *Work and Freedom.* Unlike the Stalinist ideologists, he does not deny that "alienation" exists in Soviet society: "It is hypocrisy to say that it is solved in contemporary Soviet society," he frankly acknowledges. In his view, this is a problem common to both twentieth-century capitalism and Soviet society; it arises in any society where centralized planning plays a determining role. The problem would long ago have been discussed, he states, "but the cult of personality tore apart the tradition of Soviet philosophy." He rejects as a Marxist the Western existentialist approach: "Existentialism is either inner emigration or Don Quixotism." Yet his own preoccupation, he grants, is with the "problematics" which the existentialists have raised. In philosophy, it is the posing of a problem, the recognition of a new question, which often defines the rise of a new movement; the problem itself may be soluble by no human method.

The Biblical metaphor abounds in Davydoff's conversation. He was explaining to me that he did not use "freedom" in the Hegelian sense of "recognition of necessity." He remarked by way of illustration: "When in the Bible it is said that Abraham knew Sarah, it doesn't mean he got acquainted with her, and similarly with my use of freedom." At the end of our discussion, I recollected that I had forgotten to ask his age. When I inquired, he replied: "Old enough to go to my Golgotha." A grim metaphor, suggesting the terms on which the struggle for freedom has been waged in the Soviet Union.

On another occasion, at the Institute's celebration of International Women's Day, I got into discussion with a woman Soviet existentialist. We watched the skits which were being performed by the *sotrudniki* of the Institute of Economics—songs in praise of women to the tune of "Mack the Knife" by eight young men who would have fitted into fraternity theatricals in the United States. Somehow we got talking about the Bible; it turned out that she was a close student of the Book of Job. "It deals with the problem of why good men suffer; God did not answer Job, and in real life, the problem has no answer too," she said. By our standards, this was an entirely familiar observation, but it constituted a major philosophical break with the official Soviet total pseudo-optimism. Soon there may be a Soviet Voltaire writing a new *Candide* about the bland-speaking Soviet Dr. Panglosses with their mellifluous phrases about how everything is historically necessary in this best of all dialectical worlds.

The existentialists in the Soviet Union attract at the

present time a more general interest than the scientific realists. In discussion, the existentialists claim that if the latter drew the consequences of their position, they would be positivists. The scientific realists insist, however, that they acknowledge the existence of the physical external world. As a joke, some one will say "I am my world" or "I have only my sensations," but it remains strictly a joke; as one scientific realist put it, "the influence of the official philosophy makes any positivist development unlikely." Soviet alienations will thus not take a solipsistic form.

The existentialists and scientific realists do not, of course, exhaust the modes of philosophy found among young Soviet thinkers. A significant group, particularly in the social sciences, is drawn to American pragmatism. The dogmatists continue to insist that pragmatism is a form of subjective idealism, but some younger thinkers are turning to the study of Peirce and Dewey. They are concerned with clarifying such an ambiguous concept as "practice." As Marxists, they hold that the Marxist sociology of revolution is confirmed in "practice," but what does this mean? There is not a large collection of revolutions that would give meaning to probability-frequencies as the verificational basis for their assertions. Confronted by a series of ambiguities in "practice," they propose vague solutions that are remarkably akin to Dewey's logic.

The dogmatic elder Marxists, anxious to defend their doctrine, use any weapon whatsoever against the "bourgeois philosopher" to the point that they are eclectically ultra-positivist, Bergsonian, or relativist. One day at a philosophical seminar in Tbilisi a discussion of the "cult of personality" led to a criticism on my part of Plekhanov's view that if Napoleon hadn't appeared, some other French general would have done pretty much the same. This evoked a dogmatic reply from a specialist on historical materialism that Marxism was only concerned with what did happen, not with what might have happened. It was sheer ultra-positivism, and I am sure the speaker on further reflection would not have held to this position, but the combative stance of Soviet thinkers leads them to sacrifice rigorous method for dogmatic security. On another occasion at Moscow State University, I was suddenly confronted by a Marxist variant of holist intuitionism. We had been discussing the evolution of social systems and the bearing of the Soviet and American influence on "backward" areas. I noted that the necessitarian evolutionary-stage law had been abandoned, and there was now an antecedent proviso clause that allowed for human intervention to alter the evolutionary stages, as for instance, in the statement: "Provided that there is no external human intervention, the feudal Indonesian system would evolve in such and such a way." The Moscow professor of historical materialism objected to this variety of "taking things to pieces"; it was logic-chopping. One should look at the total historical process, and grasp its general movement. In defense of the Marxist law of economic evolution, the professor was prepared to speak in Bergsonian accents.

On still another occasion, in Tashkent, a professor of philosophy tried to terminate the discussion by saying they had their method, and I had mine. He saw no incongruity in a relativized Marxism.

All the varieties of dialectical materialism in the Soviet Union fasten on different texts of Marx, Engels, and Lenin for their support. The scientific realists make their appeal to Lenin's *Materialism and Empirio-Criticism*. Neo-dialecticians prefer to quote from Lenin's *Philosophical Notebooks*. The positivist-inclined cite from *Anti-Dühring* the passages where Engels speaks of the replacement of philosophy by science. The historicists quote the second Preface to Marx's *Capital*, whereas the anti-historicists cite Marx's letter to Mikhailovsky and Engels' letters on historical materialism. The pragmatists like to recite Marx's *Theses on Feuerbach*. The existentialists quote from the *Economic and Philosophical Manuscripts*. When will the revolt against canonical texts begin?

The younger sociologists have as quietly as possible discarded the dialectical methodology. According to Marx, there were no universal laws of social science; each social system had its specific sociological laws, but a law common to diverse social systems was out of the question. The Soviet sociologists, under the pressure of their actual researches, have found themselves obliged to drop this dialectical outlook. Professor Kharchev at Leningrad, for instance, found that one-fourth of the married couples were living under "abnormal housing conditions." This was a situation, he argued, common to all industrial countries; France, for example, with its "hotel families" was in a similar position. I observed that he was engaged in a revisionist enterprise, for according to the dialectical standpoint there should be a capitalist law of population and a socialist law, but not one common to all industrial societies, socialist or capitalist. Professor Kharchev, of course, denied that he was a revisionist; it would be revisionism, he said, to assert that history knows no progress, or to deny that existence determines consciousness, but it was not revisionist to ascertain a general law by means of concrete researches. Thus the dialectical method is being revised out of existence by Soviet methodologists, even as they continue to profess their unswerving loyalty. Similarly, in Moscow, one investigator has found a decline in the average size of the urban family which evidently brings it even lower than the comparable American figure. At any rate, he supports the view that a general pattern with similar birth control practices is emerging in all industrial countries, socialist as well as capitalist. But what then of Marx's attack on the Malthusian notions as arising from specific capitalist conditions? To their great good fortune, the young Soviet demographers have managed to find a canonical text, a letter of Engels to Kautsky in 1881, which acknowledges that even communist society may find itself "obliged to regulate the production of human beings," and "to achieve by planning a result which has already been produced spontaneously, without planning, in France and Lower Austria."[1] They are thus in a position to argue that a universal law and pattern of population common to both socialist and capitalist countries

[1] Cf. *Marx and Engels on Malthus* (London, 1953), pp. 108–09.

does not contravene their philosophy. Thereby the long paragraph on the dialectical method in Marx's second Preface to *Capital* is rescinded.

But Soviet philosophers cannot bring themselves to acknowledge in theory what is being done in practice. During the discussion following my lecture on the sociology of science, I stated that Marx's own practice was inconsistent with his dialectical tenet because he did formulate laws for "all classes," "all ideologies," "all exploitative systems." The chairman of the meeting, V. V. Mshvenieradze, with a straight face denied that Marx had ever opposed the possibility of general sociological laws; he told the audience the contradictions were mine, not Marx's. The text of Marx's *Capital* was summoned to the fore for a ruling against me, but the chairman, after several worried minutes, failed to report to the audience. Later, in the privacy of his office, I showed him the very clear statement in the Preface. The gap between the public pronouncement and the private conviction in the Soviet Union is an immense one.

The official conception of philosophy as ideology makes it difficult for the ideologists to understand the nature of American philosophy and society. They project the Soviet model on American thought, and regard American philosophy as a kind of official ideology akin to their own. I encountered this projection many times. For instance, when I lectured on "Contemporary American Thought," one questioner asked me about the influence of such Catholic philosophical journals as the *American Ecclesiastical Review, New Scholasticism,* and *Thought.* When I replied that their influence was small, he was extremely skeptical, and said that after all President Kennedy was a Catholic, and that consequently, the importance of Catholic ideology must have increased. I assured him that despite President Kennedy's election, I did not know a single colleague who read the periodicals he had named, that the fact that the President was a Catholic had in no way affected philosophical teaching in the United States, and that, if anything, I felt that Kennedy's election had strengthened the liberal rather than the ideological side of Catholicism. The questioner was puzzled. In the Soviet Union, the philosophical views of the head of the government do become those of the universities, and he found it hard to conceive that the religion of the American President was not reflected in the American universities.

The primary task of Soviet philosophers, in the government's eyes, is to serve as officers of ideological warfare against the West and against "ideological coexistence." The Institute of Philosophy should be renamed more accurately the Institute of Ideological Warfare. The Section on Bourgeois Philosophy and Sociology, for instance, instructs each research worker to prepare an authoritative refutation of some bourgeois representative; such "ideologettes" are in preparation against Husserl, Hartmann, Santayana, the German realists, Whitehead, personalism, French Positivism, German neo-Thomism, and Reinhold Niebuhr.

This conception of philosophy as ideological warfare enforces on its practitioners a spirit which we might call "protivism." The word "protiv" means "against"; it is the most characteristic word in Soviet philosophical essays. They are protiv existentialism, protiv pragmatism, protiv realism, protiv abstractionism, protiv whatever emanates from the bourgeois world. Whether it is a biography of Marx, a treatise on Buddhism, or an analysis of American culture, somewhere the Soviet ideologist is called upon by the institute head, or his section chief, or the party group, or the magazine editors, to sound the keynote of protivism which alone shows that the given work is helping to fulfill the role assigned to philosophy in the seven-year plan.

This protivism ramifies throughout Soviet ideology in manifold ways—choice of titles of books, choice of subjects, choice of arguments. A young scholar told me of the book he is writing on the emergent evolutionists; he would like to call it, he said wistfully, *Man and Movement*, but its title will be *English and American Philosophy in the Epoch of Imperialism*. Another scholar who has turned from contemporary philosophy to ancient Asian thought in order to escape ideological pressures told me he would probably have to compromise by studying the philosophy of Nehru. I encountered an amusing instance of protivism in the person of Professor Sokolov of Moscow State University. He had reviewed my book on Spinoza recently in *Voprosy Filosofii* on the whole favorably, while regretting my lapses into "Freudo-positivism." I mentioned to him that I had sent a copy of my book to Premier Ben-Gurion of Israel who had then responded with a friendly appreciative letter. Professor Sokolov was incredulous: "But how can that be?" he said. "Your book is against (*protiv*) the Judaistical interpretation of Spinoza. How could Ben-Gurion have written you a friendly letter?" I replied that Ben-Gurion was keenly interested in Spinoza's philosophy, and that I believed he would appreciate my study for whatever scholarly merit it might have. But Professor Sokolov remained adamant. The logic of protivism dictated that the Israeli Premier should have taken a stand against my book; my friendly philosophical correspondence with him violated the laws of ideological warfare.

The language of protivism, militant, hortatory, embattled, finally becomes a meaningless literary convention. I met a smiling young author who presented me with a passionate pamphlet protiv Sidney Hook. I looked at the author and looked at the pages, and decided one was alienated from the other. He was a protivist only when engaged in the ceremonial ritualistic exorcism of some name which was not really a name but an intimation of an unreal bourgeois ghost.

The Soviet bureaucratic ideologists, moreover, evaluate their participation in international philosophical and sociological meetings in strict protivist terms. One day I questioned an Institute official as to which Soviet philosophers were going to attend the forthcoming International Philosophical Congress in Mexico. No Soviet philosopher, of course, can decide to attend simply on his own; he has to be chosen by the Academy of Sciences, and only after having been thus chosen is he allowed to receive the cus-

tomary invitation and announcement that individual scholars receive, as a matter of course, all over the world. I
said I hoped the Academy would send some of the young
philosophers who were really interested in discussion with
Western and Asian scholars, and whose own thinking was
alive. I hoped they would not send a delegation dominated
by some of those familiar official figures who had already
made their appearance at the International Sociological
Congress. The official replied with simple, straightforward
bureaucratism. "You are wrong," he said. "Our delegation
must be made up of men who can make decisions. Perhaps
we can have some young philosophers accompany them,
but above all we need experienced men who can make
decisions." I said that no decisions were made at an international philosophical conference. The Soviet Academy,
however, regards such congresses as international ideological skirmishes in which tactical decisions have to be
made on the spot. Theirs is a delegation, not a group of
individual scholars who have decided entirely on their own
to attend and who speak for themselves only. The Soviet
delegation is organized hierarchically with a chain of command. It holds meetings at which tactics are determined,
and at which they decide against what positions and which
bourgeois thinkers they shall polemicize most strenuously,
and on the other hand, to which thinkers they shall extend
a hand of ideological comradeship. It is all thoroughly
protivist, but the consequence is that the abler Soviet thinkers generally remain at home while the bureaucrats make
the jaunts abroad.

The restless searching for a new philosophy manifests
itself in the purely voluntary student discussion groups
which have come into existence in the universities. There
is a tacit understanding within them that their discussions
are sincere and private, and not to be repeated to the authorities. I got to know one such group, and found in it
a curious mixture of political idealism and technocratic
views, and a yearning for more intellectual freedom. The
circle was composed of about twelve young instructors

and graduate students. We began one evening with a discussion of the theory that the intellectuals were the ruling class in the Soviet Union. "That is not true," said one of them; "if you examine the lists of directorships of big enterprises and leading positions, you will find that most of them are held by uneducated men. The machine-bureaucrats rule, not the intellectuals." Another continued in the same vein: "I think the intellectuals should rule. I believe in technocracy. What is scientific is moral, and what is moral is scientific. Not the voting of the uneducated and ignorant, but the rule of the scientists, that is the best." Another man, however, disagreed. Although a scientist himself, he said he remained a communist, believing that it was a question of liberalizing the system—allowing foreign papers, journals, magazines, and statistics to circulate so that they could make meaningful comparisons. This man too had a theory very much like Deutscher's, namely that the necessities of technical progress now demanded political progress. Although he had never read Deutscher, he had heard of him. Several, however, had read W. W. Rostow or accounts of his views, and they tended to accept his thesis that a test-inspection system was incompatible with the Soviet closed society. I thought that the added popularity Khrushchev would gain with such an agreement might outweigh the party machine's desire to maintain the climate of fear and residual terror. They thought, however, that if the Americans were to accept Khrushchev's offer of three inspections, Khrushchev might be unable to fulfill his promise, and would find himself repudiated by the party machine. They doubted also that Khrushchev would be able to carry out the new line against abstract art; it had caused a tremendous discussion among the youth, they said. I asked how they explained Khrushchev's policy against free art. They said that Khrushchev had led the original policy of liberalization, but that he himself was a product of Stalinist education, and was getting old. The machine bureaucrats feared that if free art were permitted, it might lead to literary and artistic criticism of the regime.

As they discussed the question of greater freedom, they spoke with an unforgettable simplicity. One man, a student of ancient languages, said: "In our country every one has two faces, one real and one official." They spoke with pride of the audiences of fifteen thousand at their poetry readings. They wanted to know all about the American beatniks, with whose anti-organizationism and disestablishmentarianism some of them clearly felt kinship. They were much interested in hearing also about the all-night student vigil after the Soviet resumption of nuclear bomb testing, and about the proliferation of student magazines. Their longing for a single free students' magazine in the Soviet Union was patent. Their ignorance of the details of international political debate was astonishing. They had no knowledge of the American arguments on the need for inspections for underground explosions. They said they had never been told when Soviet troops were sent to Cuba, but they had been told when they were withdrawn. One of them said: "it was like a robber who announces his contribution to honesty when he withdraws with his burglar's tools."

In this small group, I had the feeling that the "technocratic" liberals tended to be scientific realists; some of them who were concerned with the science of economic planning, with input-output analysis, spoke in such terms. On the other hand, the "liberal communists" seemed to take to existentialist formulations. But such judgments must be extremely tentative. What impressed me most was how even in such an intelligent circle the capacity for thinking in terms of political alternatives and concrete reforms has been rendered almost extinct. The organs of independent political reasoning have atrophied in the Soviet Union because of compulsory disuse. It struck me that the most significant practicable reform in the Soviet Union today would be a simple one: to begin the publication in the newspapers of the difference of opinion in the Central Committee, or to start the regular publication of a *Central Committee Record* like our *Congressional Record*. Then the habit of political discussion might reawaken among the

Soviet people, and they would begin to emerge more fully from their Stalinist torpor.

Late in the spring this circle discontinued its meetings. Fears were beginning to arise, and some persons thought that perhaps they should wait to see what conditions would be imposed by the next ideological plenum. Toward the end of May, I met several of them at the Lenin Library. They were much worried. They told me that agents of the State Security had apprehended fifteen persons of another circle which was more primarily devoted to freedom of art. They had been interrogated at length, and their cases were remanded to the university for action. The Moscow University Communist apparatus had decided to expel six of the students—four of whom were from the natural sciences. The students were charged, among other things, with having fallen under "foreign" influences. I was reassured that I had never met them. But we all felt it advisable not to see each other again.

The younger generation of Soviet thinkers asks above all for a final reckoning with the ethical and sociological problems of the "cult of personality." They feel themselves without the guilt that haunts the older generation which was almost universally involved in different degrees in Stalin's guilt. The older men wish to repress the problem, to make of it an "unproblem."[1] The younger generation observes the evasions and involutions of the older men; it is around this problem that the future of Soviet thought will be determined. A successful outcome will mean a Renaissance of Soviet Thought, as the burden of guilt is lifted from people's minds. A defeat will mean the repartition of guilt among the younger people, and another Time of Torpor.

The problem of the cult of personality virtually haunts Soviet social science and philosophy; the cost of its repression is the destruction of their sincerity. I asked almost all the 150 scholars I interviewed whether he or she was in

[1] Lewis S. Feuer, "Problems and Unproblems in Soviet Social Theory," *Slavic Review*, Vol. XXIII (1964), pp. 117–24.

any way concerned with the sociological and philosophical problems arising from the cult phenomena. The most frequent answer I got was "That is not my problem." A young member of the editorial board of *Voprosy Filosofii*, for instance, knows all about alienation in bourgeois society, and can discourse at length on how Jaspers and Freud show the bankruptcy of their society, but when I asked him for his explanation of the Stalinist era he took refuge in: "I am not a specialist in this field." A lecturer at the Institute of International Relations pursues his labors by reading the critiques of America by Americans, and rewriting them in the clichés of the decline of capitalist society. He too is facile in depicting the common man's alleged alienation in Western society, but when asked about the Stalinist era and present-day Soviet alienation he will just pass the former over with an unctuous phrase of how regrettably bad it was, and then go on to a glib misdescription of an all-contented Soviet citizenry.

Next to taking refuge in one's specialty, the most frequent answer I got was that the explanation for the cult of personality was well-known, inasmuch as it was based on Stalin's mistakes. How often I heard that self-exonerating phrase about the *oshibki* of Stalin. What is a "mistake," an *oshibka*? A child does an arithmetical problem for homework; it makes a *mistake*. The child wanted to solve the problem, but its skill with numbers was inadequate. Or a child makes a mistake in its spelling. The person who makes a mistake is always credited with motives that are sound; a mistake is a reminder of human fallibility; it does not proceed from vicious motive. Thus, the very use of *oshibka* implies that Stalin was trying to do the right thing. Its use is part of the continuing repression in the Soviet Union of the facts of Stalinism. One Soviet sociologist in Tbilisi said with candor that when something unpleasant has occurred, we prefer to avoid speaking about it; that was why they avoided discussing the causes of Stalinism. I replied that in America the depression was unpleasant, but that we analyzed and discussed its causes. The point, of course, is that a terrible guilt is felt about Stalinism; large

numbers were involved in its operations, and that is why
the phenomenon is repressed by making Stalin the bearer
of all that was rotten in themselves, and mitigating it all
with the mild, de-emotionalized word *oshibki*. No American
felt guilty for the advent of the depression; therefore no
one feared the analysis of its causes. The continuing use
of *oshibki* as an explanation for a whole era's distortions
is a sign that the mentality of that era persists. For there
is a callousness in equating the millions of destroyed lives
with a child's spelling mistakes through the use of the same
word.

Soviet philosophers and sociologists are vaguely appre-
hensive that there are problems whose honest study might
shake the foundations of their theoretical structure. For
the cult confronts Soviet ideology with what we might call
its "great Contradiction." On the one hand, the Soviet
ideologist can try to remain loyal to historical materialism, and explain the Stalinist superstructure in terms of
the underlying economic foundation; in that case, he finds
himself a critic of the Soviet social system, for he must
then recognize that a Stalinist totalitarianism is potential
in the Soviet economy. Or, on the other hand, he can
attribute the cult phenomena to the effects of Stalin's paranoid personality, his persecution complex, his fears, his
irrationality. In that case, he would be ascribing an importance to the historic role of an individual which trans-
cends anything Marxism would allow; for he is then explaining the whole character of an era in terms of the
causal influence of one man. Moreover, in so doing, the
Soviet ideologist would be opening the door to the use of
psychoanalytical concepts for understanding Stalin's personal irrationality as well as that of his society; he would
find himself becoming a Freudian despite himself, and
raising such embarrassing problems, furthermore, as the
factors which made the Communist party so sado-masochist
that it was ready to collaborate in and glorify Stalin's rule
during all that time. All sorts of intermediary theoretical
positions are possible, but every intermediary position
would involve an admixture of an acceptance of the totali-

tarian potentialities of the Soviet System and the crucial role of unconscious, irrational, "Freudian" factors in history.

Confronted with this dilemma, Soviet social scientists are content to shelve even their private theoretical study of the cult phenomenon. They fear lest facts mislead them into heresy. I met only one social scientist who was ready to face the question. He was a man in middle age who had been sentenced during the Stalinist era to four years of solitary confinement. His crime: he was alleged to have said that Stalin was a cruel man. I learned of his existence only through persistent questioning at the Institute of Philosophy as to the names of social scientists who had actually been condemned to Stalin's camps or prisons. The Institute staff usually professed itself ignorant on such points. When we met, I put to him my question: How would he undertake to explain the cult period? He paused for a moment, and then uttered with an almost passionate emphasis: "To explain the cult, we shall have to call on all of Freud's categories." He gave me permission furthermore to mention his name. But few social scientists as yet have the courage to delineate in this fashion the most central problem of their society.

Soviet ideologists still shrink from the serious study of Freud. They say the study of "subjective" motives is futile. Once I asked whether the motives of intellectuals in the socialist movement were those ascribed to them by the *Communist Manifesto*. I was told this was an unsound approach "because on this level an antinomy arises between ethical and material motives. The problem has to be dealt with objectively," they said. "One must study the laws of development which determine the shift of intellectuals without reference to their subjective motives which they think determine them." This repression of the "subjective" is probably the most basic reason for the antagonism to Freud in the Soviet Union. Psychoanalytical ideas are suspect because the Soviet regime wants people to accept all its propaganda on the manifest level, and never to inquire into latent meanings. Psychoanalysis threatens the official face with the underlying real face.

Thus, the Soviet regime has made it virtually impossible throughout most of the country for students to read Freud. At the library of Tashkent State University, for instance, there were no books by Freud; instead, there was a polemical work against him by an American Marxist, and another secondary manual. There have been no printings for many years of Freud's books. One meets young students who treasure tattered editions of Freud's writings. The student who persists in asking for these books runs the risk of being interrogated by the ideological control desk. This happened shortly before I left to a student who was assiduous in reading Schopenhauer. He was asked to explain why he did so in view of the fact that he had available instead some good Marxist refutations of the philosopher of pessimism. Another student I met in Tashkent was enormously interested in studying Freud. I asked him how he had learned of him. He said he had read an article in *Inostrannaya Literatura* (Foreign Literature) attacking Freud, but had found himself more drawn to the ideas of the attacked than the dogmas of the attacker. Then too, the few philosophers and psychologists of the pre-Stalinist generation willy-nilly transmit a more liberal spirit to their students. Professor V. F. Asmus, the respected historian of philosophy who spoke at Boris Pasternak's funeral, read through Freud's works when he was a student. Professor A. R. Luria recalls for his students how forty years ago when he was a young man at Kazan, he organized a Kazan Psychological Circle. He wrote to Freud who promptly sent him all his works. He is critical of Freud's method, but students envy the freedom of "ideological coexistence" which they hear once obtained. The Institute bureaucrats naturally dislike having the question raised of the suppression of Freud's works. G. Osipov, the head of the Section on Concrete Investigations of Work and Existence (the Soviet circumlocution to avoid saying the bourgeois word "sociology"), heatedly complained that they translated more American sociological books than we did Soviet works. From his desk, moreover, he drew a copy of Kluck-hohn's essays. I remarked that it would be feasible to translate Soviet sociological books if there were any good ones around. The sociological researchers, however, at the Institute had been unable to tell me the name of a single work they thought outstanding. I myself knew of no distinguished Soviet sociologist since Bukharin, and his *Historical Materialism* was available in English. I inquired whether the Kluckhohn collaborative volume *How the Soviet System Works* would be allowed to circulate side by side with his essays. Osipov began to complain that American books were so expensive. I said I was sure the United States would be glad to operate an American bookstore in Moscow comparable to the Soviet bookstore in New York.

With the governmental antagonism to "ideological coexistence," Soviet social scientists are in a situation where their freedom extends only to borrowing the *technique* of American social science; they must still beware of Western theoretical ideas. They can study statistical and survey methods, and the methodological contributions of Lazarsfeld. They can even read Merton and Parsons with security; Merton's "middle theories" they regard with some condescension as no genuine alternative to their general theory, while Parsons, apart from his obscurities, proposes no concepts which would propel a critique of Soviet society; if anything, he has a definite appeal to representatives of the status quo. It is a different story with Freud, or even Michels. Their analytic ideas would open a critique which would fasten on all the intellectual self-repressions of Soviet society. If the Soviet regime were to relax its ban against ideological coexistence, the winds that would blow through their stuffy system would clear away the myriad Leninist cobwebs.

The intellectual class itself is divided in its outlook toward intellectual freedom. The bulk of the "mediocrats," who predominate in the middle-aged echelons, stand opposed to ideological coexistence; the "superiocrats" (as we might call them), the advanced intellectuals, are small in numbers, but exert leadership on the idealistic youth.

In a bureaucratic system, the mediocracy has the tremendous advantage of conformity and adaptability. It is only in the fields of physical science where competition with the West has been the paramount concern that the superiocrats in the Soviet Union have been allowed to forge ahead. Where the bureaucratic momentum otherwise has its way, it is the mediocracy that rules. When Deutscher speaks of the gradual growth of free thought because of the increase of education, he omits the whole sociological significance of the interplay in a bureaucratic system of the different types of intellectuals, from the superiocrats to the mediocrats and inferiocrats. The Thomases, Occams, and Roger Bacons never became popes, and likewise in the Soviet Union, the mediocrats use the mantle of opposition to ideological coexistence as a way of achieving upward social mobility over the superiocrats, the advanced intellectuals.

Late in March I had the unusual opportunity to lecture at the institute on the philosophical significance of Freud's ideas, and to observe firsthand the ideologists' fear of psychoanalytical concepts. For a while after the governmental speeches against ideological coexistence, it had seemed that I would no longer be called on for lectures. After several postponements, however, I was asked to speak to institute researchers on this topic. The Section on Psychology too was interested in the subject. When I was done speaking, the chairman, V. V. Mshvenieradze, asked me if the psychoanalytical method could be applied to Hitler. I said it could be used for the scientific understanding of Hitler, but that in many cases, an illness was beyond therapeutic bounds. Whereupon he replied that this showed that the psychoanalytical method was weak, and that the method of dialectical materialism was stronger. More meaningful questions, however, followed from others such as the possible use of psychoanalysis to understand Nietzsche's character and philosophy, and the extent to which it could be applied to understand the solipsistic mentality. But then, as was customary in these post-lecture discussions, Mshvenieradze presented a formal rebuttal. It ran the gamut from methodological and philosophical points to the final outright rejection on political grounds. To begin with, he noted, psychoanalysis might be applied to all philosophies, including dialectical materialism. He said he liked the "verification" principle more than the psychoanalytical method, but that the former shouldn't be absolutized. He objected to my correlation of different philosophies with different emotional standpoints. "What philosopher," he asked, "ever says: this is real because it is good?" He denied that Lenin had ever said solipsism cannot be refuted. Then lastly: "Dialectical materialism is verified by world-historical practice, by its victories throughout the world. If you hadn't been familiar with dialectical materialism, your use of psychoanalytical theory would have had some justification. But since we have dialectical materialism which works, why bother with psychoanalysis?"

The tone of the meeting changed after this pronouncement of the official line by the institute's secretary. There were objections that the psychoanalytical method was not serious, that it lacked a truth criterion. One person said that many people in the room had different psychological backgrounds, but that they were all dialectical materialists. Another argued that psychoanalysis led to irrationalism and individualism, and that it left social factors in a little corner and had no explanation for social consciousness. A social psychologist declared that society was an organism, not a sum of individuals, and that therefore the individual psychological approach was a poor one for trying to arrive at sociological laws.

To Mshvenieradze's evident consternation, however, a solitary young Moscow University philosopher, not an institute researcher, dared speak in defense of a possible limited usefulness for the psychoanalytical method. He said: "Consider a group of people of the same socioeconomic position; they are discussing the problem, 'Can machines think?' Some say yes, others say no. Let us admit that psychoanalysis can tell us whether they answer on the basis of knowledge or because of psychoanalytical considerations." The chairman rebuked him for the way he made this point, and oddly, for saying some of it in English.

I tried to answer these objections, which ranged from important methodological issues to plain demagogy. The psychoanalytical method, I argued, was not something to be counterposed to verification; rather the psychoanalytical method was precisely a way of utilizing important items of evidence which had previously been neglected; if verificationism were narrowly interpreted to exclude such use of psychological facts, it would impede the further development and testing of generalizations; "verification" could be "dogmatized" as well as "solipsized" and "behaviorized." Above all, I tried to deal with the ambiguities of "practice." "Whose practice? The healthy man's practice, or that of an insane man who perhaps is never shaken in his practice of being Napoleon?" I tried somehow to convey the notion that it was time for Soviet Marxists to look at themselves as human beings, who were perhaps deluding themselves at times with their phrases. Inevitably, I said, the unique diversities of individuals would try to express themselves philosophically even against the countervailing presence of a common ideology; this was the law of the free striving of the intellect, the law of life in philosophy.

Almost four hours had gone by. It is customary at Soviet philosophical meetings for a decision, a conclusion, to be arrived at, and stated by the chairman. Mshvenieradze looked to the audience to gather its consensus, but it was quite clear that there was none. He said he had wanted a decision, something more than an exchange and clarification of differences, but he was nonetheless terminating the meeting. Maybe this was the first Soviet philosophical meeting in which there was no decision.

Every first meeting, whether in Moscow, Tashkent, or Leningrad, usually included a test by the assembled institute staffs of my ability to withstand a political onslaught. The Soviet philosophical bureaucrats, from their residual Stalinist standpoint, regard themselves as entitled to a double standard with regard to political considerations. They feel themselves privileged to raise them, but not so the foreigner. When I would call their attention to the fact that they were raising political questions, and that I was ready to discuss them provided that they accepted the responsibility for proposing a political discussion, they would tell me pontifically that Marxists did not separate politics from philosophy. When, however, they discovered I was not a novice in these matters, and that the discussion was raising embarrassing questions for them, they would complain that I was making political points, not philosophical or sociological ones. Moreover, I discovered that the actual ignorance on these questions on the part of their authorities was immense.

At my very first day at the Moscow Institute of Philosophy, the Institute bureaucrats began to attack the American government for its "persecution" of the Communist party. I replied that the basic issue was whether a secret political party had any place in a democratic society; I said Lenin had made a tremendous mistake in insisting as a condition for admission to the Communist International that every communist party, including those in democratic countries, have an illegal apparatus. Perhaps such means were justified under Czarist conditions, I said, but they had no place in a democracy, and history shows that no democratic society will finally permit secret parties to exist, whether they be under Jesuit, Masonic, or communist auspices. At first, several senior Soviet ideologists denied that Lenin ever imposed such a condition on communist parties, but when I referred them explicitly to the text of the third condition for affiliation, they dropped this objection. They told me that other American professors who had visited them, unlike myself, shared their views about the persecution of communists.

The Secretary of the Institute, V. V. Mshvenieradze, told me that he was working on a study of anti-communism as an ideology. It turned out that he knew some of the American popular literature on communism but none of the scholarly books on the subject; such histories of American communism as those by Draper, Howe, Coser, and Glazer were unknown to him. I urged him to read their works, and he took down the references. Our discussion of the role of the American Communist party as an apologist for Stalin led to an interchange concerning Stalin's crimes. The head of the Section on Bourgeois Philosophy, Mme. Modrjinskaya, said the Soviet people hadn't known about them. I asked: Wasn't that because you don't have freedom of criticism, because you are a one-party state with a completely controlled press? She replied that the heroism with which the Soviet people had fought the Germans proved that their system was democratic even under Stalin. I answered that the Russian people had fought heroically in 1812 against the French, and that the Germans had fought to the end for Hitler, but this was no proof that either the Czarist or Nazi societies were democratic. Mme. Modrjinskaya became incensed at this, and said I was insulting the Soviet people by placing them on the same plane as the Germans. I replied that I was the last person in the world to entertain sentimental feelings about the Nazis. My argument, I said, was a logical and sociological one concerning the evidence required to show that a society was democratic.

Subsequently, I read the Secretary's essay on anti-communism, and noted to him once more that he had dealt with popular writers and the "lunatic fringe," not with the serious scholars of the subject. At no point had he considered the most important point, namely the disillusionment with Stalinism on the part of American intellectuals as a factor in "anti-communism"—their experiences with communist deception, the Moscow trials, the pact with Hitler, the Stalinist origin of the cold war. I said too that having seen the conditions of Soviet life, his statistics on growth were not all-impressive; that Japan could claim a higher rate of growth, and all such rates had indeed to be evaluated in terms of the relative stage of economic development. Thereupon the Secretary allowed himself to become wroth. "You Americans are aristocrats," he said with fierceness. "You had a new land; we had nothing, nothing. You brought your civilization with you from Europe. Imagine if you had had to create it from the Indians. Yes, you have televisions. But you have no perspectives, no ability to mobilize people. I would prefer to be studying logics, criticizing Black, Tarski, Adjukiewicz, but I felt I had to write this essay. In America, for every five books on logic, you have five hundred on anti-communism. I couldn't keep silent. I postponed my logical works, I believe what I wrote. Nobody told me. There was no Rockefeller Fund, no Ford Fund, to tell me what to write. Many American writers are liars who have never been here, who haven't studied Marxism-Leninism. It is not our ideology to impose revolution on other people. Communism is the only theory and practice that gives real freedom, and repudiates any alienation of labor. Bourgeois sociologists, like flies on honey, feed on the early writings of Marx, and try to find contradictions. They say there is alienation in Soviet society. Leave us alone; build your society without boasting. Our ideology is our ideology, but you are criticizing us all the time."

It was from a psychological standpoint an amazing performance. The curious criterion he took for judging societies was their relative ability in "mobilizing" people. When he said the word, it was with a kind of gesture of a mechanic manipulating his material, turning the screw. Why, I wondered, should one want to mobilize people, and keep them in a state of permanent mobilization? The sadistic component in the Soviet managerial ideology seemed eloquent in his words and gestures. He professed to have left the quiet pursuit of the philosophy of logic in obedience to a moral imperative to attack anti-communism. Actually, however, he was writing on the subject that conformed most to the ideological needs of the Soviet bureaucracy, and offered him excellent prospects of rising in the academic and political machine. His writing on "anti-communism" was scarcely a philosophical or sociological inquiry but rather a propagandist diatribe. When he affected the injured tone of a person who wishes only to go his own way—"leave us alone; build your society without boasting"

—the hypocrisy was blatant; for the palpable reality was a perpetual Soviet critique of Western civilization and a never ending boasting in each day's speeches and newspapers. It all had the irrational quality of a projecting on the other person what one was doing one's self.

As the Secretary railed against Westerners, I could not help but perceive the strain which the career of an academy bureaucrat was imposing on him. His face at such moments twitched so violently that I almost felt I should discontinue the discussion. There were evidently two characters in him never wholly resolved: the open-hearted Georgian student and the new man of the Moscow echelon. The would-be hierarch won in the showdown, to the point of rejection of his Georgian past. In Georgia, the teacher whom the Secretary most admired, Tseretelli, had been persecuted during the period of the cult of personality. When I asked the Secretary about this, he answered like a true bureaucrat: he knew nothing about it. It was well for the would-be hierarch not to study injustices under Sovietism even when done to his own beloved teacher; anti-communism was so much more advantageous a subject.

Meanwhile, however, Mshvenieradze went on to defend Khrushchev's speech against abstract art: "The purpose of art is not to make life tasteless. I have studied abstractionism; it is not an art. People generally are angry with abstractionists. In America, advertising is free, and it makes the bad thing into good. Here we don't have an anti-people's freedom. Those speak nonsense who attack the Central Committee, and say: 'Let the talented say what they wish.' They don't mobilize but demobilize people. When the abstractionists make a woman, it is not a woman. If there were such a woman, I should not be married. Neither should you. I hate such art because I love people."

Such argument was quite typical of the academic bureaucrats I met. It is best described as a synthesis of Populist anti-intellectual attitudes together with its very opposite, an elitist mistrust of the people's capacity to decide wisely for itself. We might call it the ideology of Populist bureaucracy.

My last talk at the Institute of Philosophy brought forth an outburst of Populist bureaucratic denunciation on the part of the director. I was asked, now that my travels in the Soviet Union were over, to give a last report on my impressions of their philosophy and sociology, and had been reluctant to do so. I explained to the institute official that were I to speak, much that I would have to say would be unpleasant, and that perhaps it would be better if such a last report were omitted. He said they regarded me as a friend, and that the institute had had such talks in the past from visiting Americans, whom he named. The names in question, however, were with one exception those of American communists or fellow travelers, who, I suggested, had probably told their hosts what the latter would like to hear; the exception, a professor of sociology, had been in the country too short a time to have learned very much of what was going on. The official insisted, however, that it would be a worthwhile occasion especially for the audience which, he said, would be made up of the young researchers with whom I had had individual discussions several times. On the day in question, however, although the younger researchers were present, the discussion was monopolized by older ideologists, who had rarely or never participated in our previous meetings.

So the meeting began. Soviet thought, I said, was at the crossroads; its mood was best described in Turgenev's title, *On the Eve*. I proposed to raise problems to which I did not know the answer, and which I did not know how I would face were I in their place. But I had talked with scholars and students in institutes and universities in a series of interview-dialogues, the oldest philosophical method in the world. I would compare their sociological studies with work in America.

Soviet social science seemed to me to have failed to confront four important problems: First, there was no research on the conflict of generations. In America we had several studies under way on student movements. In the Soviet Union it was denied that there was any conflict of generations. I had in the course of my travels, however, found ample evidence of such a conflict. At Leningrad University, at an open meeting of the Communist organization of the Philological Faculty, students had challenged and ridiculed the apology which the editor of *Neva* tried to present for the new party line against abstract art. There were recent occurrences at Moscow State University into which I would not enter. No Soviet sociologist, however, had shown any readiness to study the phenomena of conflict.

Second, I had found not a single article or book on anti-Semitism. They denied that there was anti-Semitism in the Soviet Union but I had visited the synagogues of four Soviet cities, and everywhere had been told that the Jews lived in fear. I could not tell how much anti-Semitism there was; this was a subject for detailed investigation. But questions such as why there had been a recrudescence of anti-Semitism would have to be dealt with scientifically. In America, I added, where I believed there was much less anti-Semitism than in the Soviet Union, the problem was nonetheless studied extensively. At the University of California, several hundred thousand dollars were being spent in such an investigation. (The argument which followed, begun by the chairman calling me "an agent of the cold war," would take too long to tell; and there were several more heated interludes.)

I then spoke of the lack of any sociological article or book analyzing the cult of personality. I said that in America we devoted much time to the sociology of political leadership. In the Soviet Union, however, although they evidently knew all about racial problems in Birmingham and imperialism in Asia and Africa, they could produce no scientific study of the most important recent phenomenon of political sociology in their own country. I said I didn't mean by a scientific analysis their repeating Khrushchev's phrase about the mistakes (*oshibki*) of Stalin. I could read those speeches too. I meant a sociological analysis: How

many victims had there been, year by year? From what
social classes had they come? What varieties of accusations had there been? Who were the accusers? Had the
accusers profited by the accusations? I said they should
study, too, what happened to the children of the people
who were sent to Stalin's camps. When millions of people
had been killed and tortured, it was not sociological analysis to refer to it as *oshibki*. I had asked upwards of 150
sociologists and philosophers whether any one of them
was studying the cult of personality, and without exception they had all replied: "That is not my problem." I had
been told that historians at the Marxism-Leninism Institute
were preparing the publication of the documents on the
cult period; I had gone to the institute to confirm this report, and spoken with its secretary. He told me emphatically they have no plans whatsoever for such a publication.
I said Marx would never have concealed such documents.

I tried next to consider the sociological study of Soviet
mass culture. I said that though they criticized American
culture, they did not study their own culture as the Americans did theirs. There was no study extant of the appeal,
for instance, of American jazz to their youth. (Someone
interrupted and said they have had other things to do.)
I continued and said they had not studied the social consequences of tying their moral education to historical mod-
els—Lenin's picture as a hunter in a rifle-shop, Lenin playing chess for the chess club, Lenin with children telling
them: "study, study, and study"—and presenting Marx's
character as the model for family life. Questioned, I replied that the letters of Eleanor Marx, the daughter who
had killed herself, showed there was a deep-seated unhappiness in the family, and that one factor had probably
been the birth of an illegitimate son to Marx by the maid
of the household, Helene Demuth. I said that on my way
to Moscow I had visited the International Institute of Social History to confirm the existence of documentary evidence on this matter, and had been informed the evidence
was incontrovertible. The chairman was quite interested,
and one of his colleagues then piped up: "That accords

with Marx's saying *'Nihil humani a me alienum puto'* "—
the only Marxian joke I ever heard at the institute.

Many of those present had to leave at this time for a
candidate's examination. The chairman proposed another
meeting but I said I was leaving shortly, and would sum-
marize briefly what I had to say concerning their philosophical work. I discussed my characterization of their
philosophical attitude as protivism, and the development of
Soviet existentialism. I spoke of the interest in Freud, despite the great difficulty in securing his books. Then I went
on to develop my "law of the spectrum," the emergence
of diverse philosophies in the Soviet Union, with critical
realists in the Russell fashion, positivists, mathematical
logicians opposed to the dialecticians, and those who emphasized "practice" indistinguishable from American pragmatists. Heads were shaken in vigorous disagreement.
Finally, I said that if I had a "last message," it was that
Soviet thought now needed someone who would do for it
what John Stuart Mill did for England and Ralph Waldo
Emerson for America—to emphasize not class, not people,
but the importance of the individual.

Indeterminacy and
Economic Development

It is widely believed that a study of the dynamics of capitalist development eventuates in a determinate law of economic evolution. If we trace the origins of this assumption, we find that it stems from the influence of the Hegelian dialectic upon economic theory.[1] The metaphysic of determinism has thus obtruded its way into social science, and brought with it the corollary that economic analysis yields an insight into the necessary pattern of capitalist development.

The purpose of this essay is to show that no determinate solution of the problem of capitalist development is possible. It is our argument that the direction of technological change is a surd factor in the theory of capitalist evolution, that its impact upon outlets for investment is hence unpredictable, that there is no foretelling whether new industries with great capital requirements will be forthcoming in any given period, and that opinions one way or the other are primarily articles of faith and not propositions of economic science.

Now, the Marxian theory has been pre-eminent among those who aim to provide a determinate analysis of economic development. In particular, its law of the falling rate of profit is a model of attempts to state the pattern of capitalist evolution. We shall therefore begin with a discussion of the Marxian theory. The essential points that emerge will, however, apply to theories of economic development generally, and it is the general thesis of economic indeterminacy with which we are concerned. Let us then set forth the Marxian law of the declining rate of

[1] Cf. James Bonar, *Philosophy and Political Economy* (London, 1893), pp. 356–57.

profit as it is expounded by its leading American interpreter.[2]

To begin with, the Marxian analysis uses concepts somewhat different from the usual ones. It makes central use
of the notion of "surplus value"; this may be defined simply as the logical construct derived from the addition of
rent, interest, and entrepreneurial profit; "variable capital" may be identified with the total wages bill, and "constant capital" as the outlay for machinery, plant, and raw
materials. Then several further terms may be defined:

(1) $\dfrac{s}{v}$ = s' = rate of surplus value, where

$\quad\quad\quad\quad\quad\quad$ s is surplus value, and
$\quad\quad\quad\quad\quad\quad$ v is variable capital.

(2) $\dfrac{c}{c+v}$ = q = organic composition of capital,

$\quad\quad\quad\quad\quad\quad\quad\quad$ where c is constant capital.

(3) $\dfrac{s}{c+v}$ = p = rate of profit.

From the foregoing definitions, there follows in accordance with the rules of algebra the following theorem:

$$p = s' \,(1 - q)$$

The above equation as it stands is the tautological consequence of the definitions. To claim the status of an empirical law of development, factual values must be assigned
to the two independent variables. It is thus maintained, in
the first place, that the trend of industrial innovation is
such as to raise the value of q, the organic composition of
capital. As for s', the rate of surplus value, empirical data
indicate that it has been roughly constant through the years
of capitalist development. A. L. Bowley thus concludes
from his statistical studies that the proportion of wages to
the total national income in Britain has been "very nearly
the same percentage, 40 to 43, according to the definition

[2] Paul M. Sweezy, *The Theory of Capitalist Development* (New
York, 1942), p. 68.

of income from 1880, or even from 1860, to 1935."[3] What Kuznets calls the "marked degree of stability" in the share of the upper income groups in the total national income is equivalent in the Marxian language to the constancy of the rate of surplus value.[4]

With factual values thus assigned, the tautological formula, $p = s' (1 - q)$, becomes the empirical law of the falling rate of profit. For, with the rate of surplus value constant, and with the organic composition of capital growing, it follows that the rate of profit will be a declining ratio. Nothing in this analysis depends in any way on the so-called labor theory of value.

The decline of the rate of profit, Marx holds, is especially crucial to the existence of the capitalist system. The rate of profit, he notes, controls the rate of investment, the "new offshoots of capital seeking an independent location." And with the fall in the rate of profit and the concomitant predominance of large-scale enterprise, "the vital fire of production would be extinguished. It would fall into a dormant state. The rate of profit is the compelling power of capitalist production, and only such things are produced as yield a profit. Hence the fright of the English economists over the decline of the rate of profit."[5] With the decline of investment, there arises the phenomenon "at opposite poles, unemployed capital on the one hand, and unemployed laboring population on the other."[6] The barrier of

[3] A. L. Bowley, *Wages and Income in the United Kingdom Since 1860* (Cambridge, 1937), p. xvi. Statistical data likewise indicate an approximate constancy in the proportion of wages and salaries to the total American national income, with the exception of a pronounced rise in the former's favor during the worst years of the depression. Cf. Simon Kuznets, *National Income and Its Composition, 1919–1938* (New York, 1941), I, 217.

[4] Simon Kuznets, *National Income: A Summary of Findings* (New York, 1946), pp. 99–100. Also, cf. Lawrence R. Klein, "Theories of Effective Demand and Employment," *The Journal of Political Economy*, LV (1947), 121.

[5] Karl Marx, *Capital*, Untermann translation, III (Chicago, 1909), 304.

[6] *Ibid.*, p. 294.

the fall of the rate of profit, Marx concludes, is insurmountable within the framework of capitalist production.

Marx's law fails, however, to give a determinate solution to the problem of capitalist development. We shall try to show this by considering two aspects of the law, one pertaining to the rate of profit, the other to the trend of the organic composition of capital.

(1) Let us assume that there is a secular decline in the rate of profit. Nevertheless, this would not entail the inevitable decline of capitalism. For the capitalist system may from period to period adjust itself to lower rates of profit. A psychological element enters into the decision as to whether a given rate of profit is satisfactory, and crises, from this standpoint, are the experiences which eventuate in social readjustments to rates of profit lower than those traditionally required. So long as the rate of profit remains above zero, such readjustments are in principle possible.

Marx's law makes it clear enough that the rate of profit does not sink to zero; it remains a positive ratio. The rate of profit could reach zero only if either the rate of surplus value were zero or if the organic composition of capital were equal to one. Both these conditions are obviously excluded. So long as wages are not the only component in the national income, the rate of surplus value is some positive number. Secondly, so long as there is a wages bill, the organic composition of capital cannot equal one. Hence it is clear that the conditions are satisfied for the maintenance of the rate of profit in the domain of positive percentages above zero.

Would the declining rate of profits, however, diminish the capitalist inducement to invest? In considering this question, it must be borne in mind that the Marxian usage of the word "profits" differs from that of current economic theory. "Profits," in the Marxian sense, include the two classes of income which academic economists call "entrepreneurial profit" and "interest." For Marxian "profits" embrace every type of income except wages. A decline of profits, in the Marxian sense, would thus still be compatible with the maintenance of the inducement to invest in the Keynesian sense. For so long as entrepreneurial profit exceeds the current rate of interest, there is an incentive to invest. In other words, provided that the distribution of profits, in the Marxian sense, is such as to elevate the marginal efficiency of capital above the market rate of interest, investment may be expected to continue.[7] The devices of fiscal policy can be used to ensure that the interest rate remains at a level lower than the current rate of entrepreneurial profit. Despite then a decline in Marxian profits, the essential condition for the stimulation to invest can be fulfilled.

Within the Marxian system itself, there is no obstacle to an indefinite lowering of the rate of interest in such a way as to maintain a favorable difference for the marginal efficiency of capital. Marx held that there is no law that determines the rate of interest, and he believed there is no such thing as a "natural rate of interest." Marx regarded custom and legal tradition as equally important as competition in the determination of the actual magnitude of interest, and for this reason, held that there were no general laws applicable to the rate of interest.[8] The distinction between profits and interest, according to Marx, simply reflects the separation of money-capitalists and industrial capitalists.[9] Whereas Keynes regards the rate of interest

[7] John Maynard Keynes, *The General Theory of Employment, Interest, and Money* (New York, 1936), p. 136.

[8] "To what extent the two parties divide the profit, in which they both share, is in itself as much a purely empirical fact belonging to the realm of accident as the division of the shares of common profit of some corporate business among different shareholders by percentage." Karl Marx, *Capital*, III, 428.

[9] It is "only the separation of capitalists into money-capitalists and industrial capitalists, which transforms a portion of the profit into interest, which creates the category of interest at all." *Ibid.*, III, 435. A sociological element, moreover, enters into the determination of the rate of surplus value itself. The value of labor power is only the lower limit to which wages can be driven. The distribution otherwise between wages and surplus value "depends on the relative weight, which the pressure of capital on the one side, and the resistance of the labourer on the other, throws into the scale." *Ibid.*, I, 572–73.

and the marginal efficiency of capital as possessing something like the status of independent variables, Marx explicitly denies the independence of the rate of interest relative to the rate of profit.[10] In effect, Marx thus seeks to clarify the common social source of all exploitative forms of income. And precisely because there is no ultimate independence between profit and interest, it would on the Marxian scheme require only adjustment of custom and tradition in order to maintain a positive numerical difference between the rate of profit and the rate of interest. Keynesian fiscal policy and Marxian social adjustments would coincide in contributing to the favorable conditions for investment.

The Marxian analysis thus does not lead to any consequence of investment decline as the necessary outcome of the declining rate of profit. It entails rather the conclusion that capitalist economy need only be flexible enough to accept lower rates of profit from one period of technical development to another in order to assure its survival. Whether the capitalist order does, in fact, possess the required degree of flexibility is, of course, another matter, and one not dependent on the principles of economic theory. The rigidities and irrationalities of social institutions are extra-economic factors in theoretic analysis. Nonetheless, their role in economic development may well be decisive.

(II) There remains for us to consider the status of the other variable in the Marxian equation, the organic composition of capital. Marx took it for granted that the direction of technical development was toward an increase in the organic composition of capital. The mechanization of industry seemed to him to involve necessarily an increase in the proportion of investment in machinery and raw materials relative to the total capital outlay. Since the Marxian theory of economic development assigns primary

[10] Keynes, *loc. cit.*, p. 246. Marx, *op. cit.*, I, 428.

importance to the technical foundation, it is clear that the determination of the direction of technical evolution controls the outcome of the Marxian system. The crucial question therefore is: does the history of technology confirm the Marxian view that the organic composition of capital tends to rise throughout the stages of technical evolution?

Economic theory distinguishes between three types of invention—capital-saving, labor-saving, and neutral. In Pigou's words: ". . . an invention or improvement which reduces the ratio of capital to labour in the industry to which it applies will be capital-saving, one which increases it labour-saving, and one which leaves it unchanged, neutral."[11] The question at issue then is whether the trend of technical invention in a given historical period may be in a capital-saving rather than in a labor-saving direction. If the rate of capital-saving innovation is higher than the rate of labor-saving innovation within a given period, then the organic composition of capital will decline rather than rise. If capital-saving invention tends to predominate during a given period, then the Marxian assumption of a rising organic composition of capital is invalidated. There is no a priori determination of the mode of technical invention; the empirical facts of technical history alone can tell us the lines of technical evolution.

That capital-saving innovation was indeed dominant for considerable segments of industry during recent years is shown by statistical evidence such as the following:

The effects of increase in productivity upon investment was strikingly clear in many industries. The amount invested in plant and machinery in the automobile industry has declined since 1926. Investment in fixed capital in 1938 was 38 per cent less than in 1926, while output (of vastly improved quality) was greater by 22 per cent. In 1926, the fixed capital invested in the iron and steel industry was valued at 3.8 billion dollars; in 1937, at 3 billion dollars; yet capacity was 57.8 million tons in the former year, compared with 69.8 million tons

[11] A. C. Pigou, *The Economics of Welfare*, 2d ed. (London, 1924), p. 632.

in the latter. . . . In the railroad industry, with a $17,000,000,-000 investment in plant and equipment, creosoting has doubled the life of a tie, and heavier rails and steel rolling stock have reduced replacement costs.[12]

During the years from 1929 to 1938, the trend of innovation in a capital-saving direction was thus marked. Nor was the decrease in capital requirements accompanied by an equivalent reduction in the wages bill of the respective industries. Wages payments in the iron and steel industry, for instance, rose indeed from $1,011,000,000 in 1926 to $1,057,000,000 in 1937. The wages bill of the automobile industry rose likewise, from $793,000,000 in 1926 to $943,000,000 in 1937; there was an abnormal decline in the following year. There was during this period a considerable decrease in the wages payments of the railroad industry, years during which the value of the fixed capital remained relatively constant but in which there was a considerable reduction in the number of wage earners employed. But the decline in the railway wages bill was due primarily not to the displacement of labor by machinery but to the great fall in the physical volume of traffic from an index of 107 in 1926 to 84.9 in 1937 and 69.1 in 1938.[13]

The dominance of capital-saving innovation has been well characterized as the outcome of "a growing importance of technological changes which result in a much smaller demand for capital goods although their effect in increasing the productivity of labor . . . continues to be considerable."[14] In the past, technological progress has been largely associated with innovations that required

[12] *Savings, Investment, and National Income,* Monograph No. 37 (Temporary National Economic Committee, Washington, D.C., 1941), p. 99.

[13] For the details of this paragraph, cf. Spurgeon Bell, *Productivity, Wages, and National Income* (Brookings Institution, Washington, D.C., 1940), pp. 297, 287, 271–73.

[14] David Weintraub, "Effects of Current and Prospective Technological Developments upon Capital Formation," *American Economic Review,* Vol. XXIX (1939), Pt. 2, Supplement, p. 15.

heavy expenditures on capital goods; such were the requirements of the great new industries, the railways, iron and steel, electric power, motor transportation. Capital-saving invention, on the contrary, is designed primarily to improve the existing technology rather than to render obsolete the given industry or equipment. Among such technological changes are included the use of industrial measuring and controlling devices, the improved composition of metals in machine construction as, for instance, the use of chromium plating in tool and die making, the consequential trend toward more durable machinery, the greater employment of roller bearings and conveyors. The productivity of labor is increased in ways that involve less than a proportionate capital expansion; productive capacity is increased in ways indeed compatible with a curtailment of demand for capital goods. An inexpensive controlling device can enhance effective capacity and, at the same time, reduce capital requirements.

It is clear then that no law can be set down stipulating that technological change must always tend to raise the organic composition of capital. The Marxian theory assumed that all invention was labor-saving, and that technological change would increase the proportion of constant capital relative to total capital outlay. But economic theory, on its own ground, cannot determine whether technological innovation will take a labor-saving or capital-saving form during any given historical period. It is of course true that the relative dearness of a factor of production will tend to direct innovation toward reducing its required supply. The relative prices of factors of production do not, however, provide the basis for a necessary law of economic development. During the thirties, wage rates were low, but so likewise was the rate of interest, the price of borrowing capital. That innovation then took a capital-saving form was a development not deducible from the principles of economic theory. The Marxian theory with its universal law of technological change overlooks the indeterminacy as to its direction. Technological innovation can both increase or decrease the organic composition of capital; to this extent, the Marxian law of the declining rate of profit is founded on an unwarranted, arbitrary choice of one of the alternative lines of evolution.

The stagnationist school of American economists holds indeed that a defining characteristic for the maturity of our economy is precisely the fact that invention now tends to be capital-saving rather than capital-using. Their analysis is thus contrary to the Marxian account, which holds that capitalist maturity is characterized by the growing organic composition of capital. Alvin Hansen wrote in this vein:

> The nineteenth century witnessed not only the widening of capital (to use Hawtrey's phrase) incident to an expanding demand, but also a deepening of capital, the use of more and more capital per unit of output. . . . It appears that the great advance made in the productivity of manufacturing in the United States in the decade of the 'twenties was made by reason of innovations in methods of production that to a large extent did not involve the use of more capital . . . but it is a grave question whether inventions and innovations are not likely in the future to be less capital-using than in the nineteenth century. In contrast, while we were in process of changing over from a direct method of production to an elaborate capitalistic technique, innovations perforce had to be capital-using in character.[15]

The stagnationist school tends, however, to transform its own descriptive analysis into a principle of economic metaphysics. Its use of the organic metaphor of "maturity" leads to the prejudging of the issues of economic development. Hansen thus inclines toward affirming as a law of

[15] Alvin H. Hansen, *Full Recovery or Stagnation?* (New York, 1938), pp. 314–15. Also, cf. Hansen's judgment that for the economy as a whole, "there is no good evidence that the advance of technique has resulted in recent decades, certainly not in any significant measure, in any deepening of capital. . . . Though the deepening process is all the while going on in certain areas, elsewhere capital-saving inventions are reducing the ratio of capital to output." "Economic Progress and Declining Population Growth," *American Economic Review*, XXIX (1939), 7.

technological evolution that the trend of invention is from
capital-using to capital-saving. The former, he avers, prevails during the transformation of rural economy to capitalism; the latter characterizes "the further evolution of a
society which has already reached the status of a fully-
developed machine technique." Like the proposed Marxian
law, the stagnationist alternative law also imposes an arbitrary pattern of development on a system that is not economically determinate. It is thus altogether possible that
the construction of synthetic oil and atomic energy plants
will once more call forth a wave of capital-using innovation. No formula of technical change can constrain the
possibilities of history. Hansen's notion of a "fully-
developed machine technique," in other words, is ambiguous, and not a scientific, operational concept, for there is
no way of deciding when a machine technique is so "fully
developed" that it excludes new momentous developments.
Laws of technological development substitute verbal or
metaphysical device for empirical proof. Marx's use of organic metaphors is from the standpoint of scientific logic
akin to Hansen's metaphor of maturity.[16] When Marx,
for instance, avers that "no social order ever disappears
before all the productive forces for which there is room in
it have been developed," the scientific economist properly
asks for some operational criterion that will enable him to
adjudge whether all the technical innovations that a given
economy can sustain have or have not been forthcoming.[17] Otherwise, the meaning of the statement becomes

[16] Karl Marx, *A Contribution to the Critique of Political Economy*, Preface, in *Selected Works* (New York, n.d.), I, 356–57.

[17] It is unwise therefore to attach too much significance to the
decline in the rate of growth of some single industry in the capitalist
economy. Varga, for instance, emphasizes that during the period
from 1913 to 1930, "the rate of growth of railways has diminished
considerably all over the capitalist world." Cf. E. Varga and L. Men-
delsohn, *New Data for V. I. Lenin's Imperialism* (New York, 1940),
p. 211. This same period, however, saw the tremendous expansion
of the automobile industry. Any judgment as to the decline of the
capitalist system is limited by the indeterminacy of the factors that
control the net rate of capital formation.

vacuous, or reduces to an ex post facto tautology that defines an economy's maximum potential technical development as that which obtained when the society did as a matter of fact disappear. Tautologies are not, however, an adequate substitute for a determinate theory of economic development.

(III) There is adumbrated, however, in the Marxian theory another doctrine which assigns only a subsidiary place to the organic composition of capital as the basis for the necessary decline of capitalism. According to this next standpoint, the central factor in capitalist evolution is the decline of the socially necessary labor force. From this viewpoint, the distinction between a capital-saving and a labor-saving invention has only a limited significance, for it pertains only to the impact of the invention upon an industry taken in isolation from the rest of the economy. From the standpoint of the economy as a whole, innovations both capital-saving and labor-saving are, in the last analysis, labor-saving.

Within an isolated industry, then, it will make sense to differentiate between inventions that reduce either the outlay on capital goods or the wages bill. But any given capital-saving invention, according to the present approach, will be seen as we trace its effect to involve the reduction of society's labor requirements. For such an invention, by decreasing the given industry's need for machinery and raw materials, likewise reduces the demand for the output of those industries that supply the requisite capital. The capital-supplying industries will then reduce their labor forces in accordance with the declining demand for their goods. When the raw materials stage has been reached, the effect of a capital-saving invention in any given industry will have been translated into labor-saving terms for the economy as a whole.

Thus, a decrease in the organic composition of capital would, none the less, be compatible with a decline in the socially necessary labor force. A typical capital-saving innovation might, for instance, change a given industry's organic composition of capital $\left(\dfrac{c}{c+v}\right)$ from $\dfrac{50}{50+50}$ to $\dfrac{25}{25+30}$. Although with a lower organic composition of capital, such a situation (according to the classical Marxian law of profit) should ease the economic strain, nevertheless it may well, in point of fact, accentuate the economic "contradictions." For the socially necessary labor force of the economy as a whole, of the labor requirements of all industries added together, would be declining. In the cited example, the capital-saving innovation would have reduced the total labor units required from 100 to 55.

On the present model, then, capital-saving invention would always tend to increase the number of unemployed workmen.[18] This would then be followed by a relative decline in consumption. The market for consumers' goods is then found inadequate, and a "realization-crisis" ensues, a failure on the part of capitalist economy to realize its surplus value because of a narrowed market. These difficulties are intensified by the fact that calculations concerning anticipated profits are normally based on market prices and conditions prior to the impact of technical innovation. Underconsumptionist crisis can thus be interrelated with the organic composition of capital, though not in the manner Marx foresaw; a declining organic composition of capital could, in the present analysis, make for disequilibrium in the capitalist system.

But even such a theory as we have now outlined does not entail the conclusion of a necessary decline of the capitalist system. Technological innovation does indeed tend, on the one hand, to decrease the socially necessary labor requirements. But, on the other hand, it may also set in motion forces that can more than counteract any tendencies to underconsumptionist disequilibrium. For technical invention may also create new industries, and with their emergence, the otherwise "redundant population," the industrial reserve, is summoned to active employment.

[18] Karl Marx, *Capital*, I, 444–45.

Emergent industries upset the dialectic pattern of economic laws. Their labor and capital requirements supervene as it were from the outside on the previously defined stage of industry and organic composition of capital. Labor needs then rise to a maximum, and the new wage bills more than suffice to eliminate underconsumptionist pressure which might have become operative apart from technologic development. Our problem therefore shifts to the most basic factor in determining the stability and development of the capitalist system—the indeterminacy of the emergence of new industries.

(IV) There is a basic cleavage among economists in their outlooks with respect to the future of the American capitalist system. William James once observed that fundamental philosophic differences were founded on temperamental discordance; and economic theory, in this regard, is much like philosophy. On one side, we have the economic pessimists, those who believe that the capitalist economy has reached its maturity, that left to its devices, its foreseeable future is now one of stagnation. On the other side, there are the economic optimists, those who believe that there are new horizons and unsuspected frontiers for capitalist development, those who have faith in the resources and initiative of free enterprise. To what extent are either of these views founded on scientific economic analysis?

What transpires from a study of the schools of economic pessimism and optimism is that both essentially acknowledge that the development of the capitalist system has an indeterminate character. Hansen, the leading theorist of economic maturity, thus writes:

Of first-rate importance is the development of new industries. There is certainly no basis for the assumption that these are a thing of the past. But there is equally no basis for the assumption that we can take for granted the rapid emergence of new industries as rich in investment opportunities as the railroad, or more recently the automobile, together with all the related developments, including the construction of public roads, to which it gave rise. . . . And when a revolutionary new industry like the railroad or the automobile, after having initiated in its youth a powerful upward surge of investment activity, reaches maturity and ceases to grow, as all industries finally must, the whole economy must experience a profound stagnation, unless new developments take its place.[19]

The final qualification enunciates the indeterminacy that goes to the heart of any proposed theory of economic evolution. "Unless indeed new developments take its place. . . ." Remarkably enough, the school of economic optimism is in basic accord with the stagnationist school upon the logic of the matter. Terborgh, the chief advocate of the open capitalist frontier, observes that "it is notorious that technological development is unpredictable," and then asks: "who can say, for example, what might be the impact of a successful harnessing of atomic energy?"[20] So far as the confirmable statistical data are concerned, there is a large measure of agreement between the opposing schools. Both, for instance, are prepared to affirm that about 15 per cent of gross capital formation is to be attributed to the impact of new industries.[21] The essential point is that both sides to the controversy acknowledge that the advent of new industries is unpredictable.

Technical innovation thus introduces a surd factor into economic analysis. A new industry is something different from the kind of invention that perfects an existing technology subserving a given scheme of wants. A new industry, like radio, calls into existence a whole new set of consumers' desires and a whole new industrial structure. It is a qualitative innovation which renders obsolete the existent system of organic composition of capital, and begins anew a whole process of interrelations between the productive factors.

[19] Alvin H. Hansen, "Economic Progress and Declining Population Growth," *American Economic Review*, XXIX (1939), 10.

[20] George Terborgh, *The Bogey of Economic Maturity* (Chicago, 1945), p. 92.

[21] Alvin H. Hansen, "Some Notes on Terborgh's 'The Bogey of Economic Maturity,'" *Review of Economic Statistics*, XXVIII (1946), 15.

The laws then of capitalist economics must be restricted in form to the structure of hypothetical propositions; they constitute a group of "if-then" statements. But the notion that one can specify a law that will state the actual lines of economic development must be surrendered. For any proposed sequence of development is contingent upon a clause that begins with "provided that. . . ." What the directions of economic development are, whether toward stagnation, collapse, or prosperity, depends primarily upon the emergence of new industries. After the laws of economics have been formulated, laws concerning prices, wages, the rate of interest, it is still not possible to foretell what the human intelligence will discover during this stage of economic development. There was no forecast from any economic school that the fission of the uranium atom would be discovered, and that a new mode of industrial energy would become available.

We are finally left with economic creeds that partake of articles of faith rather than economic science. The economic optimists look for reassurance to the confutations that pessimism has sustained in the past. They cite lines from the well-known report of the United States Commissioner of Labor in 1886, a Cassandra whose words fell upon happy days; the report described the completion of transport expansion throughout the world, and then averred that "the discovery of new processes of manufacture . . . will not leave room for a marked extension, such as has been witnessed during the last fifty years, or afford a remunerative employment of the vast amount of capital which has been created during that period. . . . The day of large profits is probably past. There may be room for further intensive, but not extensive, development of industry in the present area of civilization."[22] But great new industries were born after 1886, and capitalist growth reached unimagined levels. Nonetheless, the stagnationist can still challenge us with his query: "Such industries *can* develop but *will* they?"

[22] Terborgh, *op. cit.*, pp. 93–94.

The school of economic optimism appeals in the last resort to what Schumpeter has called "the creative response" in economic history.[23] Such a response is said to occur when industry moves "outside of the range of existing practice." Creative response, Schumpeter affirms, "cannot be predicted by applying the ordinary rules of inference from pre-existing facts." It evokes social and economic situations of a radically novel kind, and as an essential element in the historical process, "no deterministic credo avails against this."

Economic optimism itself, however, becomes a determinist creed of a metaphysical kind when it decrees that the resources of creative response will always overcome contingencies and crises. The rhythms of technical and scientific creativity bear no necessary relation to the laws of capital availability. Although there may be a plethora of idle capital upon the market seeking new outlets for investment, nevertheless no new capital-using industry may be forthcoming to meet the demand. During the depression years of the thirties, men looked with hope for the emergence of that great new industry which would do for that decade what the expansion of the automobile industry had done for the twenties. Their hope remained unfulfilled. There is no necessary law which elicits a satisfactory creative response to the challenges of the investment market. Technical innovation depends upon noneconomic factors. It is founded upon the conditions of the sciences in question, and the degree to which practical applications are feasible at this given stage in the history of the science. It is founded on obscure considerations concerning the theoretic difficulties of dominant problems, and the degree to which they permit of cooperative efforts toward solution. Creative response, as a social phenomenon then, introduces variables that do not fall within a determinate set of economic equations. A surd factor enters into the course of technical evolution. The directions of economic devel-

[23] Joseph A. Schumpeter, "The Creative Response in Economic History," *Journal of Economic History,* VII (1947), 150.

opment therefore cannot be predicted from the principles of economic theory. The system of economic laws is incomplete when measured against the standard of economic realities. The dispute between economic pessimism and optimism has justly therefore been called "the great guessing game."[24] A dearth of great new industries that are capital-using leads to the decline of capitalism; their emergence means its revival. But there is no basis on grounds of economic theory to forecast one or the other.

(v) We have throughout the foregoing analysis assumed that the emergence of new industries is the precondition for the maintenance of investment. The question is naturally raised: why may not investment persist in terms of existing needs and technology? Why, in other words, may there not be an indefinite growth of investment which is of the "widening" kind, and not of the "deepening" kind? Surely, it is argued, there is a huge demand among the world's peoples for products that are now available for manufacture, and these potential markets would for a long time to come be a sufficient outlet for investment. And here we come to the essential point of socialist criticism that the maldistribution of income precludes the indefinite continuance of investment of the widening kind.[25]

The inducement to invest is the prospect of profit, the incentive of a favorable schedule for the marginal efficiency of capital. The schedule of prospective profits is, however, depressed by the class distribution of income. For the prospective yield of capital refers to anticipation as to the state of the market for the commodity in question. The existing structure of consumers' demand is molded by

[24] David McCord Wright, " 'The Great Guessing Game': Terborgh versus Hansen," *Review of Economic Statistics,* XXVIII (1946), 19.

[25] As Joan Robinson has noted, Marx does not have a systematic theory as to the relation of investment to the workings of the economy. Cf. *An Essay on Marxian Economics* (London, 1942), p. 56. The limitation which the class distribution of income imposes on investment is implicit, however, in much of his analysis.

the distribution of income in proportions which are class differentiated. The anticipated effective demand therefore is constricted by the bounds of class income. Profit expectations are reduced when they bear in mind the large number of consumers who are outside the effective market. Within a limited period, the decline of the marginal efficiency of capital is ordinarily due to the satisfaction of the existent demand for a given commodity added to the increase in its supply price in accordance with diminishing productive returns. The general structure, however, of the curve of profit expectations is relative to the given system of class distribution of income; the equation of a demand curve for a given commodity is an expression of the economy's socio-economic relations.

An indefinite widening of investment then, as a real economic possibility, would presuppose expectations as to the continual elevation of standards of living. Only thus would the structure of demand curves be changing in a way commensurate with the requisite expansion in investment activity. But this eventuality is precluded by the conditions of profit-making in a capitalist economy that is not creating new industries. For, in a stationary situation, that is, when no new capital-using industries are emerging, the maintenance of profit rates presupposes that the total wages bill will be lower than the total prices of consumers' goods (minus the consumers' purchases of non-wage earning groups). The condition of profit-seeking, in the absence of new industries, then constricts the domain of effective demand, for the wages payments are inadequate to the purchase of the available output of consumers' goods. In a non-expanding economy, the dilemma of underconsumptionism is thus a real one. Crises cannot be avoided through a widening of investment in terms of existent needs. Class distribution of income so depresses the schedule of the marginal efficiency of capital that a capitalist economy cannot subsist on the basis of widening of investment without the emergence of new industries.

The problem of underconsumptionism becomes all the more serious when effective demand is further reduced by a declining population. For, in addition to the results of a dearth of new industries, there is then superimposed a decline in profit expectations due to the contraction of markets for existing commodities. Investment activity then suffers an intense decline, because the demand for capital goods, already adversely affected by the lack of new industries, is reinforced by reduced demand from existent industries. The consequent unemployment unbalances further the whole social structure.

Keynes, in considering this question, therefore urged that in an era of declining population and growing capital-saving innovation, it is essential that capitalist economy undertake to achieve a more equal distribution of incomes, and thereby, to achieve a more considerable effective demand. Keynes noted the trend toward capital-saving invention: "Many modern inventions are directed towards finding ways of reducing the amount of capital investment necessary to produce a given result," and he did not believe that "we can rely on current changes of technique being of the kind which tend of themselves to increase materially the average period of production." He then concluded: "Now, if the number of consumers is falling off and we cannot rely on any significant technical lengthening of the period of production, the demand for a net increase of capital goods is thrown into being wholly dependent on an improvement in the average level of consumption or on a fall in the rate of interest." The dilemma of underconsumption in a period of capital-saving innovation goes to the heart of capitalist socio-economic relationships. "If capitalist society rejects a more equal distribution of incomes and the forces of banking and finance succeed in maintaining the rate of interest somewhere near the figure which ruled on the average during the nineteenth century. . . , then a chronic tendency towards the under-employment of resources must in the end sap and destroy that form of society."[26]

[26] J. M. Keynes, "Some Economic Consequences of a Declining Population," *Eugenics Review*, XXIX (1937), 14, 17.

The Keynesian analysis however does not give sufficient weight to the causative role of the dearth of new industries in producing capitalist decline. This is because Keynes's analysis is founded on the concept of "period of production," which refers to the "interval which elapses between the work done and the consumption of the product." Now, by and large, it is true that a capital-saving innovation tends to lower the period of production. But a new industry that creates new articles of consumption cannot be said with much significance to be lowering or raising the period of production. For calculations of the latter's trend assume as their base a fixed set of commodities whose period of production then rises or falls, but the addition of a new commodity with new capital requirements deprives the period of production index of significance.

To put the matter in more practical terms, we might assume the emergence of new industries whose period of production was lower than or equal to the average period of production of existent industries. Even with a decline in the period of production, the advent of new industries would afford the required channels for investment activity. It follows therefore that the "period of production" of capital technique is not the controlling factor. What is crucial is whether new industries emerge at the required time and with the requisite intensity to absorb the available productive energies of society. And the dependence of capitalist survival on this indeterminate factor is all the more marked during a period of declining population.

If new capital-creating industries are forthcoming, the economic influence of a declining population is not, for the while, unfavorable. For wages then tend to rise, and there is a consequent widening of investment in terms of an increased standard of living for the employed population. In the absence, however, of great new industries, capitalist economy can only undertake to widen investment by the redistribution of incomes. But to do this on the scale which Keynes requires, capitalist economy would have to cease being capitalist. For to achieve equilibrium, incomes of the lower groups would have to be raised to a point where they would be sufficient to absorb the output of the available investment capacity. Capitalist economy to survive would then have transformed itself particularly in a socialist direction.

Finally, it may be argued that the line of demarcation between a new industry and the extension of a capital-saving innovation is so fine that perhaps the latter might well afford the basis for an indefinite capitalist expansion. It is noted, for instance, that the consequences of an invention like the "trackless trolley" are akin to those of a new capital-using industry. For, although the "trackless trolley" requires less fixed capital, it may however lead to the extending of service to new routes made possible by cheaper costs. There would then follow an increased demand for capital requirements. It is argued therefore that capital-saving innovation automatically opens required new channels of investment.

What this argument overlooks is that one cannot confidently expect that capital-saving inventions will open investment channels in anything like the breadth essential for full employment of resources. The first effect of capital-saving innovations is to make available new quantities of surplus capital. The problem of investment outlets is, of course, at once intensified. It is too much to expect that existing industries will all expand production at the reduced prices necessary to open up maximum new markets.[27] The quest for the conventional rate of profit is one limiting factor in the expansion of investment, and it once more constricts the ready absorption of surplus capital. Moreover, it is indeterminate whether the particular capital-saving innovations will occur in industries that permit of indefinite expansion of commodities. There is the factor of inelasticity in the markets for many commodities to be

[27] After considering all the possible direct and indirect results of the introduction of the trackless trolley, Weir M. Brown justly concludes, . . . "who is prepared to say whether, for the economy as a whole, this is a 'capital-saving' or a 'labor-saving' change?" " 'Labor-saving' and 'Capital-saving' Innovations," *Southern Economic Journal*, XIII, 111.

considered.[28] If reduced prices will not materially enhance the demand for a given commodity, then the outcome of capital-saving innovation will be the contraction, not the expansion, of capital requirements for the given industry. In the last analysis then, the automatic widening of capital-saving innovation is too uncertain in character. Reliance must be placed on new, emergent industries to supply the requisite outlets for investment, but here too, as we have seen, the pattern of development is insecure and indeterminate.[29]

(vi) The fact that there is no law of the necessary decline of capitalism does not mean that the advantages or disadvantages of a socialist economy are any the more or less. Indeed, it is precisely the indeterminacy of its pattern of development that is the most probably compelling argument against the capitalist system. The continued stability of the capitalist economy depends upon the most uncontrollable of factors, human creativity, something not in the purview of any scheme of economic laws. Whether there will be opportunities for investment depends within the capitalist system on the emergence of new industries. When such innovations are forthcoming in the required quantity, the capitalist order remains in equilibrium. But the equilibrium is always unstable. It is founded on an unpredictable, fortuitous line of technical development.

The strange thing about the capitalist system is that it

[28] William Fellner, "The Technological Argument of the Stagnation Thesis," *Quarterly Journal of Economics,* LV (1941), 651.

[29] What the effects of capital-saving or labor-saving invention on the distribution of national income will be is likewise dependent upon the advent of new industries. Pigou has proposed the view that a capital-saving invention diminishes the ratio of labor to capital in industries other than the improved one because of the release of a quantity of surplus capital. He then argues that capital-saving invention tends therefore to lower the marginal productivity of capital relative to labor, and that consequently, the distribution of national income is altered in favor of labor. The whole argument however assumes an abundance of investment outlets which only new industries can provide. The industrial structure does not automatically absorb the surplus capital liberated by capital-saving invention.

can survive only if it is ever fecund, if its creativity and resourcefulness never flag. More than this, its fecundity must keep pace with the excess funds made available for investment by the continual growth of capital-saving innovations. The capitalist system to survive must, in Marx's language, continue to be a progressive system in an accelerated way, ever expanding at a growing rate the scope of human satisfactions. The capitalist system is unique among possible economies in that it alone cannot be a "stationary system." For if investment falters, the economy becomes unsteady, and there ensues the sequence of crisis and unemployment.

Is it too severe a strain to impose upon any system that the condition for its equilibrium be an unending creativity? To make the well-being of the masses of men dependent on so tenuous a factor as "creative response" would be to abandon all hope of controlling the workings of economy to assure the stable basis of life for all. The uncontestable advantage of a socialist economy is that it can travel at ordinary and slow speeds. It can even enter upon a stationary phase, and know that its methods of economic planning will work nonetheless. It does not impose the demand of incessant invention which the capitalist order always bears. Perhaps in the end the basic "contradiction" of capitalist economy is precisely this, its dependence on the law: Innovate or Decline. There is, of course, presumable a third alternative: War. All societies in distress, whether feudal, capitalist, or socialist, have tended to seek a new equilibrium in war, but wars under such conditions have shown themselves self-destructive of the social formation.

The scientific socialism of Karl Marx was founded on the doctrine that the system of economic laws was a dialectic one in the sense that its own operations led necessarily to the advent of a novel system. Socialist ideas were thus linked to the view that economic science could provide a fully determinate theory of economic development. Marx, in his actual economic research, could not consistently adhere to the dialectical standpoint. He acknowledged, for instance, that a state of equilibrium within a capitalist economy is possible, though not to be counted upon, for . . . "a balance is an accident under the crude conditions of this production."[30] This possible equilibrium simply as a logical fact is sufficient proof that the laws of capitalist economy do not take the form of a dialectic system.

Socialist theory would do well then to abandon the last residues of Hegelian metaphysics, and to place its proposals solidly on the basis of verifiable fact. Socialist theory can then recognize that much of social science takes an indeterminate form. Marx himself made the sound logical observation that "no equation can be solved unless the elements of its solution are involved in its terms." Where a question was in the logical clouds, where the equations were not sufficient to determine the terms, all science could undertake was "the criticism of the question itself."[31] And this we have tried to do with the theory of economic evolution by showing that it fails to satisfy the conditions of determinate solution. Men's social choices must then be guided by the recognition of the indeterminacy of the directions of capitalist development.

We have thus tried to show that the theory of economic development has three basic aspects of indeterminacy:

(1) The fall in the rate of profit entails no necessary consequence of capitalist decline unless extra-economic rigidities are added to the laws of economic theory.

(2) There is no foretelling in the capitalist economy whether innovation will be predominantly of a capital-saving or labor-saving form. And a determinate theory of economic evolution cannot be founded on an indeterminate pattern of technical development.

(3) Most important, there is no way of foreseeing whether a given era will be marked by the dearth or the emergence of new great industries. It remains indeterminate therefore whether investment waves will be forthcoming that would enable the capitalist system at any given

[30] Karl Marx, *Capital*, II, 578.

[31] *The Correspondence of Karl Marx and Friedrich Engels*, trans. Dona Torr (London, 1936), p. 386.

period to surmount the pressures of underconsumptionist disequilibrium. The content of socialist proposals, from this standpoint, is an attempt to reduce the impact of economic indeterminacy on men's lives. There remains, however, the great question as to the extent to which an over-determined, over-planned, and over-socialized economy can frustrate other components in men's psyches. Socialist intellectuals unfortunately have tended not only to project a dialectical myth on capitalist evolution; they have also projected a myth of transfiguration on the workings of socialist society. They have contrived a "repressive ideology."

A Brief Bibliographical Note

The most authoritative biographies of Karl Marx are Franz Mehring, *Karl Marx: The Story of His Life*, translated by Edward Fitzgerald (New York, 1935); Otto Rühle, *Karl Marx: His Life and Work*, translated by Eden and Cedar Paul (New York, 1929); and Boris Nicolaievsky and Otto Maenchen-Helfen, *Karl Marx: Man and Fighter*, translated by Gwenda David and Eric Mosbacher (Philadelphia, 1936). Mehring, a distinguished German literary critic and pioneer historian of Marxism, was an intensely involved left-wing Social Democrat. His portrait of Marx is a sympathetic one, but also one that softens the lines of his character. Rühle appreciated the power of Marx's achievement, yet at the same time tried to illumine what he regarded as Marx's sense of inferiority. Boris Nicolaievsky, the indefatigable archivist, scholar, and Russian democratic socialist, probably knew the sources better than anyone in the world; he also had a discerning perception of Marx's traits as a man. To understand Marx's character, and the loyalty he inspired, one should still read the essays by his friends, Wilhelm Liebknecht and Frederick Lessner; his son-in-law, Paul Lafargue; and his daughter, Eleanor Marx. Much of this material is assembled in the volume *Reminiscences of Marx and Engels* (Moscow, n.d.). The Soviet collection, however, censors these essays whenever they prove embarrassing to the official Soviet ideology. It deletes, for instance, the section where Lafargue describes Marx's deep admiration for Balzac's short story, *The Unknown Masterpiece*, and likewise suppresses Liebknecht's recollection of how he and Marx got into a chauvinistic brawl with Englishmen in a London public house, and how Marx then vented his frustrated aggressions by joining in the breaking of four or five street lamps ("in order to cool our heated blood") at two o'clock in the morning, until several policemen chased them; "Marx showed an activity that I should not have attributed to him," recalled Liebknecht. The interested reader can find the uncensored texts in such older editions as Wilhelm Liebknecht, *Karl Marx: Biographical Memoirs,* translated by Ernest Untermann (Chicago, 1901). David Ryazanoff, the most learned of the first generation of Soviet scholars of Marxism, edited the useful collection, *Karl Marx: Man, Thinker and Revolutionist* (New York, 1927).

Gustav Mayer's book, *Friedrich Engels: A Biography,* translated by Gilbert and Helen Highet (New York, 1936), is the best source on Engels' character and life; there are also vivid portraits of Engels in Eduard Bernstein, *My Years of Exile,* translated by Bernard Miall (London, 1912), and Ernest Belfort Bax, *Reminiscences and Reflexions of a Mid and Late Victorian* (London, 1918). Henry Mayers Hyndman, the English socialist, in his *The Record of an Adventurous Life* (London, 1911), wrote a chapter on Marx that is a needed counterweight to the large body of adulatory writing.

Edmund Silberner's essay, "Was Marx an Anti-Semite?" *Historia Judaica,* Vol. XI (1949), pp. 3–52, still remains the most complete discussion of Marx's emotional attitudes toward the Jews. The recent Soviet biographies of Marx actually omit mentioning the fact of Marx's Jewish ancestry. Solomon F. Bloom's *The World of Nations; A Study of the National Implications in the Work of Karl Marx* (New York, 1941), is a useful survey of Marx's feelings and opinions concerning various races, nations, and peoples; Max Nomad's essay on Marx in *Apostles of Revolution* (revised edition, New York, 1961) is also well worth studying.

Among the recent books on Marxism, the most outstanding in my opinion are Bertram D. Wolfe, *Marxism: One Hundred Years in the Life of a Doctrine* (New York, 1965), and Robert C. Tucker, *Philosophy and Myth in Karl Marx* (New York, 1961). Most of the other books that have appeared add little to the earlier interpretations and criticisms made by Sidney Hook and Max Eastman.

Hook's work *From Hegel to Marx* (New York, 1936) is a study in the history of ideas that has not been superseded. Max Eastman, in *Marxism, Is It Science?* (New York, 1940), and his still earlier *Marx and Lenin, the Science of Revolution* (London, 1926), and Will Herberg, "The Christian Mythology of Socialism," *Antioch Review,* Vol. III, No. 1 (1943), pp. 125–32, clarified the nonlogical components in Marxism with a lucidity and originality that have not been surpassed in later studies.

The volumes of Karl Marx and Friedrich Engels, *Historische-Kritische Gesamtausgabe,* begun under the editorship of David Ryazanov, which appeared in Berlin before the advent of the Nazi dictatorship, are invaluable for the scholar. They contain their writings in the original languages, English, French, and German. Unfortunately this proposed complete edition of the works of Marx and Engels remained unfinished. A German edition of the *Werke* of Marx and Engels has been published in Berlin during 1961 to 1968 in forty-one volumes thus far. Marx's articles for the *New York Tribune* have never been printed in their original entirety, though selections from them have been published in such books as *The Civil War in the United States, Revolution in Spain, On Britain, Marx on China,* and *The Russian Menace to Europe,* as well as the recently published *Karl Marx on Colonialism and Modernization,* edited by Shlomo Avineri. Marx's and Engels' principal works are all available in English translations, and require no citation. The student who wishes to search into their more fugitive writings will find invaluable the *Bibliographie des Oeuvres de Karl Marx* (Paris, 1956), and its *Supplément* (1960), by the painstaking French scholar Maximilien Rubel. There is no complete edition in English of the correspondence of Marx and Engels, but three selected collections have been published, in New York, 1935, and Moscow, 1955 and 1965; the last is the most inclusive.

Marx himself had little interest in questions of philosophy and tended to repress questions of the grounds of moral decision. Consequently, when Marxists have written on such issues, they have tried to combine Marxism with their own individual or cultural standpoint. Sorel joined Marxist ideology to Bergson's philosophy, Eduard Bernstein tried a combination with Kantian ethics, Antonio Gramsci gave Marx a Crocean overtone, G. D. H. Cole made him an English realist, Sidney Hook fashioned a close linkage with Dewey's pragmatism, Austro-Marxists synthesized Marx with Mach, Lenin turned Marx into a simple nineteenth-century Russian materialist, and Sartre has terminated the existentialist search in a Marxist commitment. What this variety of philosophical "foundations" for Marxism testifies is that Marx essentially repressed any questioning within himself with respect to philosophical ultimates and decisions. The large literature on the philosophy of Marx is evidence that even among Marxists human nature abhors a philosophical vacuum.

ANCHOR BOOKS

Drama (continued)

MUSIC

ANCHOR BOOKS

ANCHOR BOOKS